W9-BXT-210

Educational Entrepreneurship

Realities, Challenges, Possibilities

Educational Entrepreneurship

Realities, Challenges, Possibilities

Edited by

Frederick M. Hess

HARVARD EDUCATION PRESS
CAMBRIDGE, MASSACHUSETTS

Library of Congress Control Number   2006930071

Paperback ISBN   1-891792-25-3
Library Edition ISBN   1-891792-26-1

13-Digit Paperback ISBN   978-1-891792-25-0
13-Digit Library Edition ISBN   978-1-891792-26-7

Published by Harvard Education Press,
an imprint of the Harvard Education Publishing Group

Harvard Education Press
8 Story Street
Cambridge, MA 02138

Cover Design: Alyssa Morris

The typefaces used in this book are ITC Stone Serif for text and ITC Stone Sans for display.

BK   ROTH
$59.95

For Todd, the first entrepreneur I ever knew

Contents

Acknowledgments

I am indebted to a number of individuals who were crucial to the compilation of this volume. Primarily, I thank the contributing authors who wrote the conference papers that were presented at the American Enterprise Institute (AEI) on November 14, 2005, and then revised them into the chapters that follow. My estimable colleague at AEI, Morgan Goatley, compiled and edited the papers meticulously, and Rosemary Kendrick and Hilary Boller, also of AEI, offered invaluable editorial guidance and conference assistance. Joleen Okun and Bridget Hahn were also of much help in the editing stages.

As always, my grateful thanks go to the American Enterprise Institute, and especially its president Christopher DeMuth, for unwavering support and resources. Funding for this project was generously provided by the Ewing Marion Kauffman Foundation, and for it, I offer my sincere gratitude. Finally, Harvard Education Press has been a valuable partner for several years, allowing for the rapid publication of several previous volumes. I thank its director Doug Clayton and production manager Dody Riggs, who have facilitated these smooth publication processes.

Entrepreneurship, Risk, and Reinvention

Frederick M. Hess

This is the era of educational entrepreneurship, to an unprecedented degree. Dynamic, unconventional thinkers have waded into the world of K–12 schooling, founded influential organizations, and upset established conventions. They have developed new models for delivering instruction or recruiting teachers and applied old-fashioned practices with inspired fidelity. While these ventures face intense resistance and constitute a still-minuscule portion of schooling, they are also responsible for the most exciting developments in twenty-first-century education.

These ventures include the most discussed names in contemporary school reform; many are also among the most respected or most controversial. They include the KIPP Academies, K12 Inc., Teach For America, the Edison Schools, New Leaders for New Schools, National Heritage Academies, Catapult Learning, Aspire Public Schools, and The New Teacher Project. Wireless Generation is a New York-based firm that provides schools with diagnostic software that operates on handheld computers, allowing teachers to diagnose student needs and chart progress while circling their classroom. Growing Stars is a California-based firm that tutors U.S. students using dozens of instructors based in Cochin, India. Able to hire educated Indians at rates steeply lower than their American counterparts, Growing Stars and its competitors are charging Americans $20 an hour for personal tutoring, less than half of the prevailing rate in much of the United States. Discovery Communications, Inc., has launched Cosmeo, a Web-based homework aid that delivers an online video encyclopedia to families for $9.95 a month. This is the home version of a service Discovery provides to more than seventy thousand schools. The screen resembles a handheld game, and the site features video clips and interactive games.

What is educational entrepreneurship and what does it look like—both inside and outside of school districts in the profit and not-for-profit sectors? Who are the educational entrepreneurs and what motivates them? What tools do entrepreneurs need to be successful, and what policies or practices enable or impede entrepreneurship? What would it mean to open up the education sector to more entrepreneurial activity? What roadblocks and risks lie ahead if we take that course? These are questions this volume addresses.

WHAT EXACTLY *IS* ENTREPRENEURSHIP?

Entrepreneurship is a famously slippery notion. There is no universal agreement on how it should be defined or understood. J. B. Say, the French economist, offered one of the earliest definitions of entrepreneurship, explaining two centuries ago that "the entrepreneur shifts economic resources out of an area of lower and into an area of higher productivity and greater yield."[1] In American culture, entrepreneurship is often used as a catch-all label to denote those who launch and operate small business enterprises. A more useful definition is classically sketched by economist Joseph Schumpeter, who suggested that entrepreneurship is the implementation of change via the introduction of new or better quality goods, new methods of production, new sources of supply, or the reorganization of an industry. Schumpeter recognized that successful ventures would displace less productive ones, creating a vigorous and adaptive climate marked by "creative destruction."[2]

With due credit to Peter Drucker, author of the seminal *Innovation and Entrepreneurship*, it may be most useful to think of educational entrepreneurship as a process of purposeful innovation directed toward improving educational productivity, efficiency, and quality. As Drucker has explained, those who open a new "greasy spoon" in a suburb are rarely entrepreneurs. However, the creation of McDonald's was entrepreneurial because it pioneered or applied new management techniques that standardized delivery, processes, and tools in order to drastically upgrade cost-effectiveness, serve new needs, and create a new market.[3] In education, entrepreneurs seek to teach children who have been ill served, improve the quality of teachers and school leaders, give educators more effective tools, and deliver services in more useful and accessible ways. In short, they seek to tackle the same problems as other educators; the difference is in how they go about it.

Rather than accept the condition of an industry or a sector as a given, entrepreneurs rethink fundamental assumptions about what works or what is possible. Business scholars W. Chan Kim and Renee Mauborgne have noted that entrepreneurial individuals often ask some variation on four questions: "Which of the factors that our industry takes for granted should be eliminated? Which factors should be reduced well below the industry's standard? Which factors should be raised well above the industry's standard? Which factors should be created that the industry has never offered?"[4] This may mean harnessing a new innovation, but it might also mean making use of tools, ideas, or approaches that are underused or overlooked. Politically constrained and uncomfortable with the notion that some activities should be cut back or eliminated in order to permit investment elsewhere, public school officials have tended to do a little bit of everything. Because they bet on a given strategy and target a particular niche, entrepreneurs find it much easier to maintain coherence and direction.

Determining the extent to which entrepreneurs are born rather than made has occasioned much discussion among business thinkers. For our purposes, such debates are more distracting than illuminating. On the one hand, there are clearly personality traits, including increased tolerance for risk and a high internal locus of control, that tend to characterize entrepreneurs. On the other, entrepreneurs are inevitably a product of their environment; they require the opportunity and the resources to act. In the end, an entrepreneurial environment attracts entrepreneurial personalities, cultivates entrepreneurial habits of thought, and supports entrepreneurial ventures.

Now, it's a mistake to wax rhapsodic about the entrepreneurial process. The expectation is not that the typical venture will improve upon the status quo, only that some will do so. Some ideas won't pan out and many ventures will fail. In fact, management scholars have estimated that 60 percent of all product-development efforts are abandoned before they ever reach the market, and nearly half of those that do reach the market fail.[5] The entrepreneurial presumption, however, accepts that the path of improvement is neither straight nor self-evident. Given the lack of an omniscient planner to foresee what will work, entrepreneurs become the engines of progress. Entrepreneurs have the flexibility and incentive to seek out new solutions, make judicious use of available data, and adapt as obstacles and opportunities dictate. While the plight of any given venture is uncertain, the entrepreneurial process itself ensures that potentially good ideas are constantly surfaced and then sifted.

Historically, educational entrepreneurship has been most notable for its absence. A search of the *New York Times*, the *Washington Post*, *USA Today*, the

Los Angeles Times, and the *Chicago Tribune* found that the phrases "education entrepreneur" and "educational entrepreneurship" appeared just forty-nine times between 1996 and 2005. Other than Edison Schools founder Chris Whittle's *Crash Course* and Teach For America founder Wendy Kopp's *One Day, All Children*—books that touch on their experiences and questions of educational entrepreneurship in the context of broader discussions—and more scholarly volumes edited by Marilyn Kourilsky and William Walstad and by Paul Hill and James Harvey, almost nothing has been written on the subject.[6] For comparison's sake, it may be worth noting that in early 2006, Amazon.com listed more than eighteen hundred titles on entrepreneurship, including *Entrepreneurship, Beyond Entrepreneurship, Handbook of Entrepreneurship Research*, and *Entrepreneurship for Dummies*.

The entrepreneurial process is fundamentally unlike the flavor-of-the-month reform that permeates so much of American schooling. Whereas public districts require officials to force change through resistant bureaucracies, or individual teachers and principals to freelance within indifferent organizations, entrepreneurship permits innovators to construct new organizations focused on devising answers to clearly articulated problems. From this perspective, the efforts of The New Teacher Project to attract talented college graduates into schooling, National Heritage Academies to provide a rigorous "back-to-basics" education to elementary and middle school students, or Catapult Learning to use tutoring to help students overcome achievement deficits are distinct from more typical reform efforts.

WHY ENTREPRENEURSHIP IS IMPORTANT IN EDUCATION

The case for educational entrepreneurship is rather simple. Our schools today confront challenges that our education system isn't equipped to answer. Erected haphazardly over the course of two centuries, our system of schooling has been configured to process large numbers of students for lives in an industrial nation. Given the realities of globalization and the demands of a knowledge economy, arrangements that may have worked passably well 35 years ago are no longer adequate. Moreover, there is no evidence that our educational system has the ability or the know-how to embrace a reconfigured model commensurate with its changed mission. In fact, decades of earnest efforts to reform public schools through conventional means have shown remarkably little ability to substantively alter routines or results.

We readily recognize the risks and problems posed by entrepreneurial activity. It means that some new schools and providers will prove ineffective or unsustainable, that some will go out of business at disruptive times, and that some children and families will be buffeted by these developments. However, while noting these dangers, we routinely fail to fully acknowledge the perils implicit in the status quo. Editorial Projects in Education has calculated that the national graduation rate is only 69 percent. It is just 55 percent for Latinos and 53 percent for African Americans. In major cities like Indianapolis, New York City, Milwaukee, Denver, Philadelphia, Dallas, and Oakland, the graduation rate is less than 50 percent.[7] On the National Assessment of Educational Progress, more than half of fourth graders in cities like Atlanta, Los Angeles, and Washington, D.C., score "below basic" in reading.[8] Meanwhile, blacks graduate high school four grade levels behind whites, and American students of all races lag internationally on the most reputable international assessments, such as PISA and TIMMS.[9] Despite educators' claims, the professional education community has not demonstrated that it knows how to educate every child or erect school systems that work well for nearly all children. School systems have been unable to respond in a timely fashion to changing student demographics or take advantage of resources in the larger society. In short, the status quo is inadequate and riven by pockets of stark failure. Standing pat is hardly a risk-free alternative.

Nonetheless, today's system of schooling is inclined to stand pat. Public school officials, enmeshed in a public bureaucracy, governed by elected representatives, and scrutinized by anxious parents and civic leaders, have traditionally been averse to risk or disruptive change. Licensure requirements prevent nontraditional aspirants from becoming teachers or school leaders. Financing systems, charter school laws, and existing regulations make it arduous and fiscally perilous to open new schools. State law and collective bargaining thwart efforts to reward the best and hardest-working educators. Teachers, principals, and district officials work in an environment where excellence is rarely rewarded, where those who do more or devise new approaches are often stymied by rule or routine, and where keeping one's head down and following procedure is the surest path to professional success. Entrepreneurs swim upstream in organizations that do little or nothing to cull the mediocre. The best educators, especially those in low-performing schools and troubled districts, have come to accept the burdens of struggling with bureaucracy and shouldering less effective colleagues as their due. In short, existing arrangements foster a culture of stagnation.

Entrepreneurship is valuable because, left to their own devices, organizations are reluctant to upset established routines. Given a natural distaste for the inconveniences of change, inertia prevails. Consequently, efforts at "reform" tend to be shallow and symbolic. Combating this tendency requires the discipline of Schumpeter's "creative destruction"—namely, the capacity of new enterprises to emerge, challenge, and displace the old. The entrepreneurial presumption is that the risks of inaction outweigh those of reinvention—even with all the attendant disappointments and confusion. As for whether this reinvention ought to occur inside or outside of school systems, or whether it ought to involve for-profits—these are open questions.

For instance, although our cities are filled with human talent and educational institutions like universities, churches, and museums, these "outsiders" are invited into schooling only in the most unusual circumstances. Entrepreneurship not only makes it easier for new talent and new approaches to emerge, but also for them to pursue cost efficiencies and achieve scale. Entrepreneurial enterprises do not inherit the cost structures, collective bargaining agreements, and organizational models of existing providers. This enables them to seek new efficiencies and, when successful, pressure the old-line providers to adjust accordingly. Given a hospitable political environment, entrepreneurial ventures can rapidly extend successful services to vast numbers of clients in multiple jurisdictions. In other words, in lieu of efforts to "reform" each of America's fifteen thousand K–12 school districts, a single entrepreneurial venture might suffice to dramatically improve instruction, teacher recruitment, data analysis, or school management across hundreds or thousands of districts.

Some critics worry that the entrepreneurial model is at odds with democratic values or the nature of public education. They suggest that democratic schooling requires all schools to be organized by uniform processes and staffed by public employees, and that allowing multiple education providers to proliferate and compete is at odds with the American tradition. Such fears are misplaced. As Paul Hill, director of the Center for the Reinvention of Public Education, has argued, "Defining democracy as centralized deliberation leading to uniform coercive results is surely perverse. When controlled by policy, public education is defined by the relative strength of interest groups and their ability to control how issues are resolved in election, legislatures, and courts." On the other hand, Hill explains, "A Jeffersonian version of democracy . . . expects arrangements to be temporary, and institutions to be re-thought fundamentally as times and needs changed."[10] It is the Jeffersonian vision that best fits the challenges posed by education. No uniform process, especially one shaped by the compromises of public policy, can prescribe models well-suited to the needs of a diverse student population or anticipate the demands of a changing society.

Other critics claim that the prominent participation of for-profit ventures in education is morally problematic. The logic behind this assertion has never quite been clear. For one thing, as various contributors to this volume note, we have a long tradition of for-profit ventures supplying pencils, paper, desks, copiers, computers, buses, facilities, professional training, and a host of other products and services to schools. For another, as previous scholars have noted, "It is almost a paradox of American culture that we applaud entrepreneurs who make their fortune with frivolous produces, such as the 'Pet Rock,' but chastise those who would make the same profit . . . trying to make the world a better place."[11]

FROM AN INDUSTRIAL TO AN ENTREPRENEURIAL SOCIETY

Why is educational entrepreneurship, largely ignored for so long, now deserving of our attention? For starters, there is nearly universal recognition that entrepreneurial energy has been the key to American success in recent decades. Observers of various stripes acknowledge that, whatever its failings, the astonishing performance and adaptability of the broader American economy has been fueled by a high rate of entrepreneurship, a welcoming regulatory climate, and the constant creation of new ventures.[12] During the 1950s and 1960s, the American economy was driven by large businesses and expanding government. Since the 1970s, however, the traditional giants have slashed tens of millions of jobs, and growth has been fueled by a raft of new ventures, great and small.

This technological and managerial entrepreneurial revolution has become an organizing principle of American public policy and social life. Surveying the terrain, former Harvard University president Larry Summers has suggested that "the world is experiencing the third biggest economic revolution of the past millennium alongside the Renaissance and the Industrial Revolution."[13] The American landscape has been swept by the entrepreneurial imperative, including once-stodgy sectors like banking, telecommunications, and air travel. Even popular culture is now awash with entrepreneurs.

In the 1970s, the popular face of commercial success was that of the veteran heads of America's longstanding corporate giants. In the 1990s, that changed. Today, a similar gallery of icons would feature those who built successful ventures from scratch—figures like Bill Gates, Michael Dell, Reed Hastings, Jeff Bezos, Phil Knight, and Steve Jobs. In the 1960s, the Bureau of Labor Statistics reported that the typical college graduate could expect to hold five jobs in the course of his or her lifetime. That same graduate today can expect to hold four jobs by the age of thirty. Today, talented, energetic college graduates no longer automatically queue up to start scaling the corporate ladder, and accomplished young professionals are far more likely to stray off the beaten path. In a world where old norms have frayed and expectations have changed, it has become increasingly difficult to justify the industrial-era organization of schooling.

Dramatic advances in technology, transportation, and data storage have created new possibilities for autonomy, decentralization, and customization. In 1991, when charter schools were first legislated, the Internet as we know it didn't exist. By 2004, the U.S. Census Bureau reported that 61 percent of households had Internet access. In 1993, the Census reported that just 23 percent of households owned a personal computer. By 2004, two-thirds did.[14] In 2004, there were 324 cable and satellite channels available in the United States—up from 60 in 1990.[15] The iPod didn't exist in 2000; by the end of 2005, more than 40 million had been sold.[16] In short, a technological revolution has swept through American homes, creating previously unimaginable communication, instructional, and educational opportunities.

Changes in public policy, including charter school legislation, the growth of alternative licensure programs for teachers and principals, and the supplemental services provisions in No Child Left Behind, have widened and lengthened the entrepreneur-friendly playing field. These measures have facilitated the entry of new providers and attracted individuals of an entrepreneurial bent. Meanwhile, more than one million children are now homeschooled, and as of 2002–03, more than 20 percent of public school districts had students taking online courses through their schools.[17] By mid-2005, twenty-one states had statewide online learning programs, and at least one virtual school (or cyberschool) operated in almost every state.[18] These developments have caused parents and educators to revisit assumptions about how, when, and where education should proceed.

Finally, the emergence of major new philanthropies like the Bill & Melinda Gates Foundation, The Walton Family Foundation, and The Broad Foundation has led to hundreds of millions of dollars in new giving annually, much of it used to support entrepreneurial ventures and entrepreneur-friendly public policy. Despite the limited amount of total K–12 philanthropy—estimated at between $1.5 and $2 billion of the more than $500 billion spent on K–12 public schooling in 2005—this money constitutes critical support for entrepreneurial enterprises.[19] Absent this support, Teach For America never would have been launched, and the KIPP Academies never would have grown from one school to forty-five.

Despite this raft of new possibilities, public school systems have been slow to adjust or to capitalize—especially in comparison to the educational entrepreneurs or more nimble knowledge-based sectors. Even in celebrated districts like Boston; San Diego; Long Beach, California; and Norfolk, Virginia, efforts to make use of new technologies, serve homeschooled populations, reinvent themselves through charter schooling, or reorient their cultures have been fragmentary and incremental at best.

Perhaps most significantly, the advent of meaningful accountability in education has made entrepreneurship feasible to an unprecedented degree. An entrepreneurial system requires that new providers be allowed to educate students, to hire in nontraditional ways, and to deliver education in nontraditional ways. For such arrangements to prove practicable, providers must be monitored and held responsible for the results of their handiwork. Before the spread of sophisticated testing and state accountability systems, the necessary systems simply did not exist. Today, however, the spread of these systems and continued refinements in them are increasingly providing the opportunity to relax regulations and focus on results.

SEARCHING FOR SOLUTIONS IS MESSY

Hesitant to contemplate "risky" alternatives when dealing with children, most education reformers—right and left—prefer solutions that minimize risk. This inspires calls for smaller classes, "best practices," more discipline, and other seemingly "risk-free" solutions. Even those who champion proposals like school vouchers or charter schooling typically tout the results of positive studies while minimizing the uncertainty of market-based solutions. The hostility toward entrepreneurial problem-solving in education is due in large part to an inadequate understanding of how progress unfolds in other sectors and how expertise, research, and data are used in other fields. While it's important to recognize that education is a unique enterprise in some ways, this should not become an excuse for incuriosity.

Entrepreneurship recognizes that progress is messy, in large part because workable and optimal solutions change over time. What worked in 1950 may not prove as effective in 2000. By definition, new solutions are going to be untested and, in almost every case, they are going to emerge from trial and error. Clay Christensen, coauthor of *The Innovator's Solution*, has reported that in over 90 percent of all successful new businesses, the strategy that the founders had deliberately adopted was not the strategy that led to success.[20] Ultimately, to embrace entrepreneurship is to reject the notion that we can somehow anticipate the future and then race there in a predictable or orderly fashion. One problem is that our imaginations are pretty much limited to what we've seen and what has already been tried. Chris Whittle, founder of the Edison Schools, has observed, "There was a time in aviation when the propeller was the only way to move a plane forward. Designers could not envision getting beyond a certain speed with a prop. Then came jet engines, and the speed of airplanes doubled overnight and eventually tripled."[21] The case for entrepreneurship rests on an inherent skepticism regarding the power of human foresight or consensus. There's much reason to believe that this stance is warranted.

Examples of our limited ability to anticipate or gauge the utility of new advances are legion. In 1861, German inventor Philip Reis invented a primitive version of the telephone—but gave up when no one expressed interest and he couldn't conceive of any viable commercial applications. Fifteen years later, American inventor Alexander Graham Bell had more luck solving the same problem. In 1902, Wilbur and Orville Wright were asked how long it would be before someone would first build a working airplane; they said probably twenty years. The very next year, in 1903, they were the first to fly.[22]

The Edsel may be the most famous commercial flop of the twentieth century. What many forget is that when it was first unveiled by the Ford Motor Company, the Edsel was the most carefully designed car in American automotive history. Its massive failure, despite extensive research, planning, and design, led Ford to rethink its assumptions and market segmentation. The unforeseen result of this rethinking was the Ford Mustang—one of the most successful cars of the twentieth century.

If it's tough to anticipate which inventions will prove useful, when advances will occur, or what products will be popular, it may be even harder to predict which firms will succeed. In the 1880s, about one thousand electric-appliance companies existed in the industrial world. By 1914, just twenty-five still existed. In 1910, there were about two hundred U.S. firms producing automobiles. By 1960, just four of these firms were left standing; the rest had gone under, been acquired, or otherwise fallen by the wayside. There was not a soul on earth who could have predicted in 1910 which four automakers would be standing fifty years later. These aren't isolated phenomena; just ask anyone who failed to predict in 1998 that eBay, Google, and Amazon would become corporate giants while hundreds of competitors would fold.

A telling example is provided by onetime computer industry leader Univac, which, based on expert analysis, predicted in 1950 that one thousand computers would be sold worldwide by the year 2000. Of course, the analysts had in mind the hulking, room-sized machines of their day. No one in the industry could foresee a day when personal computers, laptops, or handhelds would be casually sold at retail outlets. The notion that Michael Dell would one day revolutionize the way we buy and use computers by selling them out of his University of Texas dorm room seemed ridiculous—including to professors who passed up the invitation to invest—right up until he did.

It simply isn't possible to eliminate the risk implicit in entrepreneurial ventures. In fact, it's not possible to eliminate uncertainty in mature organizations, except at the cost of stagnation. Market and industry research firm BizMiner reports that 25 percent of all U.S. cookie and cracker makers that were in business in 2002 were out of business by 2004. Among florists, 24 percent of those operating in 2002 had failed by 2004. Among men's clothing start-ups, 50 percent of the firms that started in 2002 no longer existed in 2004.[23] In other words, even in relatively simple businesses where the production techniques are well understood, operators have a weak track record of knowing just how to ensure success.

If industries focused on producing straightforward products face such challenges, it should come as no surprise that matters get even more difficult when it comes to knowledge-based sectors that seek to inform, entertain, or educate a diverse clientele. When dealing with the special challenges of educating a diverse student population, things get more complicated still. This is hardly a novel insight. Peter Drucker observed two decades ago that knowledge-based innovation is especially tricky, noting that "even when it is based on meticulous analysis, endowed with clear focus, and conscientiously managed, knowledge-based innovation still suffers from unique risks and, worse, an innate unpredictability."[24] Policymakers and advocates have found it much easier to take refuge behind high ideals and airy aspirations than to face up to this difficult truth. It's time for a more realistic conversation. After all, if we consider other sectors driven by knowledge and information, we see massive uncertainty.

Take the book publishing industry. Today, tens of thousands of new books are published in the United States every year, and most of them lose money. As much as two-thirds of book sales are controlled by five publishers, but 78 percent of book *titles* are published by everyone else—by all of the little guys.[25] This is in large part because the dominant firms, with all of their resources and market research, have every incentive to play it safe and stick with formulas that have worked thus far. The result is that they reject a lot of books that, if the expert consensus had its way, would never see the light of day. One such example, passed on by numerous publishing houses, was *Harry Potter and the Sorcerer's Stone*, a children's book that you may have come across.

This isn't unusual. Consider the television or movie industries, other sectors where experts backed by enormous resources, equipped with the most sophisticated audience research available, and operating in an immensely competitive environment struggle to predict what will entertain or engage a target population. How do they fare? In a word, poorly. Members of the

Motion Picture Association of America (MPAA) spent an average of $98 million per movie in 2004; of that total, more than $30 million went to researching, planning, and executing multimedia marketing campaigns. Given those costs, it's not surprising that movie studios invest enormous sums in selecting stories, rewriting screenplays, studying audience preferences, and devising marketing strategies. How consistently do these efforts pay off? In 2004, there were a total of 475 new theatrical films released in the United States— 200 of them released by MPAA members. Despite an average investment of $98 million per MPAA film, just 20 of the 475 earned $110 million at the box office.[26] Even with all their expertise and resources, major Hollywood studios have trouble anticipating what Americans want to see 90 percent of the time. The fallibility of the major Hollywood studios is made clear by the megahits that have been rejected by major producers, frequently by several of them. The list includes such modestly successful films as *Star Wars*, *The Lord of the Rings*, *The Matrix*, *Back to the Future*, *The Passion of the Christ*, and *Dances with Wolves*.

The television industry is no different. Each year, the major television networks (ABC, CBS, NBC, and Fox) evaluate thousands of concepts for new series and purchase approximately six hundred pilot scripts. About 20 percent of those proposed scripts are turned into sample episodes; about one-third of these pilot episodes eventually make it to the air.[27] And of the forty or so that ever make it to the airwaves, few actually survive beyond one season. For instance, among the fifty-two primetime pilots that aired on U.S. syndicated and cable networks in 2004–05, just seventeen were still on the air in early 2006.[28] The high rate of failure isn't for lack of effort; the cost of developing a new television show is enormous. Networks spend hundreds of millions of dollars to acquire and produce their primetime schedules, including spending on underdeveloped concepts, unscripted ideas, unproduced scripts, and rejected pilots.[29] Nonetheless, for all their extraordinary efforts to measure and anticipate audience tastes, major networks were pleasantly surprised by the performance of "breakout" shows including *American Idol*, *Friends*, *Seinfeld*, *Desperate Housewives*, *The X-Files*, and *Lost* and by the failure of an armful of "can't miss" propositions. In the end, even when bolstered by experience and research, the predictive power of expertise is uneven.

Obviously, the publishing, movie, and television industries differ from schooling in important ways. I do not mean to suggest that they are similar or similarly important ventures. I do, however, want to make clear that expertise, resources, and research are no guarantee of success when it comes to predicting what will connect with, stimulate, or engage people. As Robert Laughlin, a 1998 Nobel Prize winner in physics, has admonished, "The search for new things always looks like a lost cause until one makes a discovery. If it were obvious what was there, one would not have to look for it." He warns, "The world is filled with sophisticated regularities and causal relationships that can be quantified. . . . But the discovery of these relationships is unpredictable and certainly not anticipated by scientific experts."[30] If giants in other sectors must rely on trial and error rather than prescience for their triumphs, the implications for education may be worth contemplating.

CREATING AN ENTREPRENEURIAL ENVIRONMENT

At the most prosaic level, entrepreneurship requires luring a lot of smart, motivated people to work under pressure, solve problems in a variety of ways, and be held accountable for their demonstrated results. Crucially, these individuals cannot be free-floating ions in indifferent bureaucracies, but require supportive and nimble organizations where their successes are captured, put faithfully into practice, and then replicated and expanded.

A persistent problem in education is that even policymakers and reformers heralded for their entrepreneurial bent are more enamored of yesterday's entrepreneurial successes than with nurturing tomorrow's entrepreneurs. More than a few "cutting-edge" superintendents have dealt with school reinvention by identifying some seemingly successful models and saying, "I want more of those in my district." That's laudable, of course, and it's a critical component of how entrepreneurial successes spread. However, such an approach plants no seeds. This kind of betting on the winners has its place, but it should not be confused with fostering an entrepreneurial climate.

Chris Whittle has observed that this tendency to bet on winners means that even those who fancy themselves open to entrepreneurship are often more interested in harvesting the best of "yesterday's" practices than fostering tomorrow's answers. This can impede the search for new, better solutions. Whittle has noted, "I've often said that Edison's schools are the 'best of the old world' in schools. We've successfully brought together under one school roof many of the best design elements out there. . . . But we have yet to bring about our most important innovation: a school design that provides a highly unusual student and teacher experience and radically superior results. We've been largely incremental and quantitative in our departures."[31] Similar points might be made about other widely hailed programs. While the KIPP Academies have accumulated an impressive track record and national recognition, those responsible for the program are the first to acknowledge that their greatest triumph is proficiently executing a traditional model of schooling. They have succeeded by relentlessly focusing on results, recruiting talented educators, building a strong culture, and forging an ethic of commitment and hard work—rather than devising a fundamentally more productive or efficient model of schooling. Programs such as KIPP are admirable entrepreneurial ventures, but ought to be regarded as the first glimmerings of what an entrepreneurial environment makes possible—rather than the triumph or culmination of that process.

Systematic investment in new, promising, entrepreneurial efforts is simply not part of the culture of American schooling. In the larger U.S. economy, for instance, it's estimated that more than one thousand new business ventures are born every hour of every working day.[32] Several thousand U.S. firms receive venture capital funding each year. The National Venture Capital Association reports that in 2005, 182 venture capital funds attracted $25.2 billion in new investment.[33] That's a lot of new ideas, a lot of energy, and a lot of resources. In the whole of the U.S. economy, 11 percent of jobs involve either starting or managing new businesses. Even in France, hardly a hotbed of entrepreneurship, the ratio is over 5 percent. In Slovenia, the rate is 2.5 percent. What's the comparable figure in the education sector? Well, the figure is so small that analysts tend to combine education and social services. The combined total: approximately 0 percent.[34]

A vital component of entrepreneurship is the investment in new knowledge. Health care and education are generally regarded as the two great domestic challenges confronting federal policymakers. In health services, the federal government spent $28 billion in 2005 to fund research and development through the National Institutes of Health (NIH). In the case of education, for the infant Institute of Education Sciences, the comparable 2005 investment was about $530 million. In the private sector, companies invest time and resources in research and development in order to cultivate new products. For instance, 3M has long had a "15 percent rule," under which company scientists are expected to devote 15 percent of their time to invention. In a public school district, it's hard for school officials to contemplate even a "1 percent rule," given enormous pressure from constituents and elected officials to deliver services in the here and now.

ENTREPRENEURSHIP IS NOT A QUESTION OF SCHOOL CHOICE

One common mistake is to conflate entrepreneurship with charter schooling or school vouchers. It may be easy to blithely assume that those who support school vouchers or charter schooling are in favor of markets and entrepreneurship, and that endorsing entrepreneurship can be reduced to supporting choice-based reform. But such thinking involves a fundamental misunderstanding of entrepreneurship. Ultimately, it isn't about "choices" so much as Darwinian selection and the process of creative destruction. While Belgium, for instance, has one of the most expansive choice-based systems of schooling in the world, few observers would suggest that Belgium is a hotbed of market forces or educational entrepreneurship. In fact, those who lived in Moscow in 1975 could choose among scores of grocery stores. Not many scholars or consumers would argue that this yielded a vibrant or entrepreneurial market-place for consumer goods. Why? Entrepreneurship is only tangentially con-cerned with giving consumers more choices—it's ultimately about unchain-ing producers. Entrepreneurship is focused on the supply side. It requires choices to be coupled with opportunities for entrepreneurs to enter the field, obtain resources, recruit talent, try new approaches, develop new products, compete fairly, and benefit from their successes. Choice fosters entrepreneur-ship *only* to the extent that it promotes these opportunities.

For instance, as noted earlier, while both France and the United States are market-based economies, they vary enormously in the incidence of entre-preneurial activity. Of the twenty-five largest firms in France in 2005, not a single one had been founded since 1965. In other words, every single one of France's leading firms today was already around forty years ago.[35] The Amer-ican picture is radically different. Of the nation's twenty-five biggest firms in 2005, three-quarters didn't exist in 1965. In fact, the pace of change in America has accelerated in recent decades. In 1960, if an American company was in the top fifth of its industry, there was a less than 5 percent chance it would fall from its position by 1965. In 1980, there was a 10 percent chance it would fall within five years. By 1998, there was a one-in-four chance that it would fall out of its spot during the next five years.[36]

One reason to be cautious about putting excessive faith in choice alone as an entrepreneurial engine is that the ability of consumers to guide the devel-opment of new products and services is limited by their experience. For all the useful signals it can convey, consumer choice historically has to be an uncertain spur for fundamental reinvention. Devising and introducing such innovations requires the techniques of "empathic design"—involving efforts to gather, analyze, and apply information gleaned from field observation— and entrepreneurs with the skills and resources to make it work. When first introduced, radio technology was primarily used for Morse code and limited voice communication. It wasn't until David Sarnoff's 1915 suggestion that it could be employed to broadcast news, music, and baseball games that the possibilities of the new technology were really exploited. Providers driven entirely by current consumer demand have little opportunity to anticipate unrealized possibilities. This is why smaller, newer ventures with less to lose are often the best situated to seek out new paths and pioneer untested ideas. As business scholars Dorothy Leonard and Jeffrey Rayport have explained, "No one asked for broadcasting because they didn't know it was feasible."[37] The lack of entrepreneurial vigor that characterizes private K–12 schooling should signal that choice is only a piece of a larger puzzle.

Choice-based arrangements are neither necessary nor sufficient to open the door to educational entrepreneurship. They aren't sufficient because, as several authors explain in the chapters to come, removing formal barriers to new schools is only one step toward nurturing entrepreneurial activity. Choice isn't absolutely necessary because, at least in theory, a vibrant entrepreneurial sector can deliver educational services, tools, and products in the absence of school choice. For instance, tutoring firms might compete to contract with traditional public schools, or an array of education management firms might pursue contracts with traditional schools or districts. In the final analysis, however, while choice-based reform may not be strictly necessary for an entrepreneurial environment, as a practical matter, it has proven essential.

LAYOUT OF THE VOLUME

From here, the volume will proceed in five sections. The first chapters examine the question of just what educational entrepreneurship is and who these people are. In chapter 1, Kim Smith, executive chairman of the NewSchools Venture Fund, and her colleague Julie Landry Petersen, provide an introduction to who education entrepreneurs are, the world they inhabit, and the critical resources they need. Smith and Petersen view education entrepreneurs as visionary thinkers engaged in creating for-profit or nonprofit organizations designed to have a large-scale impact. Smith and Petersen argue that these entrepreneurs redefine our sense of what is possible in public education. In chapter 2, University of Colorado professor Paul Teske, author of *Public Entrepreneurs*, and his colleague Aimee Williamson discuss the practice of educational entrepreneurship in more depth and provide illustrative cases of five prominent educational entrepreneurs. They suggest that many barriers make educational entrepreneurship difficult, but that these barriers may be beginning to weaken.

The next three chapters survey the landscape of educational entrepreneurship. In chapter 3, Drew University political scientist Patrick McGuinn explains that the ground rules for entrepreneurs are established by public policy—by laws, regulations, and government programs. Unfortunately, he notes, the impact of such policy changes on entrepreneurial activity has received little explicit attention. McGuinn sketches the key changes in the policy landscape that have nurtured entrepreneurship. He focuses on charter school laws, reforms to teacher and principal licensure, and the supplemental services provision of No Child Left Behind, before concluding with a discussion of the significance of No Child Left Behind–style accountability.

In chapter 4, Eduventures vice president Adam Newman explains that while the concept of an education industry may be relatively new, the practice of running a revenue-generating education business is not. As long as students have needed classroom supplies and instructional materials, organizations have existed to deliver those products and services. Focusing on for-profit educational entrepreneurship, Newman offers a framework for understanding the K–12 and postsecondary sectors. He closes by examining the private investment capital secured by entrepreneurs and companies in recent years and considering the role of mergers and acquisitions in transforming the market landscape. In chapter 5, Alex Molnar, director of the Education Policy Studies Laboratory at Arizona State University, looks in more depth at the for-profit firms that have proliferated in the past decade. Molnar takes a dim view of their track record, arguing that there is little evidence these ventures have yielded successful business models or improved academic performance.

Chapters 6 and 7 look at entrepreneurs inside and outside of traditional public school districts. In chapter 6, Joe Williams, author of *Cheating Our Kids*, considers the nature of "intrapreneurship" in school districts like New York City, Milwaukee, and San Diego. Williams depicts six types of "inside" entrepreneurs, arguing that they are often identifiable by the degrees to which they are comfortable breaking the rules and the extent to which their efforts may have systemic implications. In chapter 7, Villanova University's Robert Maranto and April Gresham Maranto profile a number of entrepreneurial ventures outside of traditional school districts. Noting that these enterprises must combine centralized values with decentralized management, they find a compelling paradox: the entrepreneurial models that can expand most rapidly are the ones that offer the most limited prospects for success. Those most capable of achieving breakthroughs can expand only gradually and exert only limited influence on traditional public schools. They conclude that the greatest gains from these ventures will take decades rather than years.

Chapters 8 and 9 explore the question of why educational entrepreneurship is so difficult. In chapter 8, Henry Levin, a professor at Columbia University Teachers College, suggests that it is not due to a lack of ideas or will on the part of would-be change agents, but to intrinsic features of the American educational system. These include cost structures, the risk aversion of school leaders, parental preferences, and institutional conservatism rooted in the need of schools to depend upon other organizations for resources. As a closing caution, Levin reminds us that resistance to change can be a valuable safeguard against poor policies and bad ideas.

In chapter 9, Steven Wilson, former CEO of Advantage Schools and author of *Learning on the Job: When Business Takes on Public Schools*, considers the relative success of entrepreneurial initiative in higher education and preK. He then asks why it has so far proved a disappointment in K–12. Focusing on the illustrative case of education management organizations, he asserts that the deeply embedded norms of the public school culture impair the ability of entrepreneurs to deliver improved academic results or to operate profitably. Wilson calls for entrepreneurs to boldly challenge norms regarding localism, teacher quality, class size, and pedagogy that hinder their ability to succeed.

In the final chapters, veteran scholars take contrasting views of the significance and the promise of today's entrepreneurs. In chapter 10, John Chubb, chief education officer of the Edison Schools, considers what the new entrepreneurship could mean for education—and what it will take to foster a truly entrepreneurial environment. Focusing on the case of charter schooling, Chubb argues that political compromises have produced a cottage industry, with thousands of small schools struggling alone and therefore unable to deliver meaningful benefits in efficiency or performance. Chubb recommends that charter policy be made more entrepreneur-friendly by relaxing restrictions on the operations of for-profit operators and freeing operations to grow in scale, while establishing strict expectations for performance accountability.

In chapter 11, Stanford University professor Larry Cuban examines today's entrepreneurs with a historian's eye and comes away unimpressed. Looking back to the progressive reformers of the early twentieth century, he finds them to be kindred spirits of today's entrepreneurs. Cuban argues that both generations brought notable changes to U.S. public school goals, governance, organization, and curriculum, but did little to substantially or permanently alter classroom regularities or the academic achievement of low-income students. Cuban further suggests that current entrepreneurial efforts to radically change the governance and preparation of school leaders have ultimately served to preserve organizational structures and school practices in urban schools.

Ultimately, as I suggest in the concluding chapter, the decision to embrace educational entrepreneurship requires an informed decision to rethink familiar policies and practices. For that reason, entrepreneurship provides a useful lens for thinking about the rules and routines that govern teacher or administrator licensure, teacher and principal compensation, financing systems, accountability, and the rest of the architecture of public schooling. In the end, serious consideration of educational entrepreneurship entails asking, In the twenty-first century, is it possible to educate children in radically more effective ways? If so, can we identify and adopt those methods using our longstanding structures and systems? If familiar arrangements do not serve, who are the pioneers willing to stumble forward in the dark to find better answers, and how willing are we to provide the opportunities, tools, and support they may need?

CHAPTER 1

What Is Educational Entrepreneurship?

Kim Smith and Julie Landry Petersen

When Fred Smith created Federal Express in 1971, few thought it was possible to ship a package overnight without paying a fortune. Smith had a vision for an express delivery service that would operate differently than the current postal system, and would also light a competitive fire under the sluggish U.S. Postal Service. Nearly everyone thought what he wanted to do was impossible—even the professor who gave him a C on the paper he wrote outlining the concept as an undergraduate at Yale University, allegedly noting, "The concept is interesting and well formed, but . . . the idea must be feasible." Federal Express went on to become a successful shipping company that changed customer expectations by demonstrating that overnight delivery was possible. And the Postal Service responded by introducing similar services much more quickly than they would otherwise have done.

Fred Smith is a quintessential entrepreneur: He had a vision for a new approach to solving a problem and created a new organization to carry out that vision. In doing so, he redefined our sense of what is possible and changed the dynamics of an entire industry. This chapter will focus on education entrepreneurs who share many of these characteristics but who do so in the hope of catalyzing massive improvement in K–12 public education. Based on more than fifteen years of experience with these education entrepreneurs, we will share our perspective on the role, the potential to have an impact, and the unique needs of education entrepreneurs. We will define education entrepreneurs as visionary thinkers who create new for-profit or nonprofit organizations from scratch that redefine our sense of what is possible. These organizations stand separate and independent from existing institutions like public school districts and teacher colleges; as such, they and the entrepreneurs who start them have the potential to spark more rapid, dramatic change than might otherwise be created by status quo organizations.

Sustainable transformation of public education will also require the work of other important change agents—including "intrapreneurs," who create new entrepreneurial approaches *within* a system. However, this chapter will focus exclusively on education entrepreneurs who operate *outside* the system because of the unique nature of the resources and support they need to be successful in this endeavor. Whether they are creating new services, schools, or tools, education entrepreneurs—particularly those who seek to have a major impact on the system itself—are worthy of our consideration because they are motivated by a novel vision for how public education could be a different and better system and they create new organizations to carry out that vision. If they receive the appropriate resources, education entrepreneurs may very well lead the public education system toward vastly improved outcomes.

WHAT IS AN EDUCATION ENTREPRENEUR?

The reasonable man adapts himself to the world; the unreasonable one persists in trying to adapt the world to himself. Therefore, all progress depends on the unreasonable man.
—George Bernard Shaw[1]

Historically, much of the scholarship on entrepreneurs blurs the distinction between innovators and entrepreneurs, who share many characteristics. For the purposes of this chapter, we will define education entrepreneurs quite narrowly as a rare breed of innovator whose characteristics and activities may lead to the transformation—not merely the slight improvement—of the public education system. This definition is grounded in author Kim Smith's experience as an entrepreneur and funder in the nonprofit and for-profit sectors for the past fifteen years. We believe it is important to understand (1) the qualities that define entrepreneurs in general, (2) those that distinguish social entrepreneurs, and (3) those that make social entrepreneurs such a potentially powerful force within public education today.

Entrepreneurs
In general, it is important to understand that entrepreneurs have a vision for a better way of doing things, thinking beyond the constraints of current rules and resources. Perhaps more importantly, they have the passion and sense of

urgency that literally compels them to take the risks necessary to realize that vision. They create new organizations to make the changes they want to see in the world—and by doing so, they inspire others to follow.

Be visionary thinkers. Entrepreneurs' most unique characteristic is that they are able to think beyond the current rules and resources to see a different way of working. One of the classic entrepreneurship textbooks, *New Business Ventures and the Entrepreneur*, points out that while most leaders plan around the resources that are currently available, entrepreneurs are driven by their perception of opportunity, irrespective of resources.[2] As such, in the words of successful Silicon Valley venture capitalist John Doerr, "entrepreneurs do *more* than anyone thinks possible with *less* than anyone thinks possible." Where many would ask *"Can* this be done?" entrepreneurs are hardwired to ask instead *"How* can this be done?" As a consequence, entrepreneurs have the power to fundamentally redefine our sense of what is possible.

Start new organizations. Good entrepreneurs are both *mavericks* and *institution-builders*, as technology entrepreneur and former president of the California state board of education Reed Hastings has noted. For entrepreneurs, innovative ideas simply aren't enough: Their sense of urgency and drive to achieve leads them to take action by creating new organizations that will make their vision a reality. Here, our definition differs from that offered by other chapters in this volume. Although "intrapreneurs"—who have a vision for changing an organization from the inside—can also be incredibly important change agents, they are different from entrepreneurs. The single greatest distinction between them seems to be their tolerance for risk and for frustration. Intrapreneurs tend to have a lower risk profile but a higher tolerance for the frustration caused by trying to create change within a status quo organization. In contrast, entrepreneurs have a lower tolerance for this sort of frustration and a higher tolerance for risk, leading them to strike out on their own.

Believe they can change the way things are done. Psychologist Martin Seligman has found that certain people have developed "learned optimism," in which they believe successes are the result of their own hard work while seeing setbacks as external and temporary hurdles they need to overcome.[3] This trait often goes hand in hand with an "internal locus of control," or belief that one can control his or her own fate, rather than feeling controlled by circumstance. Taken together, these characteristics allow entrepreneurs to face the potential failure inherent in creating a new organization by focusing on likely success and overcoming all hurdles that stand in the way.

Social Entrepreneurs

Within the realm of entrepreneurship, the social entrepreneur has particular potential for transforming public education. The social entrepreneur's vision is not merely to create something new in the pursuit of fame or fortune, but rather to do so in the quest to make the world a better place. These entrepreneurs may create social-purpose ventures through either a for-profit or nonprofit structure, but having a positive impact on society is a top priority.

A leading thinker on social entrepreneurs, professor Greg Dees of Duke University's Fuqua School of Business, notes that social entrepreneurs adopt a mission to create and sustain social value (not just private value), and that they exhibit heightened accountability to the constituencies served and for the outcomes created.[4] The social entrepreneurs in education under consideration in this chapter have great potential to have an impact today because they are focused on making a significant difference on outcomes of the K–12 system *as a whole,* particularly for those students and communities who are currently underserved, rather than just for a limited set of students.

Social entrepreneurs in education are also highly focused on outcomes. Although their organizations sit "outside" the public education system, education entrepreneurs are still accountable to it; they may need to attract students to a new public charter school, entice principal candidates to apply for a new preparation program, or deliver improved outcomes in order to maintain a district as a customer. As such, they have a customer-focused orientation and a consistent focus on outcomes, critical factors that allow them to compete with existing providers for attention, funds, and sales.

Social Entrepreneurs in Education

Within education, social entrepreneurs create many different types of organizations that seek to have a positive impact on the broader system. Some do this by creating a new supply of public schools and school systems. For example, across the country a number of nonprofit charter management organizations have cropped up to address the diverse needs of underserved urban communities by creating new centrally managed networks of small public charter schools. Other education entrepreneurs instead create organizations that seek to enhance the capacity of the existing public school system. These include developers of alternative preparation or support programs for teachers and leaders, as well as creators of products and services that help teachers and leaders with instruction, administration, and management.

The power of these entrepreneurs in education is not only as developers of alternative sources of teachers, leaders, schools, and tools, but also as change agents whose efforts spur change in the larger system. As Harvard Business

School professor Clay Christensen has found in his studies of business, "an organization cannot disrupt itself." In other words, organizations charged with serving a current customer base can only "sustain" and take change so far, while new "disruptive" innovations are the ones that move industries forward by quantum leaps.[5] This explains why, despite the best of intentions, educators and policymakers have found it impossible to achieve better outcomes within a bureaucratic structure designed more than a century ago.

At this critical point in public education, entrepreneurs have three crucial roles:

As change agents. Entrepreneurs can demonstrate what is possible when resources are used differently and point the way toward how policy and practice might be changed in light of what they accomplish. As such, their work has a direct impact, as well as a "catalytic impact" that reverberates throughout the system. For example, Teach For America has directly affected the lives of more than a million students and of the fourteen thousand corps members it has trained to serve as teachers in high-need schools. But its success has also reshaped broader policy conversations around the recruitment and preparation of teachers for high-need urban and rural settings. Another way to consider this is as "co-opetition"—a combination of competition and cooperation in which entrepreneurs create additional capacity for school systems (cooperation) while also applying pressure for change within the system (competition).

As venues for new skill sets and mindsets. The organizations that entrepreneurs create often have the kind of culture that draws and retains achievement-oriented employees who might not otherwise be involved in the more bureaucratic public education system. In exchange for a merit-based culture where they can see significant results from their efforts, these people are willing to give up the security of seniority-based progression within the traditional school system. "I have all the agility in the world—and I have nobody to blame but myself if I don't succeed," says Larry Rosenstock, a former urban public school principal turned entrepreneur who founded High Tech High Learning, a nonprofit charter school management organization based in San Diego.

As developers of learning laboratories where experimentation and ongoing learning are encouraged. As problem-solvers, entrepreneurs are constant learners who regularly review progress and correct course. Since this ongoing learning process is exactly what we are asking our public schools to embrace today, entrepreneurial organizations can demonstrate how this new dynamic might work in a school system. For example, entrepreneurs that create national or regional systems of charter schools are both increasing the supply of high-quality public schools and learning important lessons about designing aligned systems of schools as they create them from scratch.

WHAT CREATES OPPORTUNITY FOR EDUCATION ENTREPRENEURS?

The individual entrepreneur is a person who perceives opportunity,
finds the pursuit of opportunity desirable in the context of his or her life
situation, and believes that success is possible.
                              —Howard H. Stevenson and William A. Sahlman[6]

Entrepreneurs can be important change agents for large, complex systems that need dramatic improvement. But what specifically opens the door for entrepreneurs to make this difference? In general, something changes suddenly or slowly over time, requiring new problem-solving approaches. In most cases, many changes are happening simultaneously, creating a swirling eddy of both challenges and opportunities for entrepreneurs. Here, we attempt to detail the different types of change so that we can better understand what resources education entrepreneurs need.

Change in Expectations

The current system of K–12 public schooling was created in a social and economic context that was entirely different from our current one. Compulsory public education arose in the early 1900s as a way of ensuring that the massive influx of immigrants would be good American citizens and productive workers in the country's emerging industrial economy. At the time, the national population was less than seventy-five million people, with only a small portion of school-aged children attending school and an even smaller fraction of those completing high school or college.[7] The economy was driven by agriculture and industry, which offered the opportunity for a variety of skill levels to earn a living wage, often without a formal education.

On every front, this picture has changed dramatically. The national population has tripled to nearly three hundred million, with forty-eight million students in public schools.[8] Prompted by the triumphs of the civil rights movement, we expect more of our public schools today: it is no longer sufficient for a small percentage of children to be prepared for success in college. Our nation's postindustrial and increasingly global economy is now driven by knowledge and by higher-order skills like symbolic reasoning, analysis, and communication.

In other words, the public's expectations of the system have ballooned, such that public schools are now expected to serve all children equally and well. This change in expectations demands innovative new approaches. Many expect that nearly all high school students should graduate ready to attend college, for example, which would be more than triple the current rate of 30 percent.[9] But it's not likely that we have—or should have—the political will to triple spending in order to triple effectiveness, notes Kevin Hall, a former entrepreneur who is now at The Broad Foundation. "The delivery system simply has to change to be more productive," says Hall. "Entrepreneurs can either access new resources or put resources together in different ways to get to different outcomes." In other words, this enormous challenge has created opportunities for entrepreneurs to find more efficient, effective ways of ensuring that all students receive a high-quality public education.

Change in Market Structure

Because public education is a public-sector institution charged with serving the public good, public policy is the most common tool for changing its structure. Whether at the federal, state, or local level, public policy shifts can create entrepreneurial opportunity by requiring the people within a system to think differently, and also by creating new "turf" to which nobody has yet laid claim.

One of the most significant policy shifts over the last several decades has been the movement toward standards and accountability. As the expectations for public schools have increased, so have the mechanisms for specifying what students should know and be able to do (in the form of state standards), measuring whether they reach those standards (assessment), and, more recently, imposing sanctions on schools and school systems that fail to improve student outcomes (accountability).

Accountability policies have introduced a number of opportunities—some might say "pain points"—that entrepreneurs can address. For example, the No Child Left Behind Act (NCLB) has created opportunities for entrepreneurs to provide supplemental education services for students whose schools have not achieved adequate yearly progress (AYP) for three years in a row. At the state level, policies that mandate the turnaround of chronically failing schools have created demand for additional capacity to manage these schools. In Philadelphia, state-level accountability has led to a change in the structure of the entire school system to support a portfolio of entrepreneurs. Since the state took over the district in 2001, its School Reform Commission has contracted with a variety of entrepreneurial education providers to manage the city's lowest-performing schools.

Because the standards and accountability movements have begun to define desired learning outcomes and freed up the means for getting there, policymakers have created opportunities for entrepreneurs to develop new approaches to schooling. State charter school laws allow individuals and groups to create new public schools that are supported with public dollars but managed independently. By specifying the expected school performance in the school's "charter," these policies encourage entrepreneurship by allowing charter school operators to use their own approach to achieve those goals. These policies have spawned an entire subindustry of nearly 3,500 charter schools in forty states and the District of Columbia, serving nearly one million students.[10] The first wave consisted largely of individual charter schools, but these have been joined by a diverse array of entrepreneurs who seek to build systems of multiple charter schools.

Policies that specify outcomes but allow different approaches have also enabled entrepreneurs to create alternative programs for teacher certification and school leader licensure. One of the best-known examples of entrepreneurial innovation in this area is Teach For America, founded in 1989 by Wendy Kopp to recruit and prepare bright college graduates for two years of teaching in high-need classrooms. Because alternative credentialing regulations allowed for different approaches to preparation, Teach For America was able to develop innovative processes to prepare teachers—including stringent criteria for candidate selection and training curriculum targeted at teachers who will serve in low-income areas. More recently, charter school systems like High Tech High and KIPP have begun developing their own residency-based models. And New Leaders for New Schools has taken advantage of this opportunity to develop a program for preparing urban principals in major cities across the country.

Taken together, public policies like those described above have pushed public education in a new direction. Although most of our public education systems were designed to focus on *inputs* (dollars, hours, students served) and management processes evolved accordingly, the emphasis of these recent policies is now on *results* (skills achieved, content mastered, college attainment). This shift creates enormous opportunities for entrepreneurs to provide the requisite people, tools, and practices.

Change in Availability of Resources

Public policy can create new opportunities for entrepreneurs by changing the structure of the market. It can also create opportunity by reallocating resources—which usually means an increase or decrease in dollars available and who can access them. Recent examples include federal start-up grants that encourage the development of new charter schools and funds allocated for paying supplemental education service providers to tutor eligible students under NCLB.

Other forces can also constrain or expand the resources available in public education. In the late 1990s, there was a substantial increase in the dollars invested via "venture capital," in which private investment firms pool monies in support of early-stage companies in exchange for a stake in their anticipated future success. Encouraged by the success of technology businesses on the stock market, the amount of money invested by venture capitalists increased from $2.8 billion in 1990 to more than $100 billion in 2000.[11] Though much of this capital was invested in general technology infrastructure and Internet-based businesses, a great deal of new capital was available to education entrepreneurs, to the tune of $2.9 billion in 2000 (including investments in K–12, higher education, and corporate training).[12] Since 2000, however, the venture capital market has cooled in general and in education specifically, limiting the amount of private funding available to for-profit education entrepreneurs.

The spigots of philanthropic capital also open up and close off opportunities. Newer education foundations such as The Broad Foundation, the Pisces Foundation, and The Walton Family Foundation have shown a willingness to invest in new entrepreneurial education organizations. The Bill & Melinda Gates Foundation has invested more than $2 billion in transforming high schools since 2000, creating a market for entrepreneurs to create new public charter schools, develop new district schools, and break down large existing high schools into small schools.

Sometimes, entrepreneurs themselves push the structure of the market and its corresponding resources in new directions. One of the best examples here is the work of New American Schools (NAS), founded in 1992 by a former Xerox executive to encourage the development of new whole-school reform models. With more than $140 million in funding from the private sector, NAS seeded dozens of diverse new school models, including Expeditionary Learning Outward Bound and America's Choice. The effort was further leveraged in 1997 by the establishment of federal Comprehensive School Reform legislation that earmarked hundreds of millions of dollars per year to such programs. As such, New American Schools is a good example of the entrepreneurial change process: Private experiments on organizing and using resources differently lead to public recognition and support, and a shift in the way things are done with public funds (see figure 1). Ideally, public policy would include repetitions of this cycle, with new entrepreneurial experiments and lessons continuing to inform policy over time.

FIGURE 1   How Entrepreneurs Catalyze Systemwide Change

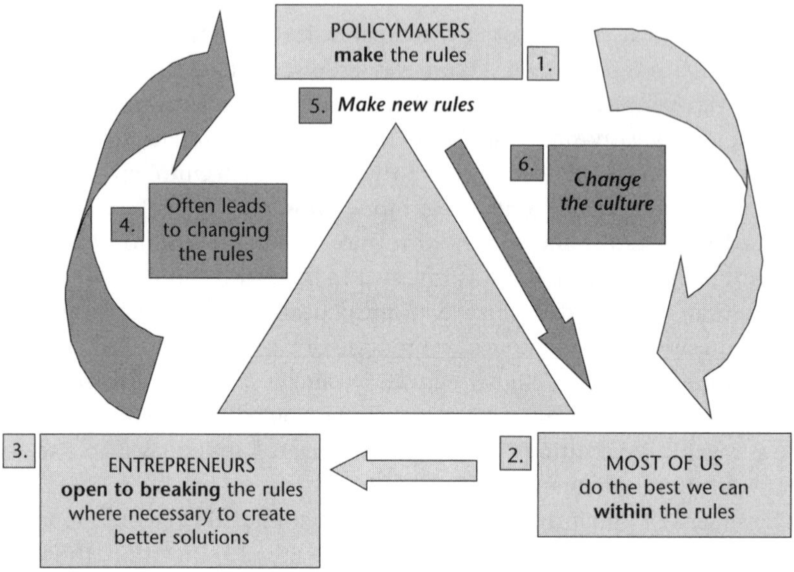

POLICYMAKERS
make the rules
1.

5. *Make new rules*

6.
*Change
the culture*

Often leads
4. to changing
the rules

3.
ENTREPRENEURS
open to breaking the rules
where necessary to create
better solutions

2.
MOST OF US
do the best we can
within the rules

Source: NewSchools Venture Fund

New Knowledge Emerges

New knowledge creates opportunity for all kinds of change in education. Sometimes this new knowledge is generated from *within* the field of education, such as when entrepreneurs create a new organization based on a new (or underutilized) approach to teaching that they find to be effective. For example, the founders of the Knowledge Is Power Program (KIPP), Dave Levin and Mike Feinberg, were heavily influenced by the no-nonsense approach of both fellow teacher Harriet Ball and successful Los Angeles teacher Rafe Esquith. Today, KIPP's model emphasizes many of the attributes that Ball and Esquith had found successful, with Levin and Feinberg turning these insights into an entire school model.

But new knowledge can also come from *outside* the field of education, such as innovations in technology. The pace of technology change has been swift, with computing power doubling every eighteen months.[13] Entrepreneurs have been quicker to take up the challenge of applying technology to the public education sector, while private companies have been quick to embrace technology as a way of making their products and services better, faster, and cheaper. Public school systems have been much slower to employ these tools.

In any sector, technology is simply a tool for doing things *differently*—and, when it works well, for doing things *better*. In public education, "better" can mean improved outcomes for students, or increased productivity in which students, teachers, or leaders do the same (or more) work in less time. Public education will need to make use of technology in both of these ways in order to achieve better results without massive infusions of people or capital.

Technology should enable teachers and leaders to use their time more efficiently, allowing them to minimize administrative tasks, maximize time spent with students, and tailor instruction and support to the specific needs of students. In order to understand the ways technology has created opportunities for education entrepreneurs, then, it is useful to consider the basic cycle of teaching and learning: assessment of student learning, interpretation of those data, planning for future action, and instruction—as well as overall management of this process itself.

Assessment. Schools and school systems have always assessed student learning through a variety of measures, ranging from homework to pop quizzes to final projects and presentations. As the standards and accountability movements have taken hold, assessment has become more formalized and standardized across classrooms, schools, systems, and states. Technology has played a substantial role in this development: Since the 1970s, the now-ubiquitous Scantron "bubble" test format has advanced the assessment of student learning in a standardized, cost-effective way that helped make the results widely available. Many public school systems have also added interim assessments throughout the year as a way to gauge student progress and inform instruction, and technology has lightened the burden of administering and scoring these tests. Targeting literacy in the early grades, for-profit start-up Wireless Generation has developed software that runs on handheld devices to allow teachers to more quickly record the results of observational assessments they conduct among students. Once the assessment information is uploaded into a computer, the software creates reports for teachers that help them target their instruction accordingly. The company's software is currently being used by approximately seventy-five thousand teachers in more than forty states. Another for-profit company, Edusoft (now owned by major publisher Houghton Mifflin), has developed scanning technology used by more than four hundred districts that allows teachers to scan multiple-choice tests on plain paper and upload results into a database for immediate analysis. Technology might also be used to create more sophisticated assessments that measure more complex skills like critical thinking, but entrepreneurs have not yet adequately addressed this area.

Interpretation. With the increasing frequency and use of standardized assessments, there has been a corresponding need for ways to make sense of all these new data. Technology entrepreneurs are beginning to fill this gap. For example, The Grow Network (now owned by major education publisher McGraw-Hill) pioneered the development of user-friendly reports on students' standardized test performance that teachers and parents can use for ongoing instruction. Through its website, Grow also provides access to recommended instructional activities based on student needs identified by test results.

Planning. One of the ways technology can be used in public education is by streamlining the way educators plan their activities. Some entrepreneurs are tackling this at the school level, providing tools for planning instruction. One such firm is Edgenuity, a for-profit start-up that has developed an instructional management system that links academic standards with curriculum, student performance data, and other information. Now in use by a handful of districts, Edgenuity's software allows teachers and principals to track the scope and sequence of their curriculum via the Internet, rather than in bulky, hard-to-access binders. Another component of planning involves linking student performance data to changes in professional development. Here, for-profit provider Teachscape offers online professional development using the video case method, allowing teachers to see how instructional strategies actually look in real classrooms—without traveling to other schools or districts.

Instruction. Despite advances in technology, the basic structure of teaching and learning itself has stayed relatively consistent: Teachers still instruct groups of students face-to-face. However, the pervasiveness of personal computers and Internet access in schools—driven in large part by the federal eRate program that has allocated more than $10 billion toward Internet infrastructure in schools and libraries—has enabled some entrepreneurs to use technology to enhance instruction. In the 1990s, former math teacher Bill Hadley blended his insights into effective algebra instruction with cognitive science research from Carnegie Mellon University to create Carnegie Learning. The for-profit company's algebra program is being used by more than 275,000 students across the country and integrates print and computer-based curricula, as well as adaptive assessments to pinpoint student mastery and learning challenges so teachers can focus on precise student needs.

Although entrepreneurs have begun to make inroads into bringing technology to bear on the teaching and learning cycle, there are a number of opportunities that remain unexploited. One area is the integration of these products and services: Because there is no soup-to-nuts solution that cuts across assessment, interpretation, planning, instruction, and management, districts must cobble together various technology products into something resembling a comprehensive approach. Furthermore, technology has the potential to transform not only teaching and learning, but also the management of school systems by providing ready access to a coherent picture of district operations.

WHAT RESOURCES DO ENTREPRENEURS NEED TO TAKE ADVANTAGE OF THESE OPPORTUNITIES?

> *The entrepreneur shifts economic resources out of an area of lower*
> *and into an area of higher productivity and greater yield.*
>
> —J. B. Say, French economist
> who is said to have coined the term "entrepreneur"[14]

An entrepreneur's pursuit starts with identifying an opportunity. But this opportunity must be matched with resources in order to have an impact. In the private sector, there is a sophisticated market of venture capital investors that differentiate themselves by industry and stage; some may provide money to very-early-stage private companies developing wireless technology, while others may prefer to invest in more mature companies developing medical devices. Because they can observe trends across the many entrepreneurial ventures they have supported, they bring great value to the entrepreneurs they support. These venture capitalists provide not only funding, but also strategic guidance; tactical assistance with building a team and board; connections to suppliers, customers, and funders; and help with identifying challenges of growth that the entrepreneur might not otherwise anticipate.

Taken together, these resources can be categorized into three groups, each of which will be discussed in detail below: financial capital, human capital, and intellectual capital. Just like any other entrepreneurs, education entrepreneurs must rely on a variety of different people and organizations in their quest for the money, people, and ideas they need to turn their vision into reality.

Financial Capital

Money is the most tangible of the resources entrepreneurs need, although it is by no means simple to obtain in the complex education landscape. Though all education entrepreneurs need financing to get started (start-up capital) and to support growth (growth capital), the capital market for for-profit organizations is markedly different from the one that nonprofit organizations can access (see figure 2). Furthermore, once an entrepreneurial organization reaches its more mature stages, it needs money to keep it going (sustaining capital), which may mean fundraising or revenue from the sale of a product or service.

Start-up capital. Education entrepreneurs creating for-profit enterprises traditionally raise their initial capital from individuals ("angel" investors) or venture capital firms. These investors put up cash in exchange for equity, or an ownership stake in the new organization, expecting that their investment will yield a financial return when the company is acquired or sells shares on the public stock market. Even though $500 billion is spent each year in K–12 public education, the challenges of operating a business in this sector mean that only a few committed venture capital firms will invest in entrepreneurs addressing this enormous market. In 2004, just over $50 million was privately invested in businesses addressing the preK–12 segment, according to market research firm Eduventures.[15] Even those education entrepreneurs who do secure venture capital funding find that there is little patience among investors for the kind of slow growth required to create a high-quality product or service and develop trust among the customer base. For-profit investors often prioritize short-term growth in revenues rather than building a sustainable company for the long term. This can be at odds with entrepreneurs' understanding of what nonprofit scholar Jed Emerson has called the "blended value proposition"—that over the long term, investments in organizations with strong results are likely to yield higher revenues and profits.

On the nonprofit side, education entrepreneurs generally raise their start-up capital from venture philanthropy firms like NewSchools, individual donors, and foundations. Only a few foundations are comfortable with taking a risk on entrepreneurial education organizations who intend to scale up their operations. Those that do make these early grants—usually multi-million-dollar grants over the course of several years—tend to be younger foundations, such as The Broad Foundation and the Bill & Melinda Gates Foundation. Until these new foundations arrived, education grantmakers tended to provide these early grants only in small increments, forcing the entrepreneur to spend enormous amounts of time and energy on fundrais-

FIGURE 2 Types of Financial Support Needed

		Start-up	Growth	Sustaining
Corporate Structure	For-profit	Equity investments from venture capital firms or "angel" investors	Equity investments from later-stage venture capital firms	Revenue from sales of product or service
	Nonprofit	Grants from individual donors, foundations, and public sources	Grants from foundations and public sources Program-related investments (loans from foundations)	Continued fundraising for grants Revenue from sales of product or service

ing from multiple donors. Nonprofit funders also tend to be risk averse, fearful of the stigma of failure that often accompanies large initiatives like the $1 billion Annenberg Challenge, a public-private partnership sponsored by the Annenberg Foundation whose mediocre results were widely characterized as ineffective. On the flip side, foundation leaders are rarely ousted for failure to have an impact. Because of this dynamic, foundation program officers find it far easier to say "yes" to a host of small grants than to go out on a limb with a few concentrated bets.

Growth capital. Finding capital to start a business is challenging, but fundraising for growth can be even more complex for education entrepreneurs. The news is better for for-profit companies that have a good track record: Venture capital firms such as Quad Ventures are willing to invest in growth for later-stage education organizations with good early results, and even venture capital firms that don't focus on education are willing to entertain the notion if they see a successful business emerging.

For nonprofits, the fundraising picture for growth is even more daunting. In some ways, growing nonprofit organizations are more appealing to foundations because they are perceived as less risky. However, in order to have a real impact on the public education system, these organizations must reach a sufficient scale in operations and staff, and that costs money. Nonprofit entrepreneurs struggle to raise the kind of large, multiyear grants necessary to support this kind of growth for the same reasons they face in the start-up stage. There is also a perverse disincentive for growing nonprofit organizations: The better the organization is doing, the more likely a donor is to drop their support, believing they have done their part or are no longer needed. As such, many foundations seem willing to support strong nonprofit organizations to expand on a limited scale, but few are willing to sustain an organization as it grows to significant scale over time.

Moreover, it is especially difficult to raise large amounts of funding from foundations through traditional means. According to federal regulations, program officers need only spend 5 percent of the foundation's total assets each year in the form of grants and other expenses. The other 95 percent of a foundation's assets are generally not used to support programs, but form its endowment, which is usually invested for the long term. Nonprofit education entrepreneurs may need to tap into these endowments in order to gain access to the sizable funds they need for scale and sustainability. One way to do this is with "program-related investments," which are loans that come from endowment funds but are expected to earn below-market rates in return for supporting social impact and programmatic priorities. For example, several foundations, including The Walton Family Foundation and The Annie E. Casey Foundation, have made program-related investments in funds that will help charter school entrepreneurs secure facilities for their schools. There is room for more such investments: Nationwide, foundations hold nearly $500 billion in their endowments, but use just over $200 million of that for charitable loans or program-related investments, according to the Foundation Center—less than one-twentieth of one percent.[16]

Sustaining capital. As figure 2 shows, entrepreneurial organizations attract capital to sustain their business by fundraising and generating revenues. Once their new organization is up and running, many education entrepreneurs bring in financial resources through earned income from the sale of products or services. On the nonprofit side, this is often problematic: Despite increasing acceptance of income-generating nonprofit organizations, few education entrepreneurs can sustain themselves on these revenues alone. Some find, for example, that the allocation of money by public school districts is rigid, with little flexible funding available for new programs. As a result, although some nonprofit education entrepreneurs can support their organization's ongoing operations through public funding—such as by per-pupil dollars that flow to charter management organizations—most must do so through ongoing fundraising from individuals and foundations. On the other hand, for-profit education ventures generally sustain their businesses exclusively through revenues, bringing a separate set of challenges. The market is fragmented, with each state, district, and school governed by its own preferences and decisionmaking processes. Education entrepreneurs must also compete against large education publishers, who have substantial teams of salespeople, big bank accounts, and decades-long relationships with district officials that often prevent serious consideration of products or services from new organizations.

For education entrepreneurs to succeed in public education, they require a more rational sales and distribution process that allows entrepreneurs with high-quality products or services to compete fairly against the publisher oligopolies. Customers within schools and districts also need help to better understand their needs and the available solutions—not to mention their future needs. In addition, small entrepreneurial organizations need assistance with navigating government relations: Large companies employ teams of people who comb through federal regulations for rules and grants that may give their business an edge, but smaller organizations can rarely afford this kind of capacity.

Human Capital

Business author Jim Collins, who has studied companies that consistently outperform their competition, found that those who did were able to get "the right people on the bus, the right people in the right seats, and the wrong people off the bus."[17] Indeed, finding and keeping the right people is the paramount challenge that education entrepreneurs—and indeed, the entire public education sector—face today.

Because their resources are often limited, all start-up organizations struggle to recruit the senior executives they need to start and manage the business. But entrepreneurs in education also face a few unique challenges, according to Amy Vernetti, an executive search specialist who has worked in both the business and education sectors. Because the existence of entrepreneurs in education is still a relatively new phenomenon, there are relatively few people experienced in starting and scaling up a new education organization. And as for experienced management talent in education more broadly, Vernetti notes, few school districts and education publishers "incubate" new management talent in the way that businesses like Procter & Gamble or Microsoft often do in the private sector. Entrepreneurs would also benefit from more executive search firms with the expertise and contacts to find senior-level managers for entrepreneurial organizations in K–12 education; the few firms who currently address this type of search within education tend to focus on higher education or on large education companies.

Although the specific mix of skills an entrepreneur needs to hire depends greatly on the type of organization being built, any new venture that is seeking social impact in public education will need what NewSchools refers to as a "hybrid team," with skills from across the education, business, nonprofit, and public sectors. Public education has as much operational and financial complexity as any business, the mission-driven character of a nonprofit, the content and social complexity inherent in education, and, of course, the need to be accountable to a diverse public. As such, education entrepreneurs need to surround themselves with skills and expertise from across these fields. For example, when lifelong educator Don Shalvey set out to create and manage Aspire Public Schools as a new system of charter schools, he needed someone to develop the systems and structures such an ambitious new organization would need to succeed. So he brought on Gloria Lee as chief operating officer; she had a hybrid background as a former business consultant, manager of a university program that trained and coached teachers and school leaders, and a dual graduate degree in education and business. Also, because Shalvey would be focused on leading the entire system of schools, he hired Elise Darwish—an experienced educator who had been a teacher and instructional coordinator—to ensure that the instructional needs of schools were met.

In addition to accumulating experience across these sectors, there are several programs that prepare people for this "hybrid" work. Mike Kirst at Stanford University was a pioneer in offering the first "dual-degree" graduate program in business and education in the late 1970s, with other universities following suit. The Broad Center for the Management of School Systems—created by The Broad Foundation in Los Angeles—has several programs that prepare midcareer professionals and senior-level executives for roles in school districts. These sources aren't enough to meet the demands of the increasing number of entrepreneurial organizations in education, though: The Broad Center programs prepare about forty-five people per year, many of whom go straight into school districts, and a large percentage of those who receive dual degrees end up at consulting firms, investment banks, or foundations. This leaves few available for hire by education entrepreneurs. More such preparation programs for hybrid leaders must be developed, especially those geared toward the demands of growing entrepreneurial organizations.

In addition to a great team, a strong board of directors is also crucial to an entrepreneurial organization's success throughout its life cycle. Legally, a board of directors is charged with overseeing an organization to ensure that laws are followed and funds are put to appropriate use. For entrepreneurial organizations, however, a board's importance reaches far beyond this basic governance role. In the start-up phase, the entrepreneur needs strategic guidance and tactical assistance from the board just to get the organization off the ground. In this formative time, for-profit organizations generally have a "venture-building" board made up of their early investors, who can make connections to potential customers, attract talent, and shape the business plan. Unfortunately, nonprofit entrepreneurs often start with either a "friends-and-family" board or one focused purely on fundraising, when what they really need is a board with expertise in new ventures. As the organization becomes more mature, nonprofit entrepreneurs usually need help with ongoing fundraising and thus may need to add board-level connections to prospective donors. Most education entrepreneurs find their board members in an ad hoc fashion through existing board members and investors; there is a need for a more efficient process, perhaps akin to boardnetUSA, a service that connects a broad range of nonprofit organizations with board members.

Intellectual Capital

Less tangible than human or financial capital—although closely tied to both—intellectual capital is equally crucial to fueling entrepreneurial success. Intellectual capital may be thought of as the ideas, practices, and policies that feed entrepreneurs' ongoing understanding of where opportunities lie, what lessons can be learned from the work that is already happening, and what changes need to take place in order to maximize success. Contributors of intellectual capital may include investors and funders who can add value by contributing experience and insight that can help entrepreneurs build their organization and prepare for the next wave of challenges. Other sources of intellectual capital may include consulting firms, evaluators, think tanks, and policymakers.

As entrepreneurs grow their organizations to scale, many have found outside consulting firms useful sources of capacity and expertise. Some of the traditional management consulting firms—including McKinsey & Company, the Parthenon Group, and The Bridgespan Group, which is a nonprofit spinoff from Bain & Company—have begun to provide these services to education entrepreneurs. For example, drawing on work it has done with nonprofit organizations in other fields, The Bridgespan Group has helped several education entrepreneurs (including Aspire Public Schools, The Big Picture Company, and Envision Schools, all of whom are creating systems of public charter schools) articulate their theory of change, which in turn has informed their growth strategies. However, it is worth noting that much of the recent influx of consulting talent into this field has been underwritten by a single source—the Bill & Melinda Gates Foundation—and so it remains to be seen whether these firms will stay and develop a broader base of expertise in K–12 public education.

Entrepreneurs also need outside evaluation firms to assess their efforts in order to establish credible evidence in support of their new approaches and learn what is (or isn't) working and why. The Center for Research on Education Outcomes at Stanford University's Hoover Institution, Mathematica Policy Research, and American Institutes for Research are among the evaluators who are currently doing such work, but there is room for additional players—especially those who can translate entrepreneurs' lessons into improved practice and policy.

Research is also a major component of intellectual capital that can fuel entrepreneurial activity. The U.S. Department of Education's research arm, the Institute of Education Sciences, has an annual budget of about $500 million and is funding some basic research with that, but more research on how to improve teaching and learning would enable entrepreneurs to leverage that knowledge by coming up with new ways to put research into practice. Some of the research that is most directly relevant to entrepreneurs' forward-thinking efforts today is coming from university centers like the Center on Reinventing Public Education at the University of Washington and the Center on Urban School Improvement at the University of Chicago. There is, however, a need for problem-based research that is not ideologically driven but instead brings cross-disciplinary researchers and practitioners to the table to understand together what approaches are working, what's not, and what is needed. Contrast, for example, the $530 million appropriated for education research under the Institute of Education Sciences in 2005 with the $28 billion allotted to the National Institutes for Health in that same period.

Research must also be converted into action through development. "As important as it is, research is generally examination, illumination, discussion," notes Chris Whittle, founder of education management organization Edison Schools, in his recent book, *Crash Course: Imagining a Better Future for Public Education.* "Development is all about solutions—execution, integration, workability."[18] Here, one model that may prove instructive is In-Q-Tel, a private nonprofit organization established by the Central Intelligence Agency in 1999. Like a venture capital firm, In-Q-Tel makes strategic investments in promising security technology start-ups and also "incubates" new organizations and products that have been identified through research as critical technologies to national security and intelligence.

As mentioned earlier, those within public education systems are unlikely to have the incentive or time to track future needs and next-wave solutions. Similarly, traditional education researchers are generally not focused on development or practical execution, with a few notable exceptions like Robert Slavin, who helped create the Success For All school model as part of his work at Johns Hopkins University, and Henry Levin, who created the Accelerated Schools model based on his research at Stanford University. As such, new research and development centers—seeded by both public and philanthropic sources and staffed with cross-disciplinary professionals—are one promising way to ensure that these new tools and approaches are developed.

Some of the intellectual capital work, though, falls squarely on the shoulders of entrepreneurs themselves. Entrepreneurial organizations are often so focused on their day-to-day work that they neglect this activity unintentionally, and few funders systematically encourage them to capture, manage, or share what they learn (although The Annie E. Casey Foundation is a notable exception). It is important for entrepreneurs to share lessons learned, so that they may avoid "reinventing the wheel" and instead learn from each other's successes and mistakes as they build brand new organizations.

These kinds of efforts are *de rigeur* in other fields where entrepreneurs flourish, such as in technology, where former employees of large companies like Microsoft swap résumés online and graduates of top-tier business schools host networking events. To this end, some foundations convene their grantees so that they may engage in this kind of collaboration. NewSchools has also created several venues for this type of work, including communities of practice for like-minded organizations and a new annual Gathering of Education Entrepreneurs in partnership with the Aspen Institute. Overall, most education entrepreneurs lack the time, money, or venue to do this sort of intentional reflection and collective learning, and could use support to make sure this happens.

Entrepreneurs must also be conscious of the need to translate their own work into system-level improvements. This may involve a whole host of tactics, including strategic communication, informing policymakers, or even spinning off new organizations. For example, Teach For America helped one of its former "corps members" create a new nonprofit, The New Teacher Project, to work with public school systems' human resources departments to apply some of the lessons Teach For America has learned over the years. The new organization complements the mission of the original entrepreneurial organization and increases the number of voices supporting that mission in the field—while still allowing the entrepreneur to maintain focus.

CONCLUSION

> *Pattern change needs two things: a new idea and a social entrepreneur*
> *who conceives, develops, and champions it over many years. Only through*
> *constant, iterative testing and improvement can a good idea become a*
> *realistic idea, then a demonstrated success, and finally . . . the accepted*
> *way society works. The faster the world changes, the greater the need for*
> *social adaptation—and therefore for social entrepreneurs."*
>
> —Bill Drayton, Ashoka[19]

In the summer of 2005, a group of entrepreneurial leaders in education con-
vened in Aspen, Colorado, to consider the question of what public education
should look like in 2030 and what role education entrepreneurs should play
in that transformation. This convening purposefully included leaders from
across the public, private, and nonprofit sectors, and also cut across the traditional silos of practice, research, policy, and philanthropy.

In those conversations, it became apparent that there are two slightly different perspectives on why education entrepreneurs matter. The first rationale is the one cited earlier as the "disruptive technologies" approach. This
view holds that the public education system must change so profoundly that
only the disruptive force of entrepreneurs—who think beyond the current
constraints and resources—can get us there. In this view, entrepreneurs are
crucial change agents at this particular moment in time, necessary to propel
us from the current system to a new model that is geared toward the needs
of the knowledge age.

The alternative—and perhaps more compelling—view on entrepreneurs'
importance in public education links them to a much larger, more far-
reaching change: a major global transformation away from slow, incremental progress and toward fast-paced, dynamic change. The industrial age was
slow-moving and focused on manipulating natural resources, its institutions
intended to operate steadily for long periods of time. As such, the public education system was designed to ensure stability for students. However, in our
current knowledge age, change is the new constant. Technology, medicine,
and other fields are now based on constantly evolving cycles of improved
knowledge. Education entrepreneurs can bring this critical "dynamic equilibrium" to public education, making them a permanent necessity rather than
merely temporary agents of change. In other words, they *are* the change we
wish to see in the sector.

This latter view is a radical concept, and one that many within public education may not agree with. But it is worth exploring in more depth six key

principles implicit in this view, and what they might imply for how we support education entrepreneurs:

Six Principles of an Entrepreneurial School System

1. *Responsive.* In a dynamic, ever-changing world, public school systems should be responsive to the changes in the needs of students, families, and communities. If schools are not permanent, but rather opened and closed based on how well they are serving market needs, the supply of schools is aligned with demand.

2. *No monopolies or oligopolies.* Monopolies and oligopolies are fundamentally closed, unresponsive systems that aggregate power and maintain it—even if results are unsatisfactory. Such inflexible practices should not be tolerated in public education, whether among school districts, teacher-preparation programs, or publishers.

3. *Customer-oriented.* Public education has many "customers," including parents, communities that provide funding, and businesses that employ schools' graduates. In order to satisfy their mission, though, public schools must focus first and foremost on the needs of *students*—not *adults* or *institutions.* As such, there must be a diverse supply of schools that address the unique learning needs of students, along with customized instruction within those schools, and mechanisms that support choice and information for parents and communities.

4. *Performance-driven.* With improved results for students as the target, public school systems must manage with an eye not only on effectiveness, but also efficiency (less time and money for the same results). There must be clear goals, alignment of resources with those goals, and constant assessment and adjustment of those goals and resources based on progress.

5. *Constant learning.* In a dynamic environment, the work of public education is never "finished." As soon as one level of performance is achieved, the next target becomes clear, with continuous improvement always a priority. This cycle of ongoing learning applies to student instruction as well as the management of schools and school systems.

6. *Culture of meritocracy.* When results are the priority, those who find a way to achieve those results are rewarded for their efforts. In other words, the "fastest learner wins"—whether an individual or a team—and others use that success to inform their own practice.

Implications

This dynamic system requires a workforce that is passionate and prepared for the hard work of educating students in this fast-changing new environment. As such, preparation, certification, and support for teachers and leaders must be transformed so that they are driven by attaining desired outcomes in K–12 rather than by maintaining the status quo within higher education. Entrepreneurs are already making inroads on this front, but a more fundamental redesign of our human capital systems is necessary to truly embrace these principles.

The public has asked their schools to prepare more children than before and to a higher standard than ever. As such, educators need *better tools and resources*—including money, technology, curriculum, and assessments—than they have today. Financial capital from philanthropic and public sources should be adequate for the task at hand, and organized in a way that enables the system to respond to—and anticipate—student needs. Technology must also be used to a greater extent than it is today; only through technology will practitioners have timely access to the detailed information they need in order to make informed decisions about instruction and management. Standards, curriculum, and assessments must also be rigorous enough to prepare students to succeed in this knowledge-driven environment.

Finally, education is a very complex, highly skilled endeavor. We must develop *new practices* that support increased productivity and responsiveness. This includes a need for more research and development on effective instructional and management approaches. We know a great deal today about fundamental areas like reading instruction, but there is much to be learned about how to manage school systems in this new environment. One critical factor is making available more transparent, timely, and relevant information about student and school progress, which would enable educators, parents, and community leaders to make more informed decisions and set the stage for entrepreneurs to create new approaches and organizations based on need.

In a system governed by the principles of dynamic equilibrium, entrepreneurs may be both important vehicles for getting there *and* permanent participants in this new environment. By imagining how education can be improved, thinking beyond the current rules and resources, creating new organizations to execute their vision, and inspiring others to follow, entrepreneurs may be agents of continuous improvement in public schooling.

CHAPTER 2

Entrepreneurs at Work

Paul Teske and Aimee Williamson

We all have a sense of what we think the term "educational entrepreneur" means, though each of us may have a quite different picture in mind. Generally, we think of someone changing the school system in some significant and fundamental way, perhaps even disrupting or transforming it. But there are many ways to try to do this, many possible types of entrepreneurs, and a broad scope of what might qualify as true entrepreneurship.

In the narrowest definition, an entrepreneur (literally, an undertaker, or one who undertakes) is a business person who successfully develops a new idea, pretty much from scratch, and creates a new business or business model. If that entrepreneur can create a big new market for the idea, he or she can become very rich. Bill Gates developed an operating system for the new market of personal computers that led to his building the largest fortune in the world, while Howard Schultz invented a "third place" (not home or business) where people would consume certain coffee drinks, the ubiquitous Starbucks.

This narrow definition restricts entrepreneurs to a small set of truly exceptional business people who are often defined by their success. A broader definition, still within the business context, could extend to any small business person trying to start a new business, even if using an established model.

More recently, students of entrepreneurship recognized that some business people play an entrepreneurial role within an already large organization by creating a new product, service, approach, or even a new industry. To distinguish entrepreneurs within large organizations, scholars coined the term "intrapreneur."[1]

All of these definitions still relate to profit-seeking businesses. The notion of entrepreneurial activities has been expanded into the public and nonprofit sectors in recent years, using the terms "public entrepreneurship," or "social entrepreneurship." This is harder to define.[2] The key is that these actors have an entrepreneurial mindset and hope to create disruptive or fundamentally transformative changes in public and nonprofit enterprises by taking a risk and seizing opportunities to provide a new service, or an existing service in a new way.

In applying the concept of entrepreneurship to education, the key element is its transformative nature—educational entrepreneurs are individuals seeking to instigate change in the public education system that will disrupt, transform, or radically alter the way education is provided. These entrepreneurs no doubt seek some individual reward beyond profits, but their activities necessarily extend into facilitating what Schumpeter called "creative destruction" in the larger system.[3]

Thus, one can think about entrepreneurs more or less broadly. We believe that a middle ground is most valuable to understanding entrepreneurship in education. Specifically, educational entrepreneurs can be businesspeople who see a new way to provide education services, create or seize an opportunity, and move to fill the gap. But, limiting education entrepreneurs solely to businesspeople is inadequate. Educational entrepreneurs can also be public leaders who seek to change or disrupt the existing system in fundamental ways from the inside (see Joe Williams, in this volume), or nonprofit leaders who create organizations on the fringes of the larger system that will try to alter the system over time. There are distinct differences between these kinds of educational entrepreneurs. However, this chapter focuses on the commonalities, viewing educational "intrapreneurs" as a subset of educational entrepreneurs.

In seeking to change the system, education entrepreneurs in all three sectors—private, public, or not-for-profit—must engage in three basic sets of tasks. All, however, are (1) alert to opportunities, (2) prepared to take significant risks to fill gaps, and (3) skilled at building organizations and networking with other people.

Entrepreneurs in any of these sectors probably share some similar characteristics. Since the 1950s, social scientists have been studying entrepreneurial personalities. Early research suggested that entrepreneurs were at the extreme end of risk takers, and that their basic personality traits, including a strong "need for achievement" and high internal locus of control, instill a sense of urgency and desire to change the status quo.[4] More recent research suggests more variation and has called into question whether or not we can develop a comprehensive list of essential personality traits or characteristics of entrepreneurs. Better empirical data has come from a Panel Study of Entrepreneurial Dynamics started in 1995, which utilizes a large sample of business entrepreneurs and a control group. These data suggest that some common assumptions are not valid: Entrepreneurs are not extreme risk takers, but they are less likely to perceive a down side to their opportunities than others and to frame risk as "potential gains." Entrepreneurs are also found to rate quite high on salesmanship ability, often higher than on risk-seeking, and they are less likely to care what other people think about them.

Financial rewards do not appear to be the main motivation of many entrepreneurs, and only private-sector entrepreneurship can provide abundant economic rewards for success. The rewards of public, nonprofit, or social entrepreneurship are more intrinsic and probably attract different types of entrepreneurs. They may also attract one person at a different point in their entrepreneurial career (a "serial entrepreneur"), after they have already earned the personal financial rewards in business and can now turn to satisfying other concerns and needs.[5]

Potential entrepreneurs can emerge anywhere, but are more likely to become actual entrepreneurs when success and rewards are possible. Consider the rapid growth of Internet start-ups in the late 1990s, where early successes attracted more risky efforts by others to duplicate those successes. The rewards potentially available to entrepreneurs interact with the institutional environment, so we need to consider how education compares to other avenues in terms of entrepreneurial energy.

Is education a sector where making a difference is understood to be important? Is there a well-paid position for the entrepreneur to take or to aspire to, one that will reward him or her for the risks taken? Is there an opportunity for national mobility for a potential entrepreneur located in a bureaucratic organizational position, such as the national market for city managers (or school superintendents)? Lacking some such set of opportunities in the environment, fewer potential entrepreneurs will actually take the plunge. Why should they, given the comparison of risk and reward in this sector, coupled with their ability to satisfy some of their entrepreneurial urges in other contexts? As scholars have noted, within the public education system "there is little reward for taking entrepreneurial risks and succeeding, while there are significant personal and professional costs associated with taking such risks and failing."[6]

But, if there are potential rewards, public and nonprofit entrepreneurs will emerge. And they do. Even in education.

It seems likely that education entrepreneurs are "born," in the sense that the key entrepreneurial personality traits must be apparent, but they are also "made" in the sense that they must envision opportunities for their entre-

preneurial energies in education. If, as discussed later, the climate for education entrepreneurship historically has been chilly, fewer potential entrepreneurs will be enticed. That chilly climate may be getting more heated now,
however.

WHY WOULD ENTREPRENEURS FOCUS ON EDUCATION AT ALL?

If we assume that potential entrepreneurs make up a small group of people,
they will have a variety of avenues they might pursue. Clearly, some entrepreneurs see education as an untapped lucrative market. Indeed, the private
sector industries that have long existed or recently emerged around public
K–12 education have obvious entrepreneurial parallels to other private sector
business enterprises. There is money to be made from new ideas about how
to provide transportation, school supplies, school facility construction and
maintenance, school food services, and now supplemental education services. Whatever his larger goals of improving education, a business person
also expects to make money, as Chris Whittle did with ventures like Channel
One and Edison Schools. But most of these basic infrastructure services have
become commodities that established firms provide to school districts.

Education has increasingly become a "multisector" service; that is, public,
nonprofit, and for-profit organizations are all involved. This is not in itself
entrepreneurial, but it broadens opportunities.

While it isn't the same as starting a new Internet firm, education has
become "sexy." More than 10 percent of Ivy League and top liberal arts
college graduates now apply to Teach For America, a kind of twenty-first-
century Peace Corps for idealistic youth. Every adult has experienced education, so every citizen has an opinion about what kinds of schooling work
best. Education shapes the future and embodies the American dream of
upward mobility. There are few more clearly worthy causes than the education of low-income children. Polls have consistently shown education to be
a major public concern.[7]

Finally, as Kim Smith and Julie Landry Petersen discuss in this volume, the
focus of private sector education philanthropy recently has been changing in
a way that supports entrepreneurial efforts.[8]

(HOW) DOES ENTREPRENEURSHIP DIFFER FROM REFORM?

Part of moving toward a better understanding of education entrepreneurship
and transformative change goals is to distinguish between entrepreneurship
and reform. The main differences are in scale and scope.

Everyone involved is in favor of some type of reform. The many problems with the current system make it difficult, though not impossible, to argue to maintain the status quo. This often leads to "policy churn," in which states and/or districts develop new ideas every few years and then abandon them, often as failures. Developing and sustaining real civic and financial capacity for continued, focused education reform is much more difficult.

In addition, some groups that benefit from the status quo have incentives to appear to favor "reform," even when they want only minor changes that do not really alter their way of doing business. By embracing what they know to be incremental change, they can endorse reform publicly but know that it will lead to a future very similar to the present. The group most often criticized for favoring incremental reform is teachers unions, but school boards, school officials, other school workers, and university schools of education also have some incentives to favor incremental reform that is not entrepreneurship.

Still, in theoretical terms it is difficult to draw a "bright line" between innovative reform and truly entrepreneurial behavior.[9] If we define educational entrepreneurship in such a way that it must promote or lead to radical transformation or disruption of the current system, that will exclude even the most entrepreneurial reformers working "within the system" and shine the spotlight on those advocating changes like choice, homeschooling, or new technological approaches like online schooling. If we include perhaps less radical or disruptive change, we might move too closely back to the category of mere incremental reform. What about system changes in teacher preparation, changes in teacher payment, or changes in principal's autonomy? These are probably good and important reforms, but only a few initial inventors or implementers of these ideas can be considered truly entrepreneurial, since they are the transformative actors, while the others coming later are simply replicating or extending the basic idea.

WHY MIGHT K–12 EDUCATION ATTRACT MORE ENTREPRENEURS NOW?

Despite these recent reform efforts, the daily delivery of most American public K–12 education still looks much like it did one hundred years ago. Teachers, who are paid pretty much the same whether or not they do a great, good, or poor job, stand in front of twenty or thirty kids seated at desks in buildings often constructed decades ago. Most students attend classes for most of 180 days a year, from about 8:00 a.m. to 3:00 p.m., with a summer break dictated by past agricultural needs, meaning that full attendance places them in school about 15 percent of their waking hours from ages one to eighteen.

While this model works adequately for some students, for many it does not result in high levels of performance, high graduation rates, or a good entrée to higher education and remunerative employment. Given the enormous changes that have created or remade other important sectors of our economy in the past century—including air travel, banking, communications, and so on—why has education been characterized by so little change?

Many believe that the constraints against entrepreneurship in the public education system are very imposing, that the system has not aimed to attract entrepreneurial talent, and that it encourages stasis and inertia. Most broadly, the American system of public education is built around a system of democracy, bureaucracy, and citizen participation that provides numerous checks, balances, and veto points, all of which greatly increase the challenges for potential education entrepreneurs. More specifically, union contracts, typical career paths for teachers and administrators, informal norms within school systems, general parental satisfaction with the current system, and the high visibility of any public decisions involving children all tend to favor inertia over change. For teachers, administrators, and staff, good and secure careers can be built by staying well within the boundaries of standard practice. Many people may be attracted to such a secure work environment, but not entrepreneurs.

Though education seems particularly challenging, other sectors of the American economy have faced similar constraints. Very often, a technological change or a sense of crisis catalyzed entrepreneurial activity in those arenas. However, at least before publication of the 1983 U.S. Department of Education report *A Nation at Risk*, the lack of a sense of "crisis" in American K–12 education made it seem there was little need for educational entrepreneurship in a system that many felt was performing adequately. Today opinion leaders are more likely to characterize American K–12 education as in crisis, since the achievement gap between low-income and/or minority students and middle- and upper-income students remains stubbornly large, and average American test scores compare poorly to international norms, especially in later grades and particularly in math and science.

Since 1983, reformers of various stripes have sought to address these problems. Unfortunately, few of these reform efforts seem to have been sustained, fewer still seem to be able to demonstrate success, and only a very small number have expanded beyond some initial small-scale success stories. This helps create a climate more amenable to consideration of truly radical reform, or entrepreneurship.

In addition to twenty years of operating with a sense of crisis, other factors make the time ripe for more educational entrepreneurship. A national market has emerged for top education leaders, especially as school boards expect to see rapid improvements from their leadership. The career rewards from being a successful entrepreneurial superintendent are more apparent. At the federal, state, and local levels, as Patrick McGuinn explains in chapter 3, public officials are creating new opportunities for those who seek to transform the existing system.

And, at the same time, there is evidence of more risk-taking and innovation in higher education, ideas that potential K–12 entrepreneurs can "arbitrage" or borrow. The higher education sector has always been more competitive for reasons Steven Wilson discusses in chapter 9. While "pay-for-performance" is a relatively new concept in K–12, university faculty pay has long been differentiated by field based upon market factors and by individual performance. Higher education has seen the emergence of private firms providing niche degrees and credentials, often with cheaper online course delivery, and continuing education programs for growing numbers of nontraditional learners. Higher education institutions have also pursued new revenue sources, including research funding and patents, and sports-related revenues such as television contracts, logo trademarks, and sponsorship. Not all of these activities are truly entrepreneurial but they are innovative, and they promote a climate ripe for new ideas.

HOW COULD ENTREPRENEURS FOCUS MORE ON K–12 EDUCATION?

While all entrepreneurs seek to be alert to opportunities, to fill gaps, and to mobilize people to make dynamic changes, educational entrepreneurs work in this highly constrained environment, making it difficult to visualize a full range of entrepreneurial efforts. Researcher Paul Hill recently identified four areas of activities that he describes as entrepreneurial and potentially significant. They mostly involve the borrowing or arbitrage of ideas from the business sector. In particular, these activities, on an increasingly ambitious scale, include providing support services, managing human resources, delivering complete courses, and operating whole schools.[10]

Common Elements of Educational Entrepreneurship

In order to effect transformative change to a slow-moving system, all education entrepreneurs—public, private, or nonprofit—must be alert to opportunities, must take risks to seize these opportunities and to fill existing gaps, and then, in the implementation phase, must be able to organize and manage other people to help carry out the vision.[11] Entrepreneurship cannot come to fruition without the involvement of many other people, especially in the public sphere. An inventor might be able to develop a new, marketable technology in her garage by herself, but someone seeking to change K–12 education needs lots of additional help. This makes the implementation phase the most difficult of this entrepreneurial sequence. Indeed, it begs the question of whether individual entrepreneurs can really change large systems, and whether they can build organizations that can maintain entrepreneurial energy beyond the charisma of the original entrepreneur, a problem common to entrepreneurial businesses.

Being alert to educational opportunities. Changes in American education have created new opportunities for entrepreneurs. In the late-1990s booming stock market years, many believed that for-profit education firms, like Edison Schools, were poised for huge growth, and their stocks rose substantially. Some perceived that new online models could radically transform education and cut costs by orders of magnitude. While some of this was due to the technology bubble and only a little of it has actually transpired, the Wall Street flame has been lit. If some firms start to earn healthy profits, more attention and capital will be attracted and more business education entrepreneurs will emerge.

Profit-seeking entrepreneurs are not the only ones who have been alert to opportunities. For example those entrepreneurs who have created alternative pathways into teaching, such as Wendy Kopp and TFA, also were alert to opportunities like the projected "teacher shortage," which suggested that demographics and labor market patterns would lead to too few teachers trained in traditional ways.

Filling a gap with a risky new education idea. There are lots of ideas in education policy, many of which have been proposed, and tried, before. Indeed, it can be hard to find truly "new" ways to deliver educational services. Often what is most innovative is a combination of programs that have not been utilized together before or delivered very well to students. For example, some charter schools serving low-income children in inner-city neighborhoods, such as KIPP (Knowledge Is Power Program), have adopted disciplined, highly focused models of learning, which are not new but had fallen out of fashion in the traditional public school sector.

The application of business innovations is another approach. NewSchools Venture Fund and New Leaders for New Schools focus on applying business concepts of entrepreneurship and leadership models, respectively, to the education sector. Other times, entrepreneurs actually develop new technologies and ideas. Chris Whittle's Channel One was an entrepreneurial venture, bringing informative televised news into the classroom (in exchange for running commercials). K12 uses new technology to operate "virtual schools," an idea that was inconceivable just a few years ago.

Other gaps are more obvious. Private tutoring firms were already providing test preparation and individual tutoring services, but mostly for upper-income clients. When NCLB mandated supplemental services to low-income students in low-achieving schools and minimized the school district's role as provider, the gap created was a no-brainer for firms like Kaplan and Princeton Review to fill.

Organizing and managing people to implement educational innovation. This is probably the hardest part of the entrepreneur's task, and almost certainly so in education. It is very hard to scale up from idea, concept, or small mode to an actual, in-place new program, school, or delivery system. While McDonald's may be quite expert at this, the franchise model has been harder to implement in education. This is especially true when Americans put so much faith in local democratic institutions, like local school boards, to run or to oversee local schools.

Some ideas require partnering with states and districts, which are often entrenched in their operations. Furthermore, the unionization of the education sector creates additional barriers and limits, especially in redeploying human resources in a system where these resources are the most important input. Securing funding for a new project—whether in the form of appropriations, charitable donations, or start-up capital—often requires extensive networking. Entrepreneurs capable of overcoming this combination of democratic, bureaucratic, union, and other barriers may be difficult to find. Indeed, there seem to be more recognizable entrepreneurs working on the fringes of the K–12 education sector at private firms and nonprofits than within the established public education system.

BRIEF CASE STUDIES

Here, we present a few brief case studies that capture some of the essential elements of educational entrepreneurship. (Other chapters provide additional examples.) All of these entrepreneurs demonstrate the psychological pattern of believing that they can succeed and of wanting to control their contribution, and thereby wreaking some "creative destruction" on the larger system.

We start with an entrepreneur operating within the public school sector, Brad Jupp. As we examined possible choices of entrepreneurial case studies, we realized that most were outside the traditional K–12 public sector; we do not think this was a coincidence, given the limited amount of true "intra-system" entrepreneurship in education, but we believe that in some extreme cases such intrapreneurship should not be ruled out as "mere reform." Next, we examine two nonprofits that are changing the landscape by expanding the pipeline of teachers and leaders, respectively, into the public school system, and are explicitly trying to help create the next generation of entrepreneurs who can change the system from within. Then we examine two private, for-profit entrepreneurial firms who seek to "do good while doing well" in education. K12 is utilizing Internet technology to develop courses and programs, while Kaplan has moved aggressively to provide supplemental services.

Brad Jupp and the Implementation of Market-Based Teacher Compensation

Many observers of K–12 education have long wondered why teachers could not be paid in a more flexible manner. Union contracts call for standardized salary schedules, usually based on seniority and formal education, making it hard for districts to attract teachers to challenging positions or even to attract top talent.

Tying teacher pay to the performance of students or market considerations seems like an obvious choice to businesspeople but has proved hard to adopt in American schools. Implementation has been the sticking point—a few experiments have proceeded, but union resistance, distrust of how merit pay is determined, budget problems that turned implementation into a zero-sum game for teachers, and other problems result in more talk than action.

Recently, however, in Denver, Colorado, the teachers union has embraced a form of pay-for-performance called Professional Compensation System for Teachers, or Pro-Comp. Brad Jupp, a teachers union negotiator, was the central player in this process, showing entrepreneurial efforts in the face of tough odds. Jupp helped start a process in the late 1990s, when traditional teacher contract negotiations were stalled, which led to a compromise four-year pilot program in which teachers were paid more for raising student test scores and for achieving a series of other goals agreed to by the teacher and the school principal.

After the successful pilot, Pro-Comp had to be approved by a majority of Denver teachers in a March 2004 vote. Early polling was negative for Pro-Comp, but a retail vote campaign led by Jupp convinced teachers that this could be a first step toward teaching getting rewarded as a real profession, similar to law and medicine. Despite national union opposition, Pro-Comp was endorsed by Denver teachers, surprising some observers. Even after the successful teacher vote in 2004, Pro-Comp still required support from Denver voters in November 2005, when they voted to authorize $25 million in new spending for the program.

For his efforts, Jupp was named innovator of the year by the Progressive Policy Institute (PPI).[12] In issuing the honor, PPI noted, "What really makes Brad an innovator is that he's a die-hard union member and was the Denver Classroom Teachers Association point person on the district-union team that designed and sold Pro-Comp to the city's teachers. . . . Pro-Comp doesn't go as far as some would like, and much farther than others want, but it would not have gone anywhere without a visionary like Brad Jupp to help lead the effort." Jupp's efforts were also profiled in the *New York Times*.[13] Jupp, a former teacher, became convinced that the unions' adherence to traditional pay scales was harmful to the development of the profession of teaching and that a program like Pro-Comp could make teaching more attractive and rewarding. He used his high level of personal energy, determination, and salesmanship to forge compromises at every juncture where Pro-Comp would otherwise have been stalled.

Pro-Comp, while hardly a new idea, has the potential to transform the current pay structure of the Denver schools, and there are already discussions of teaching candidates wanting to come to Denver to be part of it. Districts all over America are watching Denver and, if successful, the Pro-Comp model will likely be replicated elsewhere.

Teach For America and Attracting New Teachers

For her senior thesis at Princeton, Wendy Kopp developed the idea of training graduates of Ivy League-type universities to teach in low-income inner-city schools, which she believed would give future leaders insight into real "on the ground" problems. Her idea was that a formal education school degree was not necessarily important to quality teaching. She also believed she could tap the idealism and talents of these graduates and generate interest in education at this pivotal time of their career decisionmaking. After her graduation, Kopp pursued this idea by launching the nonprofit, Teach For America (TFA), which has grown steadily since 1990. In fact, more than seventeen thousand students applied in 2005, including 12 percent of the graduating class at Yale, 11 percent at Dartmouth, and 8 percent each at Princeton and Harvard.[14] The program has spawned other alternative certification programs that take capable people and prepare them for the classroom without formal education school training.

Kopp demonstrated the action orientation, extreme self-confidence, and motivation for success associated with entrepreneurs. Kopp had the idealism, and also the naiveté to buck the current system. As she wrote, "It seems to me something of a miracle that I maintained my confidence throughout that first year. . . . I think it was a blind faith in the power of the idea that kept me going. I'm not sure that the prospect of failure was real to me, although there were a few moments when it crept into my mind."[15]

Kopp sought to create a revolutionary program, not simply an innovation. She recounts the numerous times she received advice to start small and explains, "This was not going to be a little nonprofit organization or a model teacher-training program. This was going to be a *movement*."[16]

In creating this movement, Kopp overcame substantial early obstacles, most prominently the need for large sums of seed money, a task that was certainly more daunting for a fresh college graduate with no significant experience to encourage confidence in her ability to run an organization and properly manage corporate or foundation donations. She was able to succeed in an environment of uncertainty, pushing forward with organizational objectives, despite not always knowing if or when such funding would come through.

Since the launching of the movement, TFA has mostly been viewed as a success; a national study by Mathematica found that students of TFA teachers made larger math gains (with reading gains remaining even) than students of other teachers in participating schools.[17] Despite such indications of success, the program has prompted some controversy. Critics have argued that most TFA teachers do not stay in teaching very long, but move onto other things. While this is true, many education school–trained teachers do not stay in the profession very long either. Meanwhile, though most TFA teachers may not teach more than a few years, 60 percent do stay in the field of education. The 2005 National Teacher of the Year, Jason Kamras, is a TFA alumnus. And, of course, Kopp did not necessarily expect most of the TFA recruits to stay in teaching, but to gain important knowledge and insights for related careers.

Many former TFA teachers have implemented their own entrepreneurial ideas about education. For example, Kim Smith, cofounder of NewSchools Venture Fund, was one of the founding members of TFA. TFA alumni Dave Levin and Mike Feinberg founded KIPP in 1994, a program that has demonstrated significant success with low-income children.[18] After experiencing firsthand the difficulties of teaching low-income students, the two developed their own model, combining rewards and consequences to motivate middle school students. KIPP attracted financial support from Gap founders Doris and Donald Fisher, and now has thirty-eight schools serving over six thousand students.[19] Thus, TFA has steered many individuals into both teaching and educational administration, people who probably otherwise would not be in education.

Kopp certainly saw a gap and an opportunity—talented graduates who might otherwise pursue medicine, law, or business careers but had the idealism to teach for a time if they could do so without having to take several years of education school classes. She developed a summer training program that allowed them to move quickly into the classroom. Making it work required getting districts and schools to agree to work with the TFA teachers, despite early concerns that the lack of a traditional teaching degree would result in less effective teachers. Kopp also expanded TFA during a time when a shortage of teachers was looming; this made it somewhat easier to sell a shorter preparation time for bright undergraduates. TFA also faced considerable budget and development challenges during its early stages; it was by no means destined to succeed, except that Kopp maintained her entrepreneurial energy over a long period of time.

New Leaders for New Schools: Creating Future Leaders

New Leaders for New Schools (NLNS) is a nonprofit that provides training in educational leadership to promote high achievement for all children. It was founded in 2000 by Jon Schnur and other Harvard students. Schnur utilizes arbitrage as a central concept, applying business concepts to education. As an education advisor in the Clinton administration, Schnur realized that great principals make a significant difference—that exceptional principals were the common thread of effective schools. During this federal government service, Schnur decided to create a national program to recruit well-qualified individuals as principals and train them as effective leaders. But, rather than trying to be an intrapreneur, Schnur left the federal government and took this idea to the Harvard Business School, where he met others interested in his idea and developed a business plan.[20]

New Leaders are now working in over 230 schools. Participants spend six weeks at the summer Foundations Institute and attend four sessions of five or six days during the year, with a yearlong paid residency that includes a mentor principal and leadership coach. The program provides two additional years of ongoing support and a lifelong community of peers.

Schnur recognized that large percentages of current principals are near retirement and that new principals will be needed, but with a different skill set. Schnur also noticed that "you can't change a school without a great principal." He wanted to attract effective leaders, and to enable them to work more autonomously within school systems and apply sound business practices. NLNS saw opportunity in increased philanthropic funding for K–12 leadership and growing public awareness of the importance of excellent principals.

NLNS programs require funding. For example, their three-year program in Baltimore will cost $3 million, with half paid for by the school district and local philanthropies and the other half by national foundations. The primary risks involved in these programs, therefore, are to funders' money, to the reputation of NLNS, and that district funds will not be used appropriately.

It is also essential for NLNS to establish strong partnerships. The organization works with districts to share the expense of and provide training for the district's principals, and with local universities to provide certification for program graduates. NLNS will only go into districts with strong community networks of business, philanthropic, and education leaders.

NLNS describes their impact as twofold; they make a direct impact by attracting and training public school leaders, and an indirect impact by providing a model for others to follow. NLNS was the highest rated social enterprise in the United States by the Fast Company and Monitor Group's 2005 Social Capitalist Awards.[21] Other awards include Innovators of the Year from the Progressive Policy Institute (2003), being cited as one of six case studies included in a U.S. Department of Education best practices guide for school leadership (2004), being one of five organizations chosen by the Alliance for Excellent Education for demonstrating "innovative leadership that has successfully improved American high schools" (2004), and being chosen as "the only promising example" of the Teaching Commission's "recommendation to recruit, train, and empower school leaders" in 2004.

Despite demonstrated success, Schnur and his organization continue to face challenges, including recruitment needs, ongoing funding requirements, and investment in research and development, including program evaluation. Schnur's faith in his organization mission seems to fuel his determination to "foster high levels of academic achievement for *every* child by recruiting, training, placing, and supporting the next generation of outstanding principals for our nation's urban public schools."[22]

Schnur had the vision to create a new organization to provide an innovative service—teaching principals to become effective school leaders. In the process he has risked large sums of funders' money, and perhaps to a certain extent his career as a policy analyst, to leave the federal bureaucracy and pursue his concept of transforming the education system from outside government, where he saw constraints that were too strong. Schnur's vision to transform principal training, his action orientation, and his persistence against strong odds fit well the description of a successful entrepreneur.

K12: Creating Online Education

Founded by former U.S. Secretary of Education William Bennett and Knowledge Universe's Ron Packard in 1999, K12 Inc. is a for-profit company that provides an online curriculum and operates "virtual" schools, where parents can enroll students in the K12 program for a fee or, in some cases, enroll in a virtual charter school. Although K12 was not the first provider of virtual schools, it is the most prominent.

The founding of K12 reflects an awareness of opportunities for private involvement in education brought about by the emergence of charter laws, combined with the potential of new technology. K12 students typically remain at home for their schooling, using technology to tap into a different market of students than other charter schools—primarily homeschoolers. The founders realized that virtual schools would have an easier time scaling-up than other charter schools, in part because of the loosening of the space constraint. One virtual charter school can draw students from across an entire state, not just a small geographic area. This model was partly arbitraged from higher education, where the University of Phoenix and others had developed the online course delivery system.

K12 has endured extensive political and financial risk. Controversy has surrounded K12, since public funds are educating some children who may not otherwise have been in private schools. And many of K12's components are controversial—for-profit management, home schooling, virtual schools, and interdistrict schooling. Knowledge Universe Learning Group invested about $10 million to develop the curriculum, which is the firm's greatest asset. In addition, Bennett himself has proven controversial, ultimately resigning from K12 in 2005.

Although he carried some baggage, Bennett brought extensive experience and name recognition to the firm. He has spent his career as a reformer, was named one of "The 25 Most Influential People in America" by *Time* magazine, and has a demonstrated passion for education reform. By combining education and technology, K12 has demonstrated the success of a new business model.

Kaplan and the Expansion of Test-Preparation Services

Kaplan is a for-profit education company with divisions offering programs to higher education institutions, preparation for standardized testing, training for professional licenses/designations, and tutoring programs. Founded by Stanley Kaplan in 1938, it was purchased by the Washington Post Company in 1984 and has expanded significantly under the leadership of CEO Jonathan Grayer, expanding from an $80 million company in 1994, to $1.1 billion in revenue by 2004.[23]

Much of the company's expansion is due to its recognition of new opportunities for private companies in the education sector. The test-preparation division offers tutoring through its Score! Centers and within schools. The company has also entered the curriculum development market with $9 million in contracts in Philadelphia schools.[24] Kaplan also has seventy campuses and an online program serving higher education markets, competing with the University of Phoenix and others. Kaplan also networks with public and nonprofit organizations, such as Reading Is Fundamental, Inc., DonorsChoose, Watts Youth Opportunity (LA), Chicago Cares, and New York Cares, to provide services.

These new endeavors carry risks, but they are thriving. Kaplan is now the *Washington Post*'s largest revenue producing division, and will soon be its largest source of income. The major criticism of this activity has been that Kaplan's test-preparation programs, specifically those for college entrance exams, favor the higher-income students who can afford them. This criticism has been diminished by Kaplan's provision of tutoring services for low-income students in failing schools, as part of the NCLB supplemental services program.

Stanley Kaplan was clearly a private educational entrepreneur, founding his own firm in a new market he pioneered. Kaplan, Inc., has continued in this tradition, filling gaps in the education market by introducing innovative services as opportunities arise, and perhaps risking the company's reputation with each new venture. Although Kaplan has not singlehandedly transformed the educational system, it has joined others in making significant changes in such areas as higher education, tutoring, and test preparation.

CONCLUSIONS

Entrepreneurship in education is a growing force. The ongoing sense of crisis in American education and the apparent failure of incremental reforms have created a new openness to trying different ideas. Furthermore, as Patrick McGuinn notes in chapter 3, state choice laws and the federal NCLB Act have paved the way for a greater role for private and nonprofit organizations. While there are still strong barriers to enhanced entrepreneurship, the constraints are somewhat weaker than in the past.

As is typically the case when research focuses only on a handful of successful entrepreneurs, as in our case studies, it can appear that entrepreneurship is already sweeping barriers away and creating an array of new educational options. That would be an overly optimistic picture. The scaling-up problem remains to be solved for most of these ventures, which remain relatively small, particularly compared to the $500 billion American K–12 public school sector. These entrepreneurs are making changes at the fringes of the system, but will these changes really permeate through the system over time?

A concern for entrepreneurial private firms is whether they outlast their founding leadership and sustain entrepreneurial energy as they grow. At some point, do entrepreneurial organizations benefit from a different type of leader—one who is more talented at managing an established organization successfully than an entrepreneur who thrives on the initial challenge of creation? These are important questions in any entrepreneurial domain. Ultimately, do educational entrepreneurs change a few individual schools or can they really change entire school systems?

Many leading educational entrepreneurs are trying to institutionalize the entrepreneurial climate and the future supply of potential new entrepreneurs. For example, TFA, NLNS, and other groups are trying to create institutions and networks that can foster innovation beyond the original entrepreneurs. If these organizations can succeed, they will foster an environment in which smart potential entrepreneurs can and will emerge and allow them to unleash their ideas, which will lead to some "creative destruction."

Can education continue to attract entrepreneurial talent from people outside the traditional education sphere, and also "grow its own" entrepreneurs, like Brad Jupp? Both of these pipelines are probably essential to maintain a climate of continued entrepreneurship. The idea that successful entrepreneurs are characterized by action orientation, high levels of self-confidence, and persistence provides evidence that such people are born that way. But perhaps there are latent entrepreneurs waiting for support to be "made." While Wendy Kopp founded TFA fresh out of college with little experience, future educational entrepreneurs will benefit from the paths and the networks she and others have forged. NewSchools Venture Fund and KIPP already emerged from the TFA experience; all of these successful examples will encourage further entrepreneurial efforts.

Another important question is the extent to which educational entrepreneurs influence broader public policy discussions. This may be more likely for entrepreneurs within the public system of education; Brad Jupp, for example, in working to pass Pro-Comp in Denver, has clearly influenced broader policy debates about teacher compensation. K12 also takes on a public policy role to encourage state legislation allowing for the operation of virtual schools, as it did quite prominently in Pennsylvania. TFA has played a policy role, at least indirectly. By engaging future leaders in the education sector, TFA has increased the opportunities for experienced voices to be heard in the policy arena. Other organizations choose to play only minor public policy roles.

At the start of this chapter, we discussed a range of possible definitions of educational entrepreneurs. Perhaps a more concrete definition might be that a truly successful educational entrepreneur begins to change larger systems in a manner that outlasts that specific individual. Thus, while there are limits, there are also reasons to be excited about the various new entrepreneurial ventures and activities in K–12 education. Given the very long reign of business as usual in American schooling, this kind of change just might go a long way.

CHAPTER 3

The Policy Landscape

Patrick McGuinn

In recent years, American public education has undergone a remarkable transformation. Local, state, and federal reforms have been enacted to improve
student academic performance and give parents more educational choices.
Many of these reforms have been designed to encourage entrepreneurial
actors inside and outside the traditional public school system to develop and
deploy genuinely new approaches to schooling. Scholars and practitioners
are well aware that public policy—the laws, regulations, and programs insti-
tuted by governments—establishes the ground rules for educational entrepreneurship. But the actual policy landscape—the political and policy context within which educational innovators must maneuver—has received
little systematic attention.

How does policy influence the calculus of entrepreneurship in education?
What kinds of policies affect the supply, behavior, and cost-benefit decisions
of entrepreneurial actors? This chapter examines how and why states have
fostered or hindered educational entrepreneurship. It focuses on three areas
of policy that have undergone extensive change in recent years—charter
schooling, teacher and principal licensure, and supplemental services. The
chapter concludes with a look to the future of the policy landscape regarding
entrepreneurship, and in particular the impact of accountability reforms and
the federal No Child Left Behind Act (NCLB).

POLITICS AND GOVERNING THE MARKET FOR ENTREPRENEURSHIP

Understanding of the policy landscape of educational entrepreneurship in
the United States must begin with our uniquely decentralized and fragmented

system of educational governance. The nation's traditions of localism and federalism have exerted a powerful influence on the evolution of the American public education system. The day-to-day management of schools, including such matters as personnel, curriculum, and pedagogy, remained largely in the hands of local authorities (and often the educators themselves) until the middle of the twentieth century. Over time, reformers promoted bureaucratic regulation in order to combat their fragmentation. The U.S. Supreme Court's 1954 *Brown v. Board of Education* decision, the federal Elementary and Secondary Education Act (ESEA) of 1965, and a wave of school finance litigation in the 1970s forced states and the federal government to address the inferior educational opportunities available to poor students and students of color. In the equity regime that emerged in the 1960s and 1970s, the focus of state and federal governments was largely on inputs and process—on ensuring compliance of districts and schools with procedural mandates regarding student assignment and school financing. These developments produced a heavily regulated system of educational governance as local, state, and federal authorities enacted policies that impacted the day-to-day operation of the country's public schools.

The policymaking authority of these various levels of government has been used to both impede and promote entrepreneurial activity in education. There are at least three different dimensions to contemplate when analyzing governmental policies regarding educational entrepreneurship—the level of government involved (local, state, or federal); the kind of policy lever utilized (legislative, regulatory, fiscal, or judicial); and the type of sector targeted (public or private). Moreover, governmental education policies differ not just in their ends—their policy aims—but also in the means employed to achieve these aims. State and federal governments have an enormous impact on the emergence and operations of educational entrepreneurs through their funding and taxation decisions, regulatory environments, and legislative enactments.

The politics of entrepreneurship, however, is such that government is often inclined to be hostile to new players and ideas. Existing policymaking arrangements and standard operating practices are often deeply entrenched and defended by powerful interests. The most powerful political actors at the local, state, and national levels in education are the teachers unions and the variety of advocacy groups collectively referred to as the "education establishment." Due to both the dictates of self-preservation and notions of good policy, these groups generally oppose reforms that would introduce entrepreneurial approaches into the existing public school system or permit entrepreneurial actors to create alternative schools.[1] For many years, the unions were able to use their power to preserve the status quo in education by defeating—

or effectively neutering—many of the school reform proposals that emerged at the local, state, and national levels.

During the 1980s and 1990s, a variety of factors led states and the federal government to assume a greater share of education policymaking authority and to shift their focus from resources to achievement. These factors included the 1983 *A Nation at Risk* report, the larger changes in the economy, the abysmal performance of urban school systems, and the failure of additional resources to end persistent racial and class-based achievement gaps. The rise of education to the top of the public agenda at the state and federal levels during the 1980s and 1990s, meanwhile, added a political imperative to school reform efforts. State and federal governments responded by increasingly using their authority to combine deregulation with accountability and gradually opening up the educational marketplace. In this sense we may be witnessing a kind of centralized decentralization in school reform in which centralized power is used to expand the number and type of educational options for parents and children. If the political environment has grown more favorable to entrepreneurial reforms, however, the politics of education remains contentious at the national, state, and local levels. This reality—along with the incremental and conservative nature of the policymaking process more generally—has meant that most school reforms become law only after compromises have limited their size and scope and the freedom accorded entrepreneurs.

THE POLICY LANDSCAPE IN THE STATES

The developments described above helped to inaugurate a new era of accountability in education reform, and gave policymakers and school leaders both the means and the incentives to embrace educational innovation to a much greater extent. Some changes, like those in the regulations governing teacher and principal licensure, attempt to reform existing public schools from the inside by fostering public entrepreneurship. Other reforms—such as the charter movement—have encouraged the creation of new schools that operate within the public system but which utilize greater regulatory flexibility to institute different instructional and governance approaches. A third type of reform has been to increase educational innovation by embracing private entrepreneurs—either by contracting public school operations to private companies or by allowing students to use public funds to pay for private school tuition.

The major policy impediments to educational entrepreneurship have to do with three things: barriers to entry, lack of access to financial capital for new ventures, and lack of human capital—that is, an insufficient number of entrepreneurial administrators and teachers. This section explores the specific ways in which federal and state policies have shaped entrepreneurship in K–12 education within each of these dimensions.

Teacher and Principal Training and Licensure

Human capital—the accumulated skills, experiences, and attitudes possessed by employees and managers—is crucial to the success of any organization. Policymakers have an enormous impact on human capital in education through the regulations that govern who is allowed to teach in and run schools and how such individuals are recruited and trained. States and districts restrict the entrance of individuals into teaching and school administration in two important ways: first by requiring that teachers and administrators be licensed in order to work in public schools, and, second, through the requirements that they establish for licensure. Taken together, these regulations—along with compensation and hiring practices—restrict the entry of new candidates and can make mobility and risk-taking behavior among existing school personnel more costly.

These licensing processes typically include a number of curricular and experiential requirements that prospective public school educators and administrators must meet. Forty-five states (all except Florida, Maine, Maryland, New York, and Rhode Island) require prospective teachers to complete a state-approved teacher-preparation program.[2] There is considerable variation, however, across states and even across licensing institutions within states in terms of the amount and rigor of coursework required, the number and difficulty of licensing exams, and the amount of time candidates must spend student teaching. Some states require only an initial teaching certificate while others require a second- or third-stage certificate with additional course requirements. The traditional way of satisfying these requirements in most states is through completion of a teacher-preparation program run through a school of education. In 1983, only eight states reported having some kind of alternative teacher-preparation program.[3] These college teacher-preparation programs typically emphasize training future teachers to conform to existing pedagogical, curricular, and organizational practices in traditional public schools, rather than instilling entrepreneurial skills or attitudes.[4]

During the 1980s, concerns about teacher quality and projected teacher shortages led many states to focus greater attention on how teachers were recruited and trained. Some states focused their efforts on adding additional requirements to existing teacher-certification programs. In order to recruit and train more teachers and different kinds of teachers, some states also began to develop alternative teacher-certification processes that would enable prospective teachers to bypass the traditional education school programs. A 1999 study by the Thomas B. Fordham Foundation, however, concluded that these efforts remained limited and graded state efforts nationwide to create alternative pathways to teaching with a "D." They found that only fourteen states had "serious" alternative certification programs in place in 1999, and that only a few of these had produced sizable numbers of graduates.[5]

The focus on teacher quality and on alternative teacher certification received a major boost with the passage of the federal Higher Education Act of 1998 (particularly sections 207 and 208 in Title II). The act mandated that states report information on teacher preparation, certification, and licensing, including details of their alternative certification routes and the performance of teachers who use them on state licensure exams. The 2002 No Child Left Behind Act also required states to have a "highly qualified teacher" in every classroom where core academic subjects are taught by 2005–06.

These state and federal initiatives have given the alternative certification movement considerable momentum; one-third of current state alternative teacher-certification routes have been created since 2000. Data from the National Center for Education Information shows that in 2005, a total of forty-seven states (and the District of Columbia) reported that they have alternative teacher-certification programs in place. There were 122 alternative routes to teacher certification actually being implemented by approximately 619 different providers, including higher education institutions.[6] The oldest and most prolific alternative certification programs are in California, New Jersey, and Texas; these three states produced almost half of the national total of alternatively certified teachers in 2004.[7]

It is important to note that alternative certification programs vary considerably in the extent to which they produce teachers and school leaders who think entrepreneurially. Many programs merely embody a different set of requirements and timetables rather than different methods of recruiting or training that could produce a qualitatively different kind of teacher.[8] In addition, how states chose to govern and administer their teacher licensure programs has a major impact on the size and nature of alternate routes. While these programs typically run though the state department of education, some states with large numbers of teachers coming through alternative certification routes—such as California, Texas, and Georgia—have empowered separate state commissions or boards to oversee the process. Texas's Accountability System for Educator Preparation program (established in 1995) empowered multiple and varied providers of teacher preparation. By 2002, the State

Board for Educator Certification had authorized ninety-four different educator preparation programs: sixty-nine were run by colleges or universities, sixteen by regional education service centers, four by school districts, three by community colleges, and two by private entities.[9] Nationwide, about 50 percent of alternative certification programs are administered by colleges and universities, while 20 percent are administered at the school district level. In some states—such as California, Illinois, Pennsylvania, and Texas—most of the alternative teaching programs are controlled by institutions of higher education, while in other states—such as Colorado, Florida, Maryland, and Oregon—they are controlled by the school districts themselves.[10]

A number of private and public entities have taken advantage of changes in teacher and principal hiring and certification practices to recruit and train teachers and principals in different ways, targeting candidates from diverse educational and professional backgrounds who have not completed a traditional certification program. One of the most prominent of these groups is Teach For America, which began in 1990 and has placed fourteen thousand recent college graduates in public schools in poor urban and rural areas across the country. Troops for Teachers, a Department of Defense program initiated in 1994, and The New Teacher Project (1997) have also utilized alternative certification routes for nontraditional teachers. In addition, some states, such as Florida, Pennsylvania, Idaho, and Utah, have agreed to accept teachers certified through the American Board for Certification of Teacher Excellence program, which was founded in 2001 and targets nontraditional candidates. Despite the existence and growth of these programs, the number of alternatively certified teachers in the country remains quite small—by one estimate they comprised only two hundred thousand of the nation's three million total teachers in 2004.[11]

States have also begun in recent years to reconsider the process by which they recruit and train school principals and superintendents. Historically, the overwhelming majority of school leaders have risen through the ranks—beginning their careers as teachers and then moving on to become assistant principals, then principals, then up to the district office. All but two states (Michigan and South Dakota) require prospective principals or superintendents to acquire a license in school administration in order to be eligible to be hired. State principal licensure requirements typically include the following: three or more years of K–12 teaching experience, a graduate degree in educational administration, and an internship. Many states also require candidates to pass the School Leaders Licensure Assessment exam.[12] A 2003 RAND study found that "formal barriers such as certification requirements and informal barriers such as district hiring practices all but exclude those without teaching experience from consideration for administrative positions."[13] As with the standard teacher-licensing process, the typical principal and superintendent curriculum is offered through a university education school and does not emphasize the kinds of skills and attitudes that are likely to develop an entrepreneurial cadre of school leaders.[14] These requirements also likely deter many prospective entrepreneurial leaders from inside and outside of the public school system from becoming school principals or superintendents.[15]

Despite some efforts by states to revise their principal and superintendent training and licensing processes, Emily Feistritzer concluded in a 2003 report that "as yet there is no general move afoot to bring people from outside the ranks of traditional educators into school leadership positions."[16] Some large urban districts had begun to bring in different kinds of superintendents on an ad hoc basis and, as of 2003, eleven states had formal alternative routes by which principal and superintendent candidates could enter school administration positions. These alternative programs are typically run through the same education schools as the traditional programs, however, and the number of candidates moving through the alternative routes remained quite small. Seven states (Florida, Hawaii, Michigan, North Carolina, South Dakota, Tennessee, and Wyoming) and the District of Columbia do not require the certification of superintendents.[17] In these states, local districts are free to set their own requirements, but in practice these have tended to resemble the standard certification routes set at the state level elsewhere.

In a recent report entitled "Innovative Pathways to School Leadership," the U.S. Department of Education (DOE) declared that "traditional education administration programs and certification procedures are producing insufficient numbers of [effective] leaders."[18] In an effort to promote models for further action, the study provided case studies of five alternative school leadership preparation programs, which it said had taken advantage of changes in state licensing requirements to create "pioneering programs that recruit and prepare principals in inventive ways." The programs were: Boston Principal Fellowship Program; First Ring Leadership Academy (Cleveland); LAUNCH (Leadership Academy and Urban Network for Chicago); NJ EXCEL (Expedited Certification for Educational Leadership); Principals Excellence Program (Pike County, Kentucky); and New Leaders for New Schools (New York, Chicago, Washington, D.C., Memphis, and San Francisco). "These innovative and entrepreneurial programs," the report observed, "are developing new recruiting strategies to attract potential leaders from beyond the traditional pipeline of experienced teachers . . . and emphasize the principal's role as a catalyst for change."[19] While these alternative preparation programs vary in their particular origins, methods, and goals, what they have in common is their focus on producing different *kinds* of teachers and administrators by recruiting candidates with different kinds of backgrounds and by training them in innovative ways.

Charter Schooling

Amidst the reforms states have adopted in recent years, charter schools have been the most widely adopted and potentially offer the greatest avenue for introducing a more entrepreneurial spirit into the American educational system. The charter school movement is predicated on the idea of giving educational entrepreneurs the ability to operate public schools that agree to meet specified performance targets in exchange for freedom from bureaucratic rules and regulations. The first charter school law in the United States was passed in Minnesota in 1991, and the movement has witnessed remarkable growth in recent years. Charter school reforms gained significant public support and political momentum during the 1990s, when the idea was embraced by a number of Republican and Democratic leaders.

According to the Education Commission of the States, forty states had charter laws in place as of February 2005.[20] The only states without charter laws were Alabama, Kentucky, Maine, Montana, Nebraska, North Dakota, South Dakota, Vermont, Washington, and West Virginia. Gregg Vanourek of the Charter School Leadership Council estimates that the number of charter schools in operation increased from 253 in 1996 to 3,400 in 2005, and that the number of students in charters grew from three hundred thousand in 1999 to one million in 2005 (roughly 2 percent of the total K–12 student population in the United States).[21] Charter laws now cover 92 percent of the U.S. population and 96 out of the 100 largest school districts in the country, although 42 percent of charter schools are concentrated in just three states: Arizona, California, and Florida. Due to the particular design of charter laws (see below) and the problems plaguing many urban school systems, about half of all charters in the country are located in or around major cities. About 23 percent of charter schools were existing schools that converted to charter status, while 77 percent began as newly created start-ups.

It is crucial to recognize that all charter laws are not equal and all charter schools are not entrepreneurial. There is considerable variation in the extent to which state charter laws encourage the entrance and sustenance of truly entrepreneurial ventures. Charter schools have embraced a wide variety of different educational missions and approaches. While many of these may be considered pedagogically or curricularly innovative,[22] these schools do not necessarily attempt to create educational systems in which energy and fresh thinking are welcomed or constructively employed. Some charter schools, however, have taken advantage of advances in communications technology to offer educational services in radically different ways, such as through distance education programs and "virtual" schools. According to a 2002–03 survey, 3 percent of charter schools nationwide report that they rely on online instruction and do not have a physical school building. An additional 4 percent indicated that they use independent or home study. All told, there were a total of eighty-one virtual charter schools serving about twenty-eight thousand students.[23]

Another important development in the entrepreneurial landscape has been the emergence of for-profit Education Management Organizations (EMOs) and nonprofit Charter Management Organizations (CMOs). While approximately 90 percent of the charter schools in the country are independently run, about 10 percent are managed by EMOs. An even greater number of charters contract out to EMOs for the provision of particular educational services. Between 1998 and 2003, the number of states in which EMOs operated increased from fifteen to twenty-eight. While the total number of EMO-managed schools remains relatively small nationwide, they are a large presence in some states, such as Ohio, where 66 percent of charter students attend EMO-managed schools.[24] According to a report by the Commercialism in Education Research Unit at Arizona State University, 51 for-profit companies managed 376 charter schools (and an additional 87 traditional public schools) with a total of two hundred thousand students in 2004.[25]

While for-profit education companies have long played a significant role in K–12 education by providing various products and services to public schools, their entry into public school management is a recent development. Edison, Chancellor-Beacon, National Heritage, Victory, and Nobel Learning Communities are among the country's largest private managers of public schools, and they have ambitious plans for future expansion. The different missions, structures, and capacities for expansion of these for-profit EMO-managed charters distinguishes them from the majority of other charter schools, which are run by organizations such as universities or local nonprofits. But the notion of private for-profit companies managing schools is a controversial one and has generated a tremendous amount of opposition— particularly from those who believe such arrangements threaten traditional public school governance structures and funding streams.

A number of nonprofit charter management organizations have also been created in recent years. The NewSchools Venture Fund established a "charter accelerator" initiative to increase investment in charters and currently supports nine CMOs that run thirty-two schools serving eight thousand students. The Knowledge Is Power Program (KIPP) network began with schools in Houston and the Bronx, and by 2005 it had used philanthropic support to establish thirty-eight schools in fifteen states (and Washington, D.C.) serving over six thousand students. As of 2005, Aspire Public Schools had opened more than a dozen charter schools in California and plans on operating a large chain of public schools. As with independently run charters, however, the capacity of EMOs and CMOs to successfully inject entrepreneurial ideas into education is largely dependent on the extent to which they are freed from the political pressures, bureaucratic regulations, and collective bargaining agreements that limit the flexibility of public educators.

Despite the emergence of EMOs and CMOs and the rapid growth in the total number of charter schools nationwide, approximately 40 percent of charter schools report having waiting lists (which average 135 students)—an indication that the demand for charter schools has outpaced the supply. The future growth of these alternative public schools has been constrained, however, by state policies that often cap the number of charters that can be issued, provide limited charter funding, or require excessive regulation of charter schools. Approximately twenty-seven states (more than half) have some form of cap on charter schools. Some states, such as North Carolina, limit the total number of charter schools that are allowed to operate. Other states limit the number of charters that can be issued each year, or, as in Massachusetts, the percentage of a district's spending that can be directed to charters in any given year. Still other states (such as Ohio) limit the geographic range within which charters may operate.

State policies also constrain the number and type of charter schools by controlling who is given the authority to issue charters. As of 2002–03, half the states with charter schools permitted only a state agency or local school board to authorize charters. The vast majority of the six hundred existing charter authorizers—about 90 percent of the total—are the local school districts themselves. Of the remaining authorizers, 5 percent are higher education institutions, 3 percent are state education agencies, and 2 percent are other entities such as municipal or not-for-profit organizations. All told, there are only about sixty nondistrict charter school authorizers in the entire country.[26]

Placing the local school district in charge of authorizing charters is problematic for two reasons. First, districts are, not surprisingly, reluctant to expand the number of alternatives to their own traditional schools. While local districts represented 90 percent of all authorizers, for example, they authorized only 45 percent of all charter schools. State education agencies, meanwhile, which represent only 3 percent of authorizers, authorized 41 percent of all charter schools. In addition, school districts are probably more conservative about the kinds of schools and school operators that they are willing to permit. Between caps and the nature of the authorizing process, the number of new charter schools opening per year has remained largely flat since 2000, and half of the new growth over the past five years has been in only five states (Arizona, California, Florida, Michigan, and Texas). In a 2003 Fordham Foundation study of state charter authorizer practices and policy environments, none of the twenty-four states evaluated received an A, while thirteen states were given a B, eight a C, and three a D.[27]

California and Indiana have taken an unusual approach to charter authorizing, however, which could become a model for other states and encourage the growth of entrepreneurial charter schools nationwide. Indiana's 2001 charter legislation established multiple charter authorizers—including the mayor of Indianapolis, the only mayor in the country to have such power. California's 2002 charter law allows charter schools with high test scores to apply to the state's department of education for permission to expand their models statewide without local approval. In 2005, nonprofit High Tech High Learning became the first charter operation to receive such approval, and then announced plans to open two new schools a year in the state.

State laws permitting the creation of charter schools, however, are a necessary but not sufficient condition for the creation of *entrepreneurial* charter schools. Outcome clarity and operational flexibility are essential preconditions for entrepreneurship. State policies on charter financing, regulation, and accountability are enormously important in determining whether entrepreneurs open schools as well as for *how* they will operate them. The funding states provide to charter schools varies considerably, and most states provide significantly less funding to charters than to traditional public schools in the same district. Nationwide, in 2002–03, district public schools received $8,529 per pupil, while charter schools received an average of $5,688—or about 33 percent less—per pupil.[28] Chester E. Finn Jr. and Eric Osberg have remarked that "the finance ground rules appear designed to produce failure, not success, on the part of charter schools across the land."[29] Their study of seventeen states found that the per-pupil funding disparity for charters ranged from 5 percent less in New Mexico to 40 percent less in South Carolina. The gaps are even larger in most big urban school districts.[30] Research conducted by the Center for Education Reform on forty states in 2005 estimated that the charter school funding gap was 21 percent on average.[31]

The CER study identified seven major causes of the charter school funding gap: unfair bargaining relationships between charter schools and local districts, which result in an unfair allocation of local, state, and federal grants; vague language in state charter school laws; impact aid given to school districts; "hold harmless" clauses that prevent funds from following students who transfer to charter schools; denial of access to local bond measures; the withholding of funds for charters by local districts; and facilities support that is given to district schools but not charters. As of 2004, only twenty-four states (plus the District of Columbia) provided facilities assistance to charter schools: sixteen of these states provided support through grants, bond issues, tax breaks, or loan programs, while eight limited their assistance to charters to permitting them to lease public school facilities.[32] The lack of adequate support can be a powerful deterrent to prospective charter entrepreneurs and handicap existing charter schools.

A few states, such as Florida, Minnesota, and California, provide funds to charters for facilities on a per-pupil basis, much as they do for instruction. Some states allow charters to draw from state bond funds, but even in those instances they are often not allocated funds in proportion to their share of the state's public school students. The federal government initiated a number of programs during the Clinton administration to support charter schools, and the Government Accountability Office has estimated that Congress appropriated over $1 billion in federal funding to encourage new and expanding charters between 1995 and 2005.[33] With direct financial support for facilities from states and the federal government generally limited, however, charter operators often turn to the private capital markets. Federal, state, and district loan guarantees for charter schools (or "community facilities" generally), tax credits for investment in low-income neighborhoods, tax-exempt bonding authority (in Colorado and Michigan), and revolving pools of loan capital (such as the Illinois Facilities Fund) are some of the ways in which policymakers have attempted to help charters cover their facilities costs. Despite these efforts, as of 2001, fewer than 20 percent of charters owned their own facilities and almost three-quarters leased them. Some states, such as California and New York, have sought to assist charter schools by requiring that district and/or state officials lease them facilities (sometimes, as in Colorado, rent free) or provide a list of vacant public buildings.[34]

Perhaps most importantly, the creation of truly entrepreneurial charter schools requires what might be termed "entrepreneurial space"—freedom from onerous and homogenizing educational regulations. Charters need to retain a large degree of autonomy over their operations—in particular their hiring, budgets, curricula, and scheduling—because it is this autonomy that enables them to reinvent and to grow. Entrepreneurs—particularly those in the for-profit sector—also require the ability to expand the number of schools and the number of students within individual schools in order to respond to market demand and to realize operational efficiencies. One way to measure the degree of autonomy that is being granted to charter schools is to look at whether they are classified as their own local education agency (LEA) or considered part of the area's existing LEA. Currently, eight states give charters independent LEA status, sixteen include them in existing LEAs, and fifteen states grant them a kind of mixed status.[35] Placing charter schools under the regulation of the local public school district is problematic for the same reasons as making the district itself a charter authorizer—it is likely to undermine the kind of entrepreneurial behavior that charters are intended to provide.

Given these governance arrangements, it is perhaps not surprising that charter schools have not been given as much freedom from regulation as is often supposed. Vanourek's analysis of charter laws nationwide revealed that twenty-two states (about half of the total) provide some sort of blanket or automatic waiver of most regulations, six states (14%) provide a partial waiver, and fourteen states (33%) provide only for a discretionary waiver contingent on an application process.[36] In a 2001–02 U.S. Department of Education survey, 40 percent of charter schools reported not having authority over curriculum and the school calendar, while 30 percent said they did not have full authority over assessment and discipline policies. Perhaps the most essential kind of discretion for developing entrepreneurial charter schools is that over hiring, promotion, firing, and compensation for personnel. Many charter schools, however, are required to operate under the restrictions of district collective bargaining agreements, and 55 percent of charter schools reported not having full authority over teacher-certification requirements. The Department of Education study concluded that "charter schools are now held to the same requirements as other public schools in addition to measurable goals in the charter document."[37]

Another crucial public policy question related to charter school governance is how charter schools should be held accountable, for what, and to whom. How should policy straddle a desire for innovation as well as a desire for quality? In addition to being accountable internally to their own parents, staffs, governing boards, and sometimes management companies, charter schools typically face multiple layers of externally imposed accountability. Charter authorizers are typically the key player in charter school accountability. As public schools, charter schools must comply with federal health, safety, and civil rights laws and regulations as well as the provisions of No Child Left Behind. Charter schools must also adhere to many state laws and regulations governing public schools, including administering achievement tests and undergoing fiscal audits, although they are typically granted some waivers as part of their charters.

As discussed in more detail below, NCLB's public school choice provision is having a major impact on the charter school environment and has the potential to dramatically expand the size of the charter school market. The current policy environment within which charters schools must operate, however, is enormously varied both across and within states. Some states clearly offer a more hospitable policy environment for charter entrepreneurship than others, but often states that provide a more favorable policy climate for entrepreneurship in one area (such as funding) have a less favorable policy climate in another area (such as authorizing or regulation). As a result, one analysis has noted, "few states can boast a robust charter climate across the board. Almost fifteen years into the charter school experiment, it's difficult to find a place where the charter ideal has been fully developed in both policy and practice."[38]

No Child Left Behind and Supplemental Services

The No Child Left Behind Act is having a major impact on school reform across the country and can potentially provide a number of new avenues and incentives for entrepreneurial activity in education. The law's teacher-quality provision is forcing states to reconsider longstanding teacher licensure practices and may ultimately lead to the creation or expansion of alternative routes to teaching and the expansion of entrepreneurial human capital in education. The law also requires that states deal with underperforming schools by taking corrective actions such as providing extra tutoring money, giving students the option of transferring to another school, or changing school management. Under NCLB, Title I schools that have failed to meet adequate yearly progress for three or more consecutive years are required to offer supplemental educational services (typically tutoring) to students. Congress required that districts with schools in need of improvement set aside an amount equal to at least 20 percent of its Title I allocation for choice-related transportation and supplemental services (SES). The law stipulates that these services may be provided by private companies as well as the local school districts themselves.

The administration of the SES process, however, was left in the hands of states and districts, and the ultimate impact of the reform will depend on how they use this discretion. Districts vary considerably in the approach that they have taken to SES, and some have been more willing to use it than others to foster entrepreneurial activity (either within the district or in terms of outside providers). A 2005 report by the Center on Education Policy found that 10 percent of Title I districts nationwide had schools that were required to offer supplemental educational services. Approximately 1 percent of all public school students were eligible for SES in 2005, but only about one-fifth of eligible students actually received such services. A study of SES by the Association for Community Organizations for Reform Now (ACORN) found that district participation rates ranged from as high as 92 percent of eligible students to no students, and that more than half of districts enrolled less than 20 percent of their eligible students.[39] Districts report that insufficient funding is a primary obstacle to serving a greater number of eligible students and that on average they currently have the resources to provide SES to only 22 percent of all eligible students.[40]

States also control entry into the SES marketplace by establishing lists of approved providers that can offer services to students, from which parents then choose. Districts are charged with determining student eligibility for SES, informing parents about SES, managing access to school sites for SES, and establishing contracts with individual SES providers. How effectively these tasks are handled has an enormous impact on the ability of entrepreneurs to enter the SES marketplace and to deliver services to students. Siobhan Gorman has noted that "within this new marketplace, school districts hold enormous power as a result of their dual role—as both program administrator and potential provider. Districts also have little incentive to inform parents of the money available to them for tutoring, since districts get to keep any unused funds."[41] In testimony before Congress, Jeffrey Cohen of Catapult Learning noted that "providers often contend with seemingly unnecessary obstacles, including district opposition to SES, lack of information about implementation plans, and LEA regulation of state-approved programs."[42]

The newness of the SES program and the tremendous variance in the ground rules that states and districts are establishing have created a great deal of market uncertainty for potential entrepreneurs. In 2005, the U.S. Department of Education announced two significant new efforts that incorporate some of the best practices suggested by the Education Industry Association.[43] The first is a cooperative effort with the Council of the Great City Schools to enter into pilot flexibility agreements with select urban districts, the first of which was Chicago.[44] As part of the agreement, districts will have to take a number of steps that are likely to ease the entrance and activities of entrepreneurs: they must provide early notification to parents about SES eligibility; extend enrollment periods; allow private providers to use district facilities at a reasonable fee; and allow the use of an independent third party to evaluate provider effectiveness. Prior to the agreement, Chicago—like seventy-five other large and very large school districts across the country—had been declared as a district in need of improvement under NCLB and was therefore ineligible to offer SES according to the original law. The new agreement allowed the district to continue to do so. The DOE has also entered into a pilot flexibility agreement with the state of Virginia to permit the state to reverse the order in which public school choice and SES are offered in the school improvement process in four districts, allowing eligible students to receive SES one year earlier than in the original timeline of NCLB. Pilot cities and states must also commit to expanding student participation rates in SES programs. The DOE has singled out five districts for implementing SES quickly and effectively and for maximizing student participation—San Diego, Rochester, Los Angeles, Forsyth (Georgia), and Toledo (Ohio).[45] The number, size, and scope of operations of SES providers, meanwhile, continue to grow at a rapid pace.[46]

ACCOUNTABILITY AND ENTREPRENEURSHIP

Perhaps the most interesting and influential development in education in recent years has been the increased focus on accountability for academic achievement. Initiated by many state governments during the 1980s and at the federal level during the 1990s, accountability has become an even more important part of the educational landscape in the wake of No Child Left Behind. Like so many of the other reforms discussed in this chapter, accountability measures have the ability to either stifle or facilitate entrepreneurship in education, depending on how they are conceived and implemented. Historically, there has been tremendous ambiguity about how to evaluate the effectiveness of entrepreneurial ventures in education. Linking accountability to performance on standardized tests in math and reading has provided a clear measuring stick for assessing the effectiveness of alternative schools and providers. Consequences for schools and districts that fail to meet educational achievement targets may encourage policymakers and public school leaders to accept effective alternatives, even if nontraditional in design.

The accountability movement has led some states to radically alter the traditional model of district provision of education. A number of states across the country (such as New Jersey, Connecticut, Illinois, Ohio, and Pennsylvania) have assumed control of failing urban districts in recent years, and some have imposed reforms that have greatly expanded the number and type of entrepreneurial activities. The persistently poor performance of students in Philadelphia, for example, led the governor of Pennsylvania to take control of the struggling district in December 2001 and to charge a reform commission with designing and implementing a comprehensive reform plan. The commission ultimately awarded control of forty-five failing schools to seven independent operators—three for-profit firms (Edison, Chancellor-Beacon, and Victory), two nonprofit organizations (Universal Cos. and Foundations Inc.), and two universities (Pennsylvania and Temple).[47] Philadelphia marked the nation's largest state takeover of a school district, as well as the largest use of private education providers for the management of public schools in one district.

At the federal level, meanwhile, NCLB has revolutionized the ends and means of national education policy. The original federal role outlined in the 1965 Elementary and Secondary Education Act (ESEA) was narrowly targeted at disadvantaged students and focused on regulating school inputs and processes. The original ESEA was thus not intended to promote innovation in education, and indeed, many scholars believe that its numerous mandates actually served to stifle entrepreneurial thinking in the nation's poorest schools. In contrast to ESEA, however, NCLB applies to all schools and students and is focused on school outputs.[48] NCLB's impact on entrepreneurship is likely to be felt both directly through its mandates and programs and indirectly through the pressure it applies on states and school districts to improve student academic performance.

The centerpiece of NCLB is the requirement that states, as a condition of accepting federal funds, establish academic standards to guide their curricula and adopt a testing regime that is aligned with those standards. NCLB mandates that every state and school district issue a report card that details student test scores and identifies those schools that have failed to meet proficiency targets and are in need of "program improvement." States are required to establish a timeline (with regular benchmarks) for making adequate yearly progress toward eliminating racial and socioeconomic achievement gaps and moving all students to state proficiency levels within twelve years (by 2014). The law's accountability provisions require states to take a number of escalating actions with Title I schools that do not reach state performance objectives. NCLB specifies that a school that fails to meet state performance targets for two consecutive years must give its students the option to transfer to another public school in the district and pay for their transportation. Schools that fail for four consecutive years must implement corrective actions, such as replacing staff or adopting a new curriculum. After five years of inadequate progress, a school must be reconstituted through the creation of an alternative governance structure, such as reopening as a charter school or turning operation of the school over to the state. States are also responsible for overseeing districts as a whole, identifying those needing improvement, and taking corrective actions when necessary.

In sum, NCLB represents an enormous challenge to the status quo in public education and has the potential to create a major opening for entrepreneurs inside and outside of the public system. Since NCLB passed, a large number of schools across the country have been identified as "in need of improvement" for failing to meet AYP targets. An analysis of state education data by the Center on Education Policy in March 2005 found that the number of non-Title I schools identified as in need of improvement (for which states are not required to undertake corrective actions) was 2,370 in 2004–05.[49] The total number of Title I schools identified as in need of improvement has remained basically stable for the past three years, at about six thousand (or 13 percent of all Title I schools).[50] School districts across the country—particularly those in poor urban areas—have thus far been unable or unwilling to find seats in better schools for many of the students who are eligible to transfer under NCLB.[51]

The DOE has argued that seats in better schools must nonetheless be found and offered to students, and this has increased pressure on state and local policymakers to increase the supply of alternative schools such as charters. The future focus of federal education policy may well revolve around helping school districts expand the supply of choice options for students in schools identified as failing under NCLB. Significant in this regard is continued Republican support for private school vouchers. President Bush included a voucher program as part of his initial No Child Left Behind proposal, and in 2003 a Republican-controlled Congress passed a voucher program for Washington, D.C. That precedent—along with the U.S. Supreme Court's *Zelman v. Harris* decision in 2002 that the flow of public funds to religious schools does not violate the U.S. Constitution—makes expanded federal support for vouchers a real possibility.

The combination of tough federal (and state) accountability and increased transparency has clearly increased the pressure on state and local policymakers to produce tangible student achievement gains. What remains uncertain is the methods by which they will choose to do so. It seems likely that accountability pressures will lead at least some states to embrace alternative approaches to school reform and to create a policy environment that is more conducive to the entrance and sustenance of educational entrepreneurs. In addition, the new achievement-based paradigm at the heart of NCLB is having a major impact on the direction of state school finance litigation. Like policymakers, many judges have shifted their measurement of school equity from inputs to outputs. Several recent decisions have indicated that closing the resource gap is no longer sufficient to satisfy many state constitutional education guarantees if large race and class-based gaps in educational achievement continue to persist. Some state courts are now requiring that states expand the educational options available to poor and minority students, and these judicial pressures may also push states and local school districts to make policy changes that allow more entrepreneurial actors to enter the educational arena.

CONCLUSION

Education in the United States is undergoing a remarkable transformation, as longstanding policies regarding how public schools are funded, staffed, and governed are revised in an effort to improve academic performance and increase student and parental choice. The policy environment is crucial to the future of educational entrepreneurship and has become more accommodating over the past decade as a wide array of new educational approaches and reforms have been introduced, both inside and outside of the traditional public school system. Additional research is necessary to determine how individual entrepreneurs are reacting to policy shifts on the ground—how the shifting terrain of laws and regulations in schooling is affecting the behavior of the individuals and organizations in question. Many state and district policies, however, continue to constrain the potential of entrepreneurial energies to introduce, sustain, and extend innovation in America's schools. It is not the job of educational entrepreneurs to change policy, and they are often reluctant to challenge the status quo directly because they must work on a regular basis with public school leaders. But as E. E. Schattschneider famously observed, "New government policy creates new politics."[52] The existence of educational entrepreneurs—and their increasing number and activity across the country—has changed the political discourse about school reform in the local communities where they operate and in the halls of state legislatures and the U.S. Congress.

CHAPTER 4

Mapping the K–12 and Postsecondary Sectors

Adam Newman

The concept of an education industry may be a relatively new one in the public consciousness, but the practice of running a revenue-generating education business is an old one. As long as students have needed classroom supplies and instructional materials, organizations have existed to deliver those products and services to schools, educators, and students. And, along the way, entrepreneurs have emerged with new and often innovative solutions to enhance classroom instruction and student performance.

The chalkboard eraser—a fixture in classrooms across the world—was created by John L. Hammett in the 1860s. Lacking a cloth to wipe clean the slate board he was using for a presentation, Mr. Hammett picked up a carpet remnant and wiped the slate clean. Discovering that the carpet remnant worked better than the cloths generally used, he and a colleague began nailing carpet to blocks of wood and selling them to schools. By the late 1990s, the company founded in 1863 by this entrepreneur, J. L. Hammett Company, was generating hundreds of millions of dollars in annual revenues through the sale of instructional materials, school supplies, and classroom furniture and equipment.[1]

Simply defined, an entrepreneur is an individual who "organizes, manages, and assumes the risks of a business or enterprise."[2] In the case of K–12 and postsecondary education, it is an individual who assumes these risks within the second-largest segment of the U.S. economy, accounting for annual expenditures of more than $800 billion. Moreover, today's education entrepreneurs are developing solutions—and generating revenues—within the context of a well-defined set of K–12 and postsecondary markets and segments. This chapter offers a framework for understanding the markets and segments comprising the K–12 and postsecondary sectors, analysis of the private investment capital secured by entrepreneurs and companies since 1999, and the role of mergers and acquisitions in transforming the market landscape in which entrepreneurs seek to build their businesses.

K–12 SOLUTIONS SECTOR

Eduventures defines the K–12 sector by the revenues generated from the sales of products and services to public and private schools and school districts within the United States. The sector is further broken down into the three categories and nine specific markets described below.

Instructional Materials

The Instructional Materials category is composed of the sales of instructional materials into U.S. K–12 schools. The four principal markets within this category include:

- *Basal Publishing.* The sales of core curricular materials in a variety of print and electronic formats for students at the elementary and secondary school levels.
- *Supplemental Materials.* The sales of resources that augment traditional curricular products, including workbooks, instructional software, instructional manipulatives, videos, and digital video products.
- *Reference Materials.* The sales of print and digital noninstructional reference materials, including databases, encyclopedias, dictionaries, and atlases, to K–12 schools and libraries.
- *Assessment.* The sales of print and electronic testing materials and services to K–12 schools and districts.

Technology Infrastructure

The Technology Infrastructure category is composed of the revenues generated from sales of computer hardware and software solutions and services into U.S. K–12 schools. The two principal markets within this category include:

- *Computing Hardware.* The sales of personal computers, laptops, and servers; printing and imaging equipment; and hardware infrastructure for networks and interactive classrooms used for instruction and school administration.

- *Enterprise Software and Technology Services*. The sales of instructional and administrative software solutions and related technology services (e.g., systems integration) to K–12 schools and school districts.

Education Services

The Education Services category is defined by the revenues generated from sales of instruction-related services into U.S. K–12 schools. The three principal markets within this category include:

- *Professional Development Services*. The sales of services, including workshops, curriculum-training programs, conferences, courses, and related materials that help teachers and administrators improve their practice.
- *Tutoring and Test-Preparation Services*. The sales of tutoring and other supplemental academic services to schools and education agencies.
- *Outsourced School Administration Services*. The sales of services related to operating K–12 schools, including charter school management, funded by public sources.

Revenues generated by companies and organizations serving these markets are forecasted to reach $23.3 billion in 2005–06, an expected increase of 6 percent above 2004–05 figures (see figure 1).

Increased federal funding, improved state tax collections, and the resulting expenditures in support of meeting the requirements of the No Child Left Behind Act (NCLB) drive K–12 market expansion. These factors should continue to be the primary variables of market expansion, in the absence of more profound changes in the funding model for the K–12 environment.

FIGURE 1   K–12 Solutions Sector Revenues, Fiscal Years 2004–09

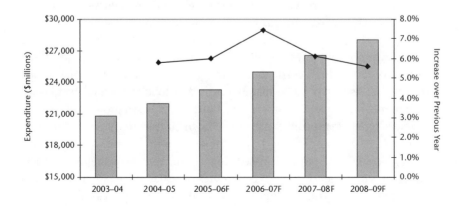

Moreover, as a result of the legislative mandates outlined by NCLB, companies delivering products and services in support of student remediation, assessment, student reporting, and school choice are contributing most significantly to growth.

Educators and suppliers in the K–12 market continue to grapple with the changes put in motion by NCLB. Provisions of the legislation relating to standardized curriculum, high-stakes testing, school accountability, and school choice influence each of the nine K–12 education markets. NCLB drives a perspective of K–12 education as an integrated process with curriculum, instruction, assessment, data management, and community involvement seamlessly interwoven. Consequently, suppliers in the industry are challenged to integrate solutions across multiple disciplines, develop new products and services that meet the newly created curriculum standards of the individual states, and adopt and integrate technology into all products and services. As the industry struggles to adapt, key trends and common themes have emerged.

- *Accountability and standards-based curriculum and assessment* drive the public K–12 market in the era of No Child Left Behind. The requirements of NCLB mandate the creation and adoption of state content standards, demand that instructional and assessment materials and professional development be aligned to those standards, and hold states responsible for reporting student academic progress. Suppliers of products and services to K–12 public institutions that best support these initiatives win in this market sector.
- *Industry consolidation* is occurring as the emergence of state standards and aligned assessments overwhelmingly favors suppliers with access to the distribution channels in each state. Long lead times and comprehensive offerings favor the large players—at the expense of entrepreneurs—with extensive product offerings. In this environment, the top ten suppliers control more than 85 percent of the $9 billion educational materials market and a significant portion of the $3 billion professional development market that is tied to standardized curriculum training. Consolidation continues in the K–12 space as instructional material providers look to leverage basal, supplemental, reference, assessment, and curriculum-based professional development purchases within the districts in which they sell.
- *Centralization of procurement* has become more prevalent with the move toward statewide standards-based curriculum and assessment. Districts and states are able to leverage economies of scale, made possible through standardized curriculum adoptions, to negotiate lower prices and to reduce

administrative purchasing overhead. These practices are forcing suppliers to reevaluate their marketing and sales strategies.

- *Student data and reporting requirements of NCLB* are driving the integration of administrative and instructional systems. Districts and schools are in the early stages of systems development that integrates communication tools, course management systems, student information systems, and traditional administrative management systems, supported by a central database. Suppliers of single applications are challenged to partner and integrate in order to compete in the market.

- *Individualized learning strategies* based on formative assessment and designed to ensure that students receive the instructional support necessary to achieve mastery of standardized curriculum are driving the development of assessment products and services. Computer technology will continue to play a critical role in the development of this new learning and instructional paradigm. In response, the dominant instructional materials providers are adding assessment products to their portfolios, primarily through mergers and acquisitions. In addition, these products are driving demand for professional development in this area. A key obstacle to the development of individualized learning initiatives continues to be the slow path to one-to-one computing.

- *Professional development* spending in the standards-driven, tight budget environment that is the K–12 sector is being redirected toward in-house programs, primarily funded through salary supplemented in-service programs. Professional development dollars allocated to third-party providers are most often spent in support of curriculum-specific development. The beneficiaries of these revenues are the major publishers and supplemental materials providers who typically bundle professional development with textbook and supplemental product adoptions.

- *Title I remediation opportunities* became a significant market driver during the 2003–04 school year and will continue to be a key factor in future expansion of opportunities for established suppliers and entrepreneurs. As schools fail to meet the growth objectives of NCLB, federal funds become available to Title I students for use in afterschool tutoring and remediation programs, an emergent market for third-party services providers.

- *School choice* is primarily manifested in the form of charter schools under NCLB Title V provisions. Parents and students are continuing to choose alternative public schools in forty-one of the fifty states. At the beginning of the 2005–06 school year, more than 3,600 charter schools would enroll approximately 1.1 million students.[3] Many of these schools are managed by for-profit companies that often provide customized curriculum to the schools. Robust growth in this area is dependent on NCLB funding and will continue to be a volatile, high-profile component of K–12 education reform.

- *Digital products and services growth* is limited by delays in achieving one-to-one student-to-computer ratios. Although several key initiatives driven by NCLB demand the increased productivity made possible through technology, full implementation of these initiatives is limited by the inability of schools to achieve a one-to-one student-to-computer ratio. The cost of computing devices when combined with the cost of network infrastructure support and maintenance continues to limit classroom penetration. The concept of a school in which formative assessment directs individualized learning plans, enriched by access to unlimited instructional materials delivered over the Internet, and supported by a new pedagogy for one-to-one and cooperative instruction, must wait for a financial model that makes this new education paradigm universally accessible.

POSTSECONDARY SOLUTIONS SECTOR

Eduventures defines the postsecondary sector by the revenues generated from the sales of education-specific products and services to nonprofit and for-profit colleges and universities within the United States. Important exceptions to this rule are the textbook and custom publishing markets, where key elements of the purchase decision are made by the institution or its agents, especially faculty, but where the purchaser is the consumer (i.e., student). The sector is further broken down into three categories and eight specific markets and segments described below.

Content and Curriculum

The Content and Curriculum category is composed of the sales of instructional materials to institutions and to consumers for use in a postsecondary program of study. The three principal markets within this category include:

- *Textbooks.* The sales of new print textbooks selected by professors or institutions and sold to students as core materials in college courses.
- *Custom Publishing.* The sales of supplemental content for higher education, such as course packs and case studies in print and digital forms, as well as custom-designed textbooks.
- *Reference Materials.* The sales of print and digital noninstructional materials, such as periodicals, journals, and subscription databases sold to college libraries.

Technology Infrastructure

The Technology Infrastructure category is composed of the revenues generated from sales of computer hardware and software solutions and services to U.S. colleges and universities. The two principal markets within this category include:

- *Computing Hardware.* The sales of personal computers, laptops, and servers; printing and imaging equipment; and hardware infrastructure for mobile computing and networks (e.g., wireless access points, routers, and switches) to colleges and universities for instructional and administrative use.
- *Enterprise Software and Technology Services.* The sales of enterprise software and services in three primary segments: enterprise resource planning software (also known as ERP, consisting of finance, human resources, development, and student information systems modules); e-learning platforms (both synchronous and asynchronous); and technology services.

  - *ERP Software.* The sales of software licenses and services directly related to the ERP offering (e.g., maintenance, support, and installation).
  - *E-Learning Platforms.* The sales of online learning technologies, as well as directly related services such as application service provider (ASP) hosting and course design.
  - *Technology Services.* The sales of services in technology consulting, systems configuration and implementation, and ongoing systems maintenance and support.

Services

The Services category is composed of the revenues generated from the administrative and professional services market, which includes a broad range of outsourced services that assist institutions with administrative operations. Areas in which external administrative and professional services firms are most often utilized include marketing and enrollment management, financial aid, technology support, and billing and payment services.

Revenues generated by companies and organizations serving these markets are predicted to reach $12.1 billion in 2005, an expected increase of 4.7 percent above 2004 figures (see figure 2).

Fundamentally, growth in the postsecondary sector is driven by increasing enrollments in postsecondary education—as colleges enroll more students, they spend proportionally more on products and services. However, while overall U.S. higher education enrollment has continued to grow at a rate of approximately 2 percent annually, many colleges and universities have seen their budgets flatten or even decline in recent years due to shortfalls in state

FIGURE 2 Postsecondary Solutions Sector Revenues, Fiscal Years 2002–07

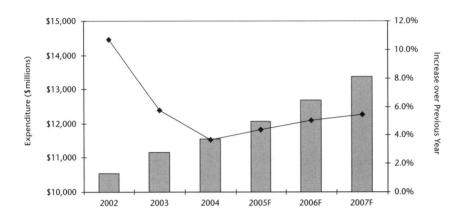

or local funding, variability in endowment returns, changes in philanthropic giving, and shortfalls in other revenue sources.

In many ways, the sector is caught in a cyclical low point between waves of adoption—in essence, a "hangover" in spending relative to the boom in 1999 and 2000. After explosive growth followed by significant resource constraints, budgets are now on their way to stabilizing, and many markets are "taking a pause" to better leverage technology and other committed investments. The notion of "e-learning" is no longer new, the digital textbook does not threaten the viability of printed texts in the foreseeable future, and there is no Y2K crisis to fuel mass upgrades of administrative systems. Rather, a number of postsecondary sector markets are characterized by relative maturity and stability—evidenced by more stable and even slowing market growth rates, consolidation among providers, the domination of markets by fewer leading companies, and fewer start-ups.

Market and segment growth rates highlighted below illustrate that the most opportunity for suppliers is being created in technology and services markets, and that the least value is being created in more mature content markets (see figure 3).

Custom publishing, which in effect combines content with a customization service, is experiencing growth as an alternative to traditional content models, while both the administrative and professional services and ERP markets are driven by institutions' needs for enhanced efficiency in allocating resources. As colleges and universities grapple with an increasing "performance" culture, key trends and common themes have emerged.

FIGURE 3   Postsecondary Solutions Growth Rates by Market Segment, Fiscal Years 2002–07

	2002	2003	2004	2005F	2006F	2007F
Content						
Textbooks	12.9%	3.6%	0.0%	1.0%	2.0%	3.0%
Custom Publishing	13.6%	13.5%	14.0%	15.0%	15.0%	15.0%
Reference	6.0%	6.0%	0.0%	1.5%	3.0%	3.0%
Infrastructure						
ERP	15.4%	8.8%	7.2%	7.1%	7.0%	7.0%
E-Learning Platforms	51.2%	28.5%	21.4%	17.9%	15.0%	13.7%
Technology Services	13.2%	9.5%	9.0%	9.5%	10.0%	10.0%
Computing Hardware	7.2%	3.0%	2.0%	2.0%	2.0%	2.0%
Services						
Administrative and Professional Services	9.5%	9.0%	9.0%	9.5%	10.0%	10.0%
Total	10.7%	5.7%	3.7%	4.4%	5.0%	5.4%

- *Online education is driving growth* across a number of market segments. Institutions desiring to scale online education programs, particularly those fully at a distance, has resulted in growth for e-learning platform companies, marketing services firms, and custom publishers, among others. As a new academic delivery model, online education is providing suppliers with an opportunity for deeper customer relationships and entirely new lines of business. Across the sector, firms with the best growth prospects tend to offer products and services related to online education.

- *Market maturity is leading to supplier consolidation.* The markets comprising the postsecondary sector share a stable of well-established leaders— large, education-focused companies that often have hundreds of millions of dollars in revenues. In recent years, these companies have maintained their market position by acquiring innovative start-ups in order to capture growth in new niches. Companies such as Dell in computing hardware; the "Big 3" publishers (i.e., McGraw-Hill, Pearson, and Thomson) in content; and SunGard, Blackboard, and WebCT in administrative and e-learning software are all firms that have market shares many multiples higher than their nearest competitors. In fact, by Eduventures' estimates, half of the $11.6 billion in 2004 sector revenues was controlled by only thirty companies.

- *Suppliers are diversifying* across markets and segments. In the enterprise software and services market in particular, software providers are moving into new niches and acquiring or developing new capabilities to play in multiple market segments. For example, SunGard SCT and Blackboard seek to offer solutions across a broad range of technologies; publishers such as Thomson Learning span textbooks, reference, and custom publishing; and eCollege offers marketing services in addition to e-learning software and technology services. The lines are blurring between product and service markets in particular, as products generate service opportunities.
- *Colleges are demanding services* to complement off-the-shelf products. This demand is strong and growing, as colleges are working with for-profit firms to host and implement e-learning and ERP systems, market to and enroll prospective students, develop online courses and custom printed materials, and administer financial aid programs. Established suppliers are expanding to meet their customers' needs, while the past decade has witnessed the emergence of numerous entrepreneurial companies to support online education.
- *"Outsourcing" is the new frontier.* As markets mature and product and service needs become more standardized, outsourcing is increasingly becoming an option for many colleges and universities looking to control costs or extend capabilities while limiting capital investment. Whether in information technology support, marketing services, content development, or administrative support services, the race is on for providers to substitute for colleges' and universities' internal structures with outsourcing arrangements.

K–12 AND POSTSECONDARY INVESTMENT AND ACQUISITION OVERVIEW

A key theme across the past decade has been the level of private investment directed to entrepreneurs and businesses across the education sectors. Companies in the child-care, K–12, postsecondary, and corporate learning sectors raised more than $9.6 billion from private equity firms and venture capitalists between 1995 and 2004 (see figure 4).[4]

More than 57 percent of this funding was directed to entrepreneurs and companies during 1999 and 2000, a watershed period for investments in the education sector, and a significant percentage of the investments in these years supported innovative—and often speculative—technology-based businesses. This period saw the emergence of investment funds dedicated to the education sector, such as DHM Arcadia Partners and Quad Ventures, as well

FIGURE 4   Private Investment in the Child-Care, K–12, Postsecondary, and Corporate Learning Sectors, 1995–2004

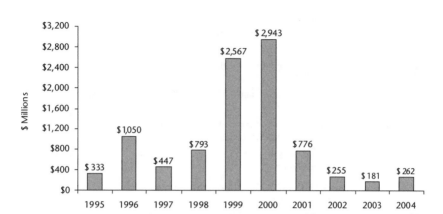

as considerable industry bets by established and well-respected firms like Forstmann Little & Co., GE Equity, Patricof & Co., and Warburg Pincus.

During this period, numerous K–12 and postsecondary companies, some with minimal or no revenues, secured single financing rounds in excess of $15 million dollars, and valuations for private companies soared (see figure 5). The private sector education industry was buzzing, and many industry players anticipated a swift and transformative shift in the educational products and services landscape, as well as the very nature of delivering education to K–12 and postsecondary students through companies delivering school management services and Web-enabled learning models.

However, like any of the bets historically placed by private equity and venture capital firms, a few paid off and many more did not. With the public markets firmly closed by 2001 to any venture funding–rich, revenue-poor companies, many investors turned their attention to mergers and acquisitions (M&A) as a way to extract a modicum of return from their portfolio businesses. M&A activity in the pre-K–12 and postsecondary sectors accelerated beginning in 2000, even as the number of private investments fell precipitously. Between 2001 and 2004, acquisitions outpaced investments more than 2.6 to 1.

K–12 SOLUTIONS SECTOR INVESTMENT AND M&A ACTIVITY

Entrepreneurs and companies targeting the K–12 sector experienced a dramatic decline in access to private investment resources after 2000, and while

FIGURE 5   Where Are They Now?

Company	Description	Total Estimated Private Investment
BIGWORDS.com	Online textbook and e-commerce destination for college students	$70–75 million
Classwell Learning Group	Online K–12 education company integrating instruction, assessment, and teacher training	$30–35 million
Epylon	Electronic procurement solutions for K–12 districts and schools	$75–80 million
HighWired.com	Online publishing tools and student community solutions for high schools	$40–50 million
Mascot Networks	Software intranet platform solution for colleges and universities	$25–30 million
netLibrary	Digital reference and resource books to college and school libraries	$100–110 million
MindSurf	Wireless computing software platform and hardware for K–12 students, teachers, and parents	$70–75 million
Schoolpop	Online fundraising and e-commerce network for K–12 schools and districts	$40–50 million

selected companies and management teams are attracting capital, many more are not (see figure 6).

In the current funding environment, many entrepreneurs and companies are focusing on building businesses by generating revenues and reinvesting profits to support incremental investments or through small "friends and family" fundraising efforts. In both cases, growth and scale are generally achieved in a more measured fashion, with an emphasis on customer acquisition, effective implementations, and high levels of customer service and support.

Education suppliers secured $50 million in private investment in 2004, with an average-value transaction of $4.5 million. Providers of supplemental curriculum, professional development services, and tutoring and test-prep services represented the focus of investment during 2004, a trend anticipated to continue as suppliers of supplemental education services, formative assessment products, and professional development services continue to leverage opportunities made possible through NCLB.

M&A activity dropped almost 30 percent in 2004 relative to 2003 levels, with fewer deals executed by the major textbook publishers and supplemental school product distributors. Although less active than in 2003, consolidation continued in 2004 as Pearson, School Specialty Discovery Communica-

FIGURE 6   Private Investment in the K–12 Solutions Sector, 2000–04

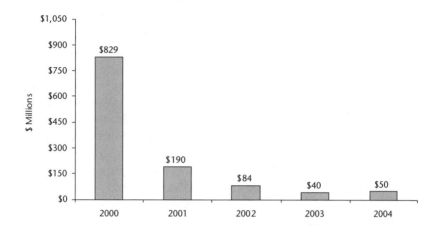

tions, Cambium Learning, and Haights Cross Communications completed two deals each. Additionally, McGraw-Hill, Thomson, and Harcourt added to their respective product and service offerings with a single transaction apiece. ProQuest Company also made two acquisitions, including Reading A–Z, a publisher of K–12 reading resource materials, and Voyager Expanded Learning, a provider of reading instruction and intervention programs. The latter acquisition in particular provided a potentially dramatic shift in business focus for ProQuest, which immediately finds itself a key player in the early literacy market, which has seen significant increases in funding as a result of NCLB's "Reading First" program. A brief summary of additional 2004 transactional trends in each sector category is included below.

K–12 Instructional Materials

More than a dozen supplemental content transactions dominated investment and M&A activity in 2004. Unlike 2003, when digital content pervaded investment activity, in 2004 traditional text products returned to favor. Several key transactions occurred during the year. Cambium Learning formed through the merger of Sopris West with the Metropolitan Teaching and Learning Company. Harcourt's acquisition of Saxon Math provided instant entry for Harcourt into the growing charter school and homeschool math markets in which Saxon had developed a strong following. Haights Cross increased its market share in the K–12 space with the acquisition of Options Publishing and Buckle Down Publishing, while Pearson acquired Dominie

Press. Consolidation activity in the content space targeted the reading and math subject areas, the primary focus of NCLB accountability efforts through 2004, with science a key untapped area that began to see activity in 2005 in anticipation of the introduction of annual statewide science assessments.

K–12 Technology Infrastructure

Investment in enterprise solutions was limited in 2004 to $4.3 million, as the Edison Fund provided TetraData funding for expansion of its existing workforce. Pearson purchased altonaEd, an ASP-based student information system serving small to mid-sized school districts. With this acquisition, Pearson continued to expand its portfolio of student data management solutions. Public Consulting Group also enhanced its position in the K–12 enterprise solutions segment with its acquisition of EDsmart. Although the enterprise solutions market was expected to see significant investment activity in 2004 as schools continued to search for data management and reporting tools, few new companies emerged as attractive acquisition candidates. Small client bases, long sales cycles, and challenging district technology budgets limited activity in this area, factors that continued to dampen demand through 2005.

K–12 Education Services

Two investment transactions in the area of professional development were executed in 2004, as ACT invested in the Teachers Support Network and ETS acquired The Pulliam Group. With districts' professional development expenditures increasingly staying in-house, little activity in this area was expected in 2005, with the exception of science-related professional development training as schools prepared to meet NCLB science requirements. On the other hand, tutoring and test preparation garnered significant attention within the investment community in 2004, as supplemental educational services (SES) funding began to filter to private providers of afterschool programs. Platform Learning, Tutor.com, and The Princeton Review received funding for the development and expansion of school-paid tutoring programs. Finally, in a single charter school management deal, Imagine Schools acquired Chancellor Beacon.

POSTSECONDARY SOLUTIONS INVESTMENT AND M&A ACTIVITY

The investment landscape for the entrepreneurs and companies selling products and services into colleges and universities has experienced a similar shift to that seen in the K–12 environment: Few announced transactions since 2001, with a considerable emphasis on mergers and acquisitions to salvage value and limited returns from venture-funded businesses (see figure 7).

This paucity of traditional investment activity, however, masks the growing investment by the postsecondary community itself in open-source technologies. In several areas, such as e-learning platforms and enterprise portals, consortia of institutions and private foundations have created open- and community-source solutions that are being considered by colleges and universities as potential alternatives to commercial software products. For investors, this trend has led to an emphasis on identifying more services-based business models that can facilitate integration and adoption of various technologies and their anticipated business process enhancements.

Private investment in the postsecondary sector in 2004 was marked by one large deal, Jenzabar's $35 million package, and several smaller ones. This trend mirrored events in 2003, when eCollege's $30.5 million represented the vast majority of investment activity in the sector. Since 2001, however, most of the transactional activity has occurred on the mergers and acquisitions front, as established companies purchased smaller technology and services businesses to augment offerings for their existing customers and to capitalize on emerging market opportunities.

FIGURE 7   Private Investment and Number of Transactions in the Postsecondary Solutions Sector, 2000–04

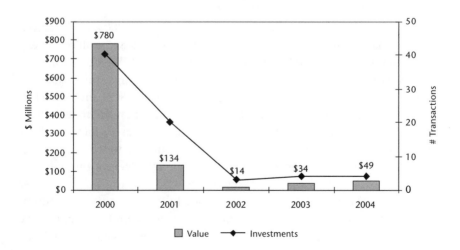

M&A activity stayed fairly consistent in 2004 relative to 2003 levels, with most deals executed in the Technology Infrastructure and Services categories. In both years, enrollment management and financial aid technology and services providers proved attractive targets, trends that should continue as colleges and universities demonstrate an increasing willingness to consider outsourcing selected administrative business processes. A brief summary of additional 2004 transactional trends in each sector category is included below.

Postsecondary Content and Curriculum

The content segment, which primarily includes textbook and digital content publishers, was quiet in 2004, as it had been the year before, with only one M&A transaction and one investment transaction recorded. Questia Media was the sole investment in the content segment, receiving $10 million during the first quarter. Copley Publishing Group, a publisher of custom textbooks for college courses, was acquired by ProQuest during the second quarter to become part of ProQuest's XanEdu product offering. Custom textbooks contain copyright-cleared material selected by faculty, as well as faculty-written sections, across academic disciplines. Relative market maturity means that the pace of change in the postsecondary content category is slow, with supplier consolidation continuing along with a steady shift to digitally delivered materials. This mature segment is dominated by a handful of large publishers—in particular, Pearson Education, Thomson Learning, and McGraw-Hill—that possess a commanding two-thirds market share combined.

Postsecondary Technology Infrastructure

Software companies continued to attract investment in 2004, as evidenced by Blackboard's initial public offering (IPO), Jenzabar's $35 million investment package, and ED MAP's $1.5 million investment package. Moreover, early 2005 saw a spate of high-profile acquisition and investment transactions in the ERP space, with Oracle, PeopleSoft, SunGard SCT, and Datatel all involved in transactions. MCG Capital Corporation, a publicly traded financial services company, invested $35 million in Jenzabar to fuel Jenzabar's accelerated growth strategy. Jenzabar applied the funding to invest in its custom-tailored solution composed of ERP, campus intelligence, Internet portal, and constituent-relationship modules, as well as consulting and other services. Blackboard's IPO marked a milestone in the evolution of an education market leader. Over the past several years, Blackboard has acquired five companies, lengthened its customer list to an estimated twelve hundred U.S.

clients, and broadened its product offerings. Blackboard is one of two dominant learning management system providers in higher education, an application that is now considered essential at most institutions.

Postsecondary Services

Postsecondary services as a category posted ten transactions in 2004, five of which affected companies that enable postsecondary institutions for e-business. Another three transactions affected companies in the educational lending space, a sign of the shift taking place as a result of the privatization of Sallie Mae (SLM Corporation). After it completed its separation from the U.S. government, Sallie Mae wasted little time in beginning its new identity as a private-sector educational lending company, acquiring the Student Loan Finance Association as other educational lenders made acquisitions to reposition themselves in this evolving market. In addition, colleges and universities that are managing supply chains, marketing and media placements, and IT outsourcing have led to investments and acquisitions in these areas—and will continue to do so—as investors see institutions' interest in applying business practices to education.

Eduventures predicts that as markets mature and product and service needs become increasingly standardized, outsourcing will become increasingly popular as institutions look to control costs or extend capabilities as they limit capital investments. Eduventures anticipates that investment in software and services to help postsecondary institutions manage their business processes will continue to be an area of growth in the next few years.

FOR-PROFIT POSTSECONDARY INVESTMENT AND M&A ACTIVITY

The for-profit postsecondary education market has been the single most attractive market for investors and strategic acquirers since 2001. Eduventures defines the for-profit postsecondary education market in terms of Title IV-eligible for-profit postsecondary institutions (i.e., those participating in relevant federal financial aid programs). These institutions, often referred to within the industry as career colleges, are accredited, private, for-profit colleges and universities—as distinct from private, nonprofit institutions (e.g., DePaul University, Harvard University) and public, nonprofit institutions (e.g., University of California, Valencia Community College). The for-profit postsecondary education market includes a broad spectrum of institutions, ranging from less-than-two-year, certificate- and diploma-granting vocational schools to degree-granting four-year and doctoral institutions.

Experienced entrepreneurs and managers have demonstrated that it is possible to grow for-profit postsecondary institutions into $500 million–$1 billion businesses. For investors, the strength of the market opportunity lies in strong demographic and labor market trends, dedicated and expanding public and private funding sources for prospective students, a well-documented earnings premium for students with postsecondary education, and access to the public markets for sufficiently scaled businesses. Moreover, most of today's leading for-profit postsecondary institutions are primarily concentrated in the highly saturated U.S. postsecondary market and have yet to tap into the tremendous demand in countries in Asia and South America.

While the number of investment transactions in the for-profit education market is much lower than that of the K–12 and Postsecondary Solutions sectors, the average annual investment value per transaction has been higher every year since 2000 (see figure 8).

Thus, investors have chosen to put more dollars to work across a smaller universe of entrepreneurial and existing postsecondary institutions, choosing to concentrate their efforts on a single institutional platform from which to drive scale. This investment approach furnished privately held for-profit institutions with capital to make acquisitions, even as several of the leading for-profit postsecondary institutions employed the currency of their publicly traded stock to engage in an acquisition binge across this period. Between 2000 and 2004, for-profit postsecondary institutions made nearly 90 announced transactions, with Career Education Corporation, Corinthian Colleges, Education Management Corporation, Kaplan, and Laureate Education (formerly Sylvan) accounting for nearly 50 percent of the announced transactions (see figure 9).

Chief acquisition drivers have been, and will continue to be, opportunities to secure a presence in new geographic markets, diversification of program areas (e.g., adding health sciences programs to an IT-heavy curriculum), and access to new, often upscale terminal degree levels (e.g., moving into bachelor's, master's, or doctoral degree programs).

FIGURE 8 Average Annual Investment Value per Transaction for Companies in K–12 and Postsecondary Solutions Sectors and For-Profit Education Market, 2000–04

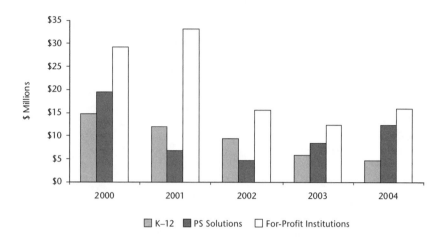

FIGURE 9 Mergers and Acquisitions in the For-Profit Education Market, 2000–04

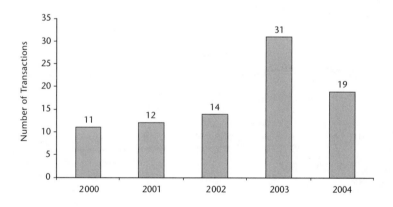

CHAPTER 5

For-Profit K–12 Education: Through the Glass Darkly

Alex Molnar

The merits of a marketplace model for public education has been among the most prominent themes in education policy discussions over the last two decades. The 2002 reauthorization of the Elementary and Secondary Education Act, popularly known as the No Child Left Behind Act (NCLB), has accelerated the trend toward private, for-profit activities in public education. These activities range from the provision of various supplementary education services to the private management of public schools. While it's true that there has been for-profit activity in education for many years, in industries ranging from publishing to construction to software, it has historically been limited to the provision of goods and services in support of schools and their programs. It is only in the past decade or so that the for-profit model has been extended into the core activities of public education. Michael Sandler, founder of Eduventures Inc., which bills itself as "the leading information services company for the education market," estimates that between 1993 and 2001, annual revenues in the "education industry" increased more than fourfold, from $24 billion to $115 billion.[1]

Advocates of market approaches to education reform contend that creating a market in educational services will foster competition among providers and thus spur delivery of better services at the same or lower cost than traditional public schools can achieve. Whether this is the case is debatable. It is clear, however, that the policy preferences of the past twenty-five years have increasingly leaned toward privatization. These preferences have been expressed in repeated efforts to promote school vouchers; in the advocacy of "strong" state charter school laws; and most recently by NCLB.

THE GROWTH AND SCOPE OF ENTREPRENEURSHIP IN EDUCATION

In education, the label "entrepreneurial" has been applied to for-profit educational services firms, nonprofit charter schools, and even new programs within traditional school districts. For the purposes of this chapter, however, I define entrepreneurship as organizing a business venture and assuming risks in hopes of earning a profit. Although entrepreneurship in preK and postsecondary education is briefly reviewed, the main discussion focuses on entrepreneurial activity in K–12 education. Within K–12 education, the discussion is confined to the management of schools or the provision of supplementary educational services.

From infant daycare to postgraduate university programs, for-profit entrepreneurship as a practice and policy now influences every level of the education system. With the rise in double-income households, early childhood education enrollment has quadrupled over the past three decades, and private providers have captured a significant share of that increase. The growth in preschool enrollment has spurred the emergence of a number of for-profit firms in this sector, such as Bright Horizons Family Solutions, Inc.; Kinder-Care, Inc., now a unit of Knowledge Learning Corp.; Crème de la Crème, Inc., which has been described as a cross between "Harvard and Disneyland";[2] Kids 'R' Kids, Inc.; La Petite Academy; and Learning Care Group, formerly Childtime Learning Centers.

At the postsecondary level, for-profit firms have a long history. The sector began with the development of trade schools, such as the ITT Technical Institute, that market training in fields as diverse as car repair, cosmetology, and computer technology and are eligible for federal grant funds when they enroll low-income students.

Enrollment in trade school has skyrocketed in recent years, with enrollment reaching six hundred thousand nationwide by 2002, a 147 percent increase from 1995.[3] (By contrast, projected enrollment in public and private colleges in 2004 was 16.4 million, up about 15 percent from 14.3 million in 1995.)

The past three decades have also witnessed an explosion of full-fledged for-profit colleges, which offer bachelor's and graduate degrees and often cater to working adults. Citing data from Eduventures, the *Wall Street Journal* reported in September 2005 that enrollment at for-profit colleges was growing four times as fast as at traditional colleges, reaching 1.7 million students—9 percent of all U.S. college and graduate students.[4]

DeVry, Inc., to some extent represents the bridge between for-profit postsecondary trade schools and full-fledged, for-profit college and university programs. Founded as the DeForest Training School in Chicago in 1931 to train technical workers in electronics and broadcast media, DeVry Institutes were accredited to grant associate degrees in 1957 and bachelor's degrees in 1969. Today DeVry, which is publicly traded on the New York Stock Exchange, enrolls a total of 53,000 students and offers associate, bachelor's, and master's degrees, primarily in technical and business fields, through both brick-and-mortar campuses and online.

DeVry has since been joined in the industry by schools such as the University of Phoenix. John Sperling, an economist, founded Apollo Group in 1973 and its principal subsidiary, the University of Phoenix, in 1976. Apollo Group, according to the firm's account of its history, was founded to provide higher education to working adults. Its University of Phoenix subsidiary offers postsecondary degrees through face-to-face and online instruction, while another subsidiary, Western International University, offers undergraduate, graduate, and certificate programs in four traditional campus settings in and around Phoenix, Arizona, with another location under construction in Peoria, Illinois. Apollo Group's view of education may best be summed up in an online promotional video for Western International: "Education is a product. At WIU we view ourselves as a business that delivers the product of education and our students as consumers of that education."[5]

The for-profit postsecondary education sector has long been plagued by allegations of financial abuse, high-pressure selling tactics, and inflated promises. A 1994 *New York Times* article reported systematic abuses in the sector, finding that "directors of for-profit trade schools and colleges have looted the budgets of these loosely regulated federal student aid programs to buy themselves Mercedes-Benzes, travel the world, subsidize a drug habit, invest in religious causes or pay themselves million dollar salaries."[6] The *Times* report observed that low-income students were hurt when they were unable to gain promised skills and then defaulted on their loans, while U.S. taxpayers absorbed the costs of the loan defaults.[7]

Audits by the New York State comptroller's office of four postsecondary institutions—two commercial schools, a public college, and a private nonprofit college—"found that irregularities in financial aid grants were more than eight times higher at the two commercial schools studied," according to the *New York Times*.[8] The *Wall Street Journal* has reported on at least a half-dozen lawsuits against for-profits by graduates claiming that traditional institutions did not recognize their degrees or college credits, and alleging that for-profits' admissions personnel misled them into thinking otherwise. Such scandals have by no means been limited to fly-by-night institutions or to the trade schools sector: In September 2004, the University of Phoenix paid $9.8 million to settle charges that it violated federal laws governing higher education aid programs, though it denied wrongdoing.[9]

Entrepreneurship in K–12 Education

Entrepreneurial activity in K–12 education is distinct from the preK and postsecondary markets in that few for-profit firms actually own private schools and charge tuition. This is largely due to the existence of a wide variety of established, well-regarded nonprofit alternatives for K–12 education, including both religious and secular private schools, as well as a free public K–12 education system. Thus, for-profit firms have found more opportunity in the K–12 arena in selling supplemental services to the public schools, such as the tutoring services now required by NCLB, as well as outsourcing management of public schools. The latter firms fall under the umbrella of what Wall Street analysts have dubbed the education management organization (EMO) industry—private corporations such as Edison Schools and Mosaica that have been hired to manage public district schools or charter schools. Although the analogy is far from perfect, Wall Street coined the term EMO as an analogue to health maintenance organizations (HMOs).

The most significant opportunity for for-profit firms in K–12 education was supposed to arise from the creation of voucher programs that would enable private schools to compete for public tax dollars. However, this market has largely failed to materialize—vouchers are still limited to a handful of programs in Milwaukee, Cleveland, Florida, and Washington, D.C. The 1992 defeat of President George H. W. Bush, whose administration had lent strong rhetorical support to voucher proposals, effectively shut down the prospects of federal support for vouchers for most of the next decade. Meanwhile, at the state level, vouchers proved to be highly unpopular with the general public, suffering repeated defeats in ballot initiatives and in state legislatures.

With vouchers gaining little political traction, the growth of the EMO industry has largely been fueled by state charter school legislation. Charter schools are schools that operate largely outside of regulations governing traditional district schools, and they have enjoyed strong bipartisan support. For-profit firms most often manage charter schools as agents of not-for-profit charter holders. Although not necessarily envisioned as such by early charter school advocates, charter school legislation has become the principal vehicle by which for-profit firms manage public schools.

Arguably the most familiar name in the EMO category today is Edison Schools, Inc. Edison was actually founded with the intent of creating a chain of private, tuition-charging schools. The company has denied that its original business plan was premised on the assumption that federal policy would encourage the adoption of voucher systems nationwide—a development that would have effectively created a taxpayer-subsidized market for the company's schools. When federal support for vouchers evaporated and its original business plan proved unattractive to investors, the company shifted its game plan, becoming instead a manager of public district and charter schools. The evolution of Edison approximates the trajectory of the EMO industry as a whole: It started by planning to open a chain of private schools; it shifted to managing schools for school districts, and then to managing charter schools; and now has moved into the provision of an array of supplemental educational products and services.

Supplemental services constitute the other category of entrepreneurial activity in K–12 education. These services are targeted at a number of specialized markets. Some are well-established, while others are just emerging, such as the market for firms offering remedial and enrichment instruction to students who are eligible for such services under the mandates of NCLB. This law has fostered a number of other markets, such as those for tutoring services, test preparation, teacher training, summer school, and curriculum development. Provisions in NCLB that call for converting schools identified as "failing" into charter schools are also likely to bolster the marketplace for school-management firms.

The Growth and Composition of the EMO Industry

The 2004–05 edition of the annual *Profiles of For-Profit Education Management Organizations*, for which I am the lead author, identifies fifty-nine education management organizations.[10] Together these firms manage 535 schools, with a total enrollment of 239,766 students across twenty-five states and the District of Columbia. This is more than quadruple the number of firms reported in the first edition of *Profiles*, which covered the 1998–99 school year, and is up from fifty-one in the 2003–04 report. Details are shown in table 1.

The National Association of Charter School Authorizers also tracks education management organizations, focusing on those holding charter school contracts.[11] The organization's website lists a total of sixteen for-profit firms with charter school management contracts, virtually all of which are also

TABLE 1   Number of Companies, Schools, and States Profiled by Year

School Year	Number of Companies Profiled	Number of Schools Managed by Profiled Companies	Number of States in Which Profiled Companies Operate
1998–99	13	135	15
1999–2000	20	230	21
2000–01	21	285	22
2001–02	36	368	25*
2002–03	54	406	26*
2003–04	51	463	29*
2004–05	59	535	26*

*Includes the District of Columbia.

Source: Alex Molnar, David Garcia, Carolyn Sullivan, Brendan McEvoy, and Jamie Joanou, *Profiles of For-Profit Education Management Organizations, 2004–2005* (Tempe: Arizona State University, Education Policy Studies Laboratory, Commercialism in Education Research Unit, 2005).

represented in the Commercialism in Education Research Unit (CERU) *Profiles* reports. All but one of these firms are privately held; the exception, The GEO Group, is a subsidiary of a publicly traded company.[12] The association lists six more firms holding charter management contracts that are structured as nonprofits.

Charter schools account for a large and growing majority of EMO contracts: 86.3 percent of the privately managed schools covered in the 2004–05 *Profiles of For-Profit Education Management Organizations* are charter schools. Overall, the fifty-nine EMOs profiled in 2004–05 account for 31 percent, or 175,350, of all students (565,648) enrolled in charter schools, and 41 percent (114,591) of all charter primary school students (277,240).[13] My interpretation of these data is that for-profit firms concentrate on primary schools because primary education is less expensive than middle and high school education (see table 2).

So-called virtual schools represent another source of growth in the EMO industry. These schools, sometimes also known as online charter or virtual charter schools, offer an Internet-based curriculum outside of the conventional brick-and-mortar setting of traditional public and charter schools, and they frequently cater to children who were previously homeschooled. Where legislation has permitted such schools, state education dollars pay for children who enroll in them. The definition of virtual schools is imprecise and, depending on the definition, the number of such schools and the num-

TABLE 2   U.S. Charter School Enrollment by School Level

	Primary	Middle	High	Other**	All School Levels
Number of Students Enrolled in All Charter Schools	277,240	43,768	119,999	124,641	565,648
Number of Students Enrolled in Charter Schools Managed by EMOs	114,591*	3,215	30,309	27,235	175,350*
Percentage of Students Enrolled in Charter Schools Managed by EMOs	41.3%*	7.3%	25.3%	21.9%	31.0%*

Note: Noncharter schools are not included in these data. Virtual charter and noncharter schools are not included in these data.

* One school, Valor Campus of Detroit School of Industrial Arts (a charter primary school managed by National Heritage Academies) has unknown enrollment. Its enrollment is not counted in these data.

**The U.S. Department of Education defines "other" schools as schools that do not fall within the grade-level configurations of primary school, middle school, or high school.

Source: Alex Molnar, David Garcia, Carolyn Sullivan, Brendan McEvoy, and Jamie Joanou, *Profiles of For-Profit Education Management Organizations, 2004–2005* (Tempe: Arizona State University, Education Policy Studies Laboratory, Commercialism in Education Research Unit, 2005).

ber of students enrolled in them varies widely. According to *Newsweek*, as of 2004, about 2,400 virtual schools served 40,000 to 50,000 students.[14] Virtual schools that purport to provide a K–12 education may be poised to generate substantially larger profits than conventional charter schools, because they receive the same amount of per-student funding as their traditional public school counterparts despite not having to finance a physical structure.[15]

Enrollment Comparisons

The 2004–05 *Profiles* defines "large EMOs" as those managing ten or more schools. Among the charter schools managed by large EMOs, 65.5 percent have enrollments exceeding the average U.S. charter school enrollment. The majority of students attending charter schools run by twelve of the fourteen large EMOs are in schools with enrollments that exceed the national average for comparable charter schools (see table 3).

These enrollment figures contrast markedly with overall charter enrollment trends, as well as with one of the ostensible benefits of charter schools. A 2000 report by RPP International found that the median size of charter

TABLE 3   Percentage of Large EMO Charter School Students Who Attend
Schools with Enrollments above the Average U.S. Charter School Enrollment

Large EMOs	Percentage
Victory Schools	100
Edison Schools	98
National Heritage Academies	96*
Charter Schools USA	95
Imagine Schools	92
White Hat Management	86
Mosaica Schools	85
Charter Schools Administrative Services	83
The Leona Group	74
Helicon Associates	64
Richard Milburn HS, Inc.	61
Sequoia Charter Schools	55
Designs for Learning	28
The Planagement Group	0

Note: Noncharter schools are not included in these data. Virtual charter and noncharter schools are not included in these data.

* One school, Valor Campus of Detroit School of Industrial Arts (a charter primary school managed by National Heritage Academies) has unknown enrollment. Its enrollment is missing from these data.

Source: Alex Molnar, David Garcia, Carolyn Sullivan, Brendan McEvoy, and Jamie Joanou, Profiles of For-Profit Education Management Organizations, 2004–2005 (Tempe: Arizona State University, Education Policy Studies Laboratory, Commercialism in Education Research Unit, 2005).

schools (137 students) was much smaller than district schools (475 students).[16] Research has generally found academic benefits associated with smaller school size.[17]

Charter schools run by large EMOs, however, tend to enroll a larger-than-average number of students. Moreover, nearly one in five of large EMO-run charter schools have enrollments above the average U.S. district school enrollment. The majority of students attending charter schools managed by Charter Schools USA, Edison Schools, and Imagine Schools are likely to be attending schools that are larger than the national average for district schools (see table 4).[18]

Funding for schools is based on enrollment, with more students resulting in more revenue per school site. Therefore, profitability concerns create

TABLE 4   Percentage of Large EMO Charter School Students Who Attend Schools with Enrollments above the Average U.S. District School Enrollment

Large EMOs	Percentage
Edison Schools	74
Imagine Schools	63
Charter Schools USA	63
Helicon Associates	46
Charter Schools Administrative Services	45
Mosaica Schools	34
National Heritage Academies	15*
The Leona Group	13
White Hat Management	3
Victory Schools	0
Richard Milburn HS, Inc.	0
Sequoia Charter Schools	0
Designs for Learning	0
The Planagement Group	0

Note: Virtual charter and noncharter schools are not included in these data.

** One school, Valor Campus of Detroit School of Industrial Arts (a charter primary school managed by National Heritage Academies), has unknown enrollment. Its enrollment is missing from these data.

Source: Alex Molnar, David Garcia, Carolyn Sullivan, Brendan McEvoy, and Jamie Joanou, *Profiles of For-Profit Education Management Organizations, 2004–2005* (Tempe: Arizona State University, Education Policy Studies Laboratory, Commercialism in Education Research Unit, 2005).

an incentive to increase enrollments, posing a potential conflict between the interests of investors on the one hand (in larger, and thus potentially more profitable, schools) and the interests of students and parents on the other (smaller, and thus potentially more educationally desirable, schools). It is not unreasonable to conclude that the larger enrollments of primary schools managed by large EMOs are the result of a strategic decision to increase profits by increasing school size at the primary level, where the cost of providing education is relatively cheaper than in the higher grades. Furthermore, Sharon Nichols, Gene Glass, and David Berliner have observed that at the primary school level, achievement outcomes are most readily influenced by standardized curriculum using drill-and-practice-oriented instruction.[19] Such methods tend to require less training and talent among staff and can produce short-term improvement in performance, regardless of long-term achievement. The resulting combination of cost-savings and appearance of quick results may render such strategies appealing to EMOs. Whether or not they produce long-term benefits for students is another matter altogether.

Taken together, these findings suggest a three-pronged strategy for for-profit school management firms to drive up test scores, win more business, and generate larger profits: implement a standardized curriculum focusing on drill and practice, increase school size, and focus on managing primary schools, where the cost of providing education is relatively cheaper than at the middle or high school levels. It is not clear, however, whether in the long term any of these strategies will yield profits for investors or significant and sustainable gains in educational outcomes.

Whatever the eventual fate or form of the for-profit management industry, there can be little doubt that privatization has been a principal focus of education reform efforts over the past decade and a half. The annual report on Trends in Schoolhouse Commercialism, also produced by the Commercialism in Education Research Unit at Arizona State University, has documented schoolhouse commercialism trends since 1990 by tracking media references that fall within eight categories, one of which is school privatization. Over the years, there has been considerable variation in the number of media references to privatization in all of its forms—voucher programs and for-profit management of district and charter schools. Nevertheless, the growth is remarkable. Between 1990 and the most recent period studied— July 1, 2003, to June 30, 2004—the number of references to school privatization had increased twentyfold, from forty-seven to eleven hundred.[20]

NO CHILD LEFT BEHIND, EMOs, AND SUPPLEMENTARY EDUCATION SERVICES

While charter school legislation has stimulated the growth of for-profit firms, NCLB may prove to be an even bigger boon to the industry. The law includes a number of provisions encouraging the growth of for-profit education enterprises, especially its requirements that school districts offer a variety of supplemental educational services (SES). These policies are not surprising, in light of explicit White House advocacy of privatization as a desired strategy for reorganizing public services.[21]

How NCLB Subsidizes Market Creation

NCLB requires schools, in return for federal education aid, to conduct standardized testing annually in grades three through eight. To achieve adequate yearly progress, or AYP, schools must raise the test scores of all their students, as well as those of subgroups of students disaggregated by gender, ethnicity, socioeconomic status, special education status, migrant status, and English-language learner status. Schools that fail to achieve AYP overall or among any one subgroup are subject to sanctions. The sanctions get progressively more stringent until, after three years of inadequate progress, schools must offer supplemental educational services to students, typically in the form of after-hours individual or small-group tutoring that is often supplied by private for-profit firms. After four years, a school that still has not made AYP must choose from several actions, including implementing a new curriculum and appointing outside expert advisers. Finally, a school that has failed to achieve AYP after five consecutive years must reopen as a charter school, replace virtually all of its staff, contract with an outside organization to manage the school, or otherwise be restructured—a provision that seems likely to further encourage the growth of EMOs.

In the wake of NCLB, for-profit education management companies have expanded and diversified, venturing into areas such as tutoring. For example, Edison Schools reports that in the 2004–05 school year, it had contracts to serve 270,000 students. But of those, just 71,000 were enrolled in Edison-managed schools; the rest were in some way involved with other Edison services. Thus, while Edison's school-management business is stagnant, the company has grown as a result of diversifying into other educational services.[22]

NCLB not only creates a market for private providers, it keeps public schools out of the lines of business it creates. The act explicitly forbids schools themselves from providing federally funded tutoring if the school has failed to achieve AYP for two consecutive years.[23] Instead, the schools are required to contract with outside providers for tutoring, effectively creating a federally subsidized market for private tutoring firms. The result has been a spur to a private tutoring industry that by one estimate was projected to generate as much as $200 million in 2005.[24]

In addition to managing schools and offering the supplemental educational services required by NCLB, private firms market a range of services tied to its testing and accountability provisions, from consulting and curriculum development to programs that purport to detect and deter cheating on tests. By one estimate, NCLB has created a $20 billion to $30 billion market for various in-school services provided by private, for-profit contractors.[25] For example, Edison Schools is marketing a product line, Tungsten Learning achievement management solutions, which targets schools seeking to raise school test scores. Tungsten's services appear to mainly involve online assessment of students, professional development for teachers, and consulting on "best practices" in education.[26] Indeed, Edison has expanded well beyond its core school-management business to offer private tutoring, operate summer schools, provide test-preparation services and programs, sell curriculum materials, offer in-service training for teachers, and, through Edison Alliance, help schools and districts meet their NCLB AYP targets.

Even as private enterprise seeks profits in tutoring, test writing, and test coaching, the specter of cheating hasn't escaped entrepreneurial attention. With an eye to reports of increased fraud since the inception of NCLB and the high-stakes testing environment it has spawned, a Utah security company, Caveon, has positioned itself as the first firm to provide security services in the field of K–12 high-stakes testing. The company has obtained contracts with at least six states to audit schools' testing procedures for security weaknesses and to recommend measures to improve security.[27]

The current policy environment has also encouraged public schools to behave in entrepreneurial ways. This is reflected in the ascendance of the marketplace model for school improvement, through open-enrollment policies, and in charter and voucher programs described as attempts to expose public schools to competition. It is also reflected in an increasing focus on "marketing," as public schools seek to brand themselves in the public mind in various ways.

A case in point is the Houston Independent School District (HISD), which brands certain products and services that it then sells to other districts. Those products include a variety of management services, such as Medicaid claims collection; employee benefits administration; curriculum and related services, including curriculum software; professional staff development services for teachers and instruction over the Internet; and sundry other services such as job-order construction, lighting retrofitting, printing, and minority- and women-owned business listings. Such efforts began as much as a decade ago, and in 2003–04 sales totaled $12.5 million.[28]

It is not clear whether schools—or, more to the point, students—will benefit as a result of adopting business models. There is no clear evidence that efforts by public school districts to become more like businesses improves the quality of education. This also seems to be the case with charter schools and the for-profit companies that manage them. Notwithstanding anecdotal reports of success and charters' popularity with some parents, the evidence does not suggest that charter students are faring better academically than their peers in traditional public schools.[29] For example, the 2005 RAND evaluation of Edison Schools reported uncertainty about whether Edison's performance was comparable or superior to matched comparison schools.[30] The continued expansion of the for-profit education management industry in the face of mediocre educational results suggests that there is no clear demonstrated link between a successful education management business model and higher student academic performance.

PROSPECTS FOR INCREASED ENTREPRENEURSHIP IN EDUCATION

Though the current policy climate appears highly favorable to the growth of for-profit activity in education, it is not clear that maintaining current conditions will promote the development of the for-profit sector in the long run. The for-profit provision of education services, especially at the K–12 level, remains controversial, and there are still significant obstacles to growth. Critics of the for-profit education sector have expressed a wide range of concerns at the trend of increased for-profit involvement in K–12 schools: possible trade-offs between profits and the best interests of students; evidence that EMOs and supplemental services firms have rarely been held accountable for achieving promised academic results; and recurring allegations of questionable relationships among politicians and policymakers and for-profit companies.[31] These concerns, if left unaddressed, could threaten the prospects of the industry.

Accountability Issues

While NCLB purports to promote a laser-like focus on performance, the for-profit firms that benefit from NCLB's provisions are frequently let off the hook. For example, a *Baltimore Sun* investigation of educational software whose marketers aggressively promoted their products as a means to comply with NCLB standards found that they relied on "dubious studies, often performed or paid for by the companies themselves" to make their case.[32] The series concluded, "While poor schools tend to buy software with repetitive math and reading exercises that produce few lasting gains, wealthier ones are using technology in ways that contribute more to in-depth learning."

Problems notwithstanding, the extent to which federal policy favors privatization was shown in 2004, when federal authorities ordered the Chicago Public Schools to stop using $53 million in federal funds to pay its own staff to tutor some forty thousand students. While private firms tutored another forty thousand at an average cost of $1,300 per student, the cost of tutoring the forty thousand for whom the district employed its own teachers was $400 per student on average. Despite the threefold higher costs, federal education authorities ordered the district to place all students into private tutoring programs, claiming that since Chicago schools were "failing," they were not qualified to provide tutoring.[33] Meanwhile, in March 2005 the Chicago school district had to discipline one firm, New York-based Platform Learning, which had a $15 million contract to tutor fourteen thousand children in seventy-six Chicago schools. Arne Duncan, chief executive officer of the Chicago Public Schools, ejected Platform from seven of those schools because principals complained of chronic absenteeism among tutors and overcrowded tutoring classrooms, where children watched movies or played games because they lacked tutors. In addition, a former Platform tutor told the *Chicago Tribune* that, contrary to a requirement that the firm develop individual tutoring plans for each child, "tutors were told to use the same plan for each child." With contracts in New York, Detroit, Atlanta, Los Angeles, San Francisco, and Newark, New Jersey, Platform is one of the largest private tutoring firms to have emerged in the wake of NCLB. Its New York contract alone is reportedly worth $35 million.[34]

The Chicago district ultimately turned down federal funds in order to continue providing its own tutoring. In the fall of 2005, the school district and the U.S. Department of Education reached a compromise that permitted the district to provide tutoring with federal funds for a year; Secretary of Education Margaret Spellings said the district's improvement justified waiving the NCLB provision.[35] Whether other school districts will be granted similar waivers remains to be seen.

NCLB assigns responsibility for evaluating tutoring services to the states, which are supposed to evaluate supplemental service providers after two years of operation. But a 2004 survey conducted jointly by the Association of Community Organizations for Reform Now, based in Washington, D.C., and the American Institute for Social Justice, based in Dallas, found that states consistently failed to hold supplemental tutoring services accountable in the way that the NCLB holds schools accountable for failing to achieve adequate yearly progress. The survey found extensive problems with the state evaluation processes, considering them untimely and inadequate to establish the actual quality of such services. The report concluded that as much as $200–$300 million had been spent in supplemental services in the nineteen surveyed districts, "with almost no scientific evidence that this spending has contributed to academic achievement." Of twenty-four states in which supplemental services had been offered for at least two years, only six states had finished their evaluations of the 2003–04 performance data, the survey found. According to the report, "This means that parents are choosing providers for their children *right now* without being able to tell if the children will be getting real help with their academics."[36]

The lack of accountability within the supplemental services sector is evident within the for-profit school-management industry as well, and the ensuing failure to ask school-management firms to make good on their often lofty promises could threaten the industry as a whole. Advocates of private management of public district or charter schools have argued that the power to cancel contracts for nonperformance allows districts to hold private management firms accountable. Certainly, some districts have exercised that power, deciding not to renew contracts with EMOs and on occasion canceling contracts midstream. Such decisions, however, are relatively infrequent. A review of charter school studies by Gerald Bracey found that the contention that charters can be held accountable because failing charters will swiftly close is not borne out by experience.[37] In addition, while an EMO may stand to lose *future* profits when it loses a contract for failure to perform, the action does not deprive it of *past* profits it gained while failing to perform. This is especially problematic in that, in the meantime, the profits a for-profit firm receives are almost certain to leave the community.

A particularly egregious example of the lack of oversight exercised by public authorities over for-profit firms is the California Charter Academy (CCA) bankruptcy. CCA, which was once California's largest chain of publicly financed charter schools, closed sixty schools while facing bankruptcy in the fall of 2004. The closures left ten thousand students without schools to attend.[38] The CCA organization was managed by the for-profit Educational Administrative Services Corp., and both were investigated by the Associated Press. The news service's report "detailed the school's questionable enrollment records, its practice of having small school districts oversee dozens of remote campuses, and its use of the private management firm to avoid disclosing school executives' salaries and other expenses."[39]

Many of the schools managed by Edison continue to fall short on NCLB's measures of academic achievement. The problem was especially acute in the Chester Upland School District, where nine of the district's ten schools were run by Edison from 2001 to 2005. The district's Pennsylvania System of School Assessment scores continued to fall throughout Edison's tenure.[40] Edison, having reportedly spent $30 million over the four years, relinquished its contract in July 2005 amid infighting among the company, the school administration, and the board of control.[41]

At another school run by Edison, West Middle School in Clark County, Nevada, 291 students have exercised their school choice option, leaving the school in 2004 after it was deemed failing two years in a row under NCLB guidelines.[42] Overall, contracts between EMOs and at least twenty-two schools ended during the 2004–05 school year. In 2004 alone, Imagine Schools stopped managing five schools, bringing the number of schools under its purview to thirty-three. Mosaica Education stopped managing four schools while adding seven, leaving it with twenty-seven.[43]

It is not always known whether the EMOs or the schools initiated the separation. Thus, some schools may have been closed, while others may remain open but no longer under contract with the EMO in question or any EMO at all. For example, Renaissance Advantage Charter School, originally managed by Mosaica, lost its charter after the school failed to meet its academic or attendance goals, to file annual reports in a timely fashion, to provide documentation to show that 75 percent of its teachers were certified, and to maintain stable staffing.[44]

Students leaving a for-profit school and schools losing their charters for poor performance would appear to give at least some support to the contention of EMO and charter supporters that the public can hold schools accountable by "voting with their feet." Even so, there appears likely to be increased pressure on EMOs themselves and on the schools or school districts that contract with them to insist on more transparent accountability. Failure to respond to such demands is likely to further stunt EMO growth, while acquiescing to them in turn may squeeze EMO profitability.

Cozy Relationships

The lack of accountability and transparency within the for-profit education sector has extended to the process by which vendors are chosen. Politics and relationships often seem to matter more than performance. For instance, politicians responsible for passing the laws that have created these new markets have been known to sit on the boards of companies that stand to profit from them, creating an appearance of self-dealing and influence peddling. An Arkansas law pertaining to K12 Inc., the private provider of online charter school curriculum materials and an organizer of virtual charter schools in a number of states, is illustrative. K12 Inc. is a partner with the Arkansas Department of Education in The Virtual School, an online academy. The school received federal grant money in the amount of $9.3 million over five years, while state legislators blocked funding from the state over a variety of concerns. In addition, the state Board of Education waived for the Virtual School a state law that ordinarily forbids public school officials from having a financial interest in the sale of textbooks or other instructional materials in the schools with which they have an official connection. The waiver reflected the fact that The Virtual School is a subsidiary of K12 Inc., which sells K–12 curriculum to the school. It is Arkansas's only such school with this type of exemption. Sitting on the school's board of directors are former state senators John Brown, John Riggs, and Kevin Smith. Former state education department employees also staff the school.[45] Their status raises the same sort of questions that arise when legislators become lobbyists and Pentagon staffers go to work for defense contractors: namely, whether the companies hiring such personnel obtain undue influence in the halls of government where decisions are made that affect their bottom lines.

Similarly close relationships are found elsewhere. Janet Aikele, a former school superintendent and state legislator, was hired in 2002 by K12 Inc. to head the Idaho Virtual Academy. The academy is an online-based charter school operated by a nonprofit board of trustees in partnership with K12, which provides the school's curriculum. The arrangement prompted the *Idaho Statesman* to urge lawmakers to "set up safeguards to make sure the people running charter schools aren't on the payroll of the schools' contractors."[46]

Sometimes for-profit companies set up nonprofit entities that appear to be little more than fronts for the for-profit firm. The links between Planagement and Eagle Academies of Texas suggest such a relationship. Eagle Academies is a nonprofit charter school chain that shares an office with the for-profit management firm Planagement. An article in the *Austin American Statesman* revealed that the two companies are often hard to distinguish, sharing, besides the office, a receptionist, a conference room, and company vehicles. While Eagle reported it retained Planagement to manage its finances, the newspaper reported that Planagement's involvement extended to recommending candidates for Eagle's board, supplying the curriculum, and rotating management between Planagement and Eagle so as to avoid violating a state law that bars charter school administrators from having a "substantial" financial interest in management companies. "Unlike public schools, Eagle and many other charter schools don't hold public elections for board positions. Parents who are unhappy with an Eagle school can't run for the board or support a favorite candidate," the article reported.[47] The same article found that Eagle spends nearly twice as much as the state average on administration while spending half as much on instruction. This kind of financial management is in direct contrast to the claims of EMO supporters, who believe EMOs can save money on administration while increasing achievement. As Eagle enters the virtual school business, doing away with the overhead involved in traditional brick and mortar, its profit margin further increases.[48] It is for these and other reasons that concern over the propriety of for-profit companies managing charter schools has led three states, Hawaii, Mississippi, and Tennessee, to pass laws banning charter schools from entering such contracts.[49]

Profitability Questions

As has already been noted, the profitability of most EMO firms remains unknown because all but one or two are privately held and therefore do not disclose detailed financial data. In fact, EMOs would prefer to keep their cost structures and profits as opaque as possible, due to the political and emotional ramifications of seeming to profit excessively from school management. To the extent that EMOs are profitable, they can be expected to spark some degree of public suspicion or resentment, particularly if those profits— or noneducational costs such as marketing, advertising, executive salaries, and the like—are seen as coming at the expense of quality instruction or of students and their communities.

The dearth of available information is a significant policy issue. For example, K12 Inc. manages the California Virtual Academies (CVA), a network of virtual public charter schools founded in the summer of 2002. The state of California pays CVA $4,700 for each enrolled student. Of that, $600 per child is paid to K12 as a management fee and another $1,800 per child is paid to K12 for curriculum.[50] That leaves $2,300 per student that apparently stays with CVA, but it is not clear where that money goes or for what it is used. At $4,700 each for the 1,200 students reportedly enrolled in CVA in 2004, the company, which does not disclose financial data, appears to have grossed $5.6 million that year.

In Massachusetts, state law requires public schools to return to municipal general revenue funds any surpluses that accumulate in the course of a fiscal year. In Springfield, Massachusetts, however, Sabis Educational Systems, the for-profit company managing Sabis International Charter School, was permitted under its contract to retain a $2.86 million surplus accumulated over three years. The company dismissed objections to the contract, arguing that it should be allowed to keep the funds because Sabis had invested money to improve the school facility. During the same three-year period, the Springfield School District was laying off 329 teachers due to funding shortfalls.[51]

Embedded in the economics of education is a question about whether schools can ever be profitable over the long term. Education is labor intensive: Approximately 70–80 percent of every school's budget goes to pay the salaries and benefits of teachers and administrators.[52] Thus the most obvious place to seek a profit is personnel costs. The simplest way to reduce personnel costs is to reduce teacher pay, which is most easily accomplished by hiring teachers with less experience and fewer qualifications. The other alternative is to increase class size. Indeed, larger classes may be on the way. Edison founder Christopher Whittle, in his new book *Crash Course: Imagining a Better Future for Public Education*, recommends *raising* teacher salaries but cutting the *number* of teachers in half and having children "working on their own" for half of the time.[53]

Assume, then, the entry of a new, for-profit firm into a particular education field. In order to hold down costs, the firm hires a cadre of young, inexperienced teachers with only the minimal level of academic qualifications. Over time, those teachers will gain experience and, presumably, qualifications (for instance, by obtaining advanced degrees or otherwise undergoing professional development training). Thus, there is a built-in escalation of costs that will, in time, erode profitability. The alternative would be to endure a chronically high level of staff turnover, which would inevitably undermine staff morale and the quality of the education program.

Such conditions set up a likely scenario in which a for-profit school can profit in the beginning—particularly in comparison with a district school carrying a staff of higher-paid, more experienced teachers—but soon lose its advantage as labor costs catch up. The only other alternative would be for the for-profit school to accept a high turnover of staff and compensate with a highly standardized curriculum—a model that closely resembles that of for-profit higher-education institutions such as the University of Phoenix.

The trends already visible in for-profit education, as noted earlier, point to this sort of strategic decision: enrolling more students and relying on more standardized curriculum. Indeed, from the entrepreneur's point of view, standardization and "branding" are likely to become values in and of themselves for their ability to draw in more students on the strength of brand reputation. Yet such an approach stands in stark contrast to the visions that animate educational entrepreneurship and that inspired the charter school movement: greater autonomy, heightened flexibility, small schools, individualized curriculum, and community control.

Virtual schools may offer other ways around the central dilemma that for-profit educational firms face: by eliminating the costs of school infrastructure and by using technology to enable an individual teacher to reach many more students. It is unknown, however, whether virtual schools will be able to expand significantly beyond the homeschool market, and whether they will succeed in diverting significant numbers of students from conventional public schools.

Moreover, the virtual school model seems especially prone to a lack of accountability and even fraud. For instance, the Ohio state education department reported that a large number of children enrolled in virtual schools in the state were not taking an achievement test mandated by the state. The Ohio state senate responded by passing an amendment to the state budget requiring that children in online schools who fail to take the test two years in a row be expelled and prevented from enrolling in another online school.[54] If other states follow Ohio's lead, the result could place a damper on virtual school growth.

The question of whether for-profit education is economically viable is completely separate from that of whether it is educationally sound. The evidence of its educational value is weak; that of its economic viability remains an open question.

CONCLUSION

Early childhood education and postsecondary education show signs of being the most promising sectors of for-profit, entrepreneurial activity in education as far as investors are concerned. Neither preschool nor postsecondary education are mandatory or universal, and regulatory oversight is correspondingly more relaxed.

Investors' enthusiasm for for-profit K–12 education firms remains more tepid. Edison Schools started as a private company in 1991, went public in 1999, and was taken private again in 2003 at a fraction of its original share price, failing to earn shareholders the sorts of returns they hoped for when they first bought the company's stock. No EMOs since Edison have sought to sell stock to the general public.

To the extent that the public perceives issues such as lack of performance, rising costs, and potential fraud, abuse, and corruption as problems, they will likely insist that policymakers bring for-profit firms under closer scrutiny. This places the for-profit industry in a difficult position. Failure to act risks discrediting private-sector entrepreneurialism in K–12 public education. Addressing the issues, however, requires increased regulatory oversight. Such oversight would have the effect of raising the cost of for-profit initiatives for taxpayers and for companies. For this reason, investors are likely to question the profit-making prospects of the enterprise and, over time, to lose interest in the sector.

Education is, as Henry Levin points out, both a public and private good. In the public interest, it prepares young people to assume adult civic roles, participate in the workings of a democratic society, and embrace the nation's values and its underlying "economic, political, and social life." In the private sphere, it offers students and their families opportunities to enhance their "individual economic, social, cultural, and political benefits."[55]

Given Levin's formulation, assessing the value of entrepreneurship in education is inherently problematic. With its emphasis on *individual* action, profit, and risk, the concept of entrepreneurship doesn't fit comfortably with education as either a public good *or* private good. The emphasis of education as a private good focuses on the recipient—the student—while the emphasis inherent in entrepreneurship focuses on the *provider* and the well-being of that provider. In order for the logic of educational entrepreneurship to make sense, it is necessary to assume that the well-being of the provider is synonymous with the well being of the student—an arguable assumption, to say the very least.

In my view, the concept of entrepreneurship is best confined to market economics. In market ideology, the individual entrepreneur bears the risk of potential loss or collects the profit. In the provision of education services, however, where the entrepreneur's efforts are subsidized by taxpayers, the risk is borne not just by the individual but by the community. Arguably, indeed, the greater the public's share of the cost, the greater the risk the public itself bears in the process.

Whether for-profit education succeeds or fails will rest on whether it demonstrates that it can provide a clear social value. It has yet to do that. Despite the accomplishments of some individual schools, for-profit education as an institution has not been able to demonstrate that it is contributing to the greater good or making a positive difference in the practical reality of children's lives.

CHAPTER 6

Entrepreneurs within School Districts

Joe Williams

It was the kind of defiant act that most school principals probably have contemplated wistfully at one time or another. Disgusted by what he and his staff considered to be poorly written, poorly stapled, and generally disorganized mandatory citywide exams sent to Fritsche Middle School by the Milwaukee Public Schools (MPS) central office in the fall of 1999, principal Bill Andrekopoulos committed an act of ownership theretofore unheard of in the one hundred thousand–student school district. Andrekopoulos and his staff stuffed the exams back into the box and shipped them back, return to sender. They included a brief message: What you produced wasn't good enough for our students. Please try again.[1]

At schools all across Milwaukee that autumn, word spread quickly about the test-box rebellion, if for no other reason than that acts of defiance were such rarities in a system where power was closely held by bureaucrats and where schools were expected to respect, honor, and obey the central office. But this wasn't just any school. Andrekopoulos and his close-knit team of teachers and parents at the south-side school had increasingly been taking advantage of every bit of autonomy and site-based control that the school system was offering amid political pressure created by threats from private school vouchers and proposed nondistrict charter schools at the time.

When a slate of voucher-supporting school board candidates swept the previous spring's elections, it created a window of opportunity for Andrekopoulos and his staff to spring into action. The previous school board resisted plans to allow any of its own schools to become "instrumentality" charter schools, or schools chartered by the district as opposed to outside entities, and the new board was eager to break down that wall. Fritsche Middle School was already doing great things for its students, and the staff there had long rallied behind Andrekopoulos's leadership. Arguing that the teachers, administrators, and parents at the one thousand–student middle school had better ideas about how their school could excel than the hundreds of bureaucrats who spent their days shuffling paper at the district office miles away, the school community asked the new school board to be left to put its plans in place without any bureaucratic obstruction. The deal was inked: Fritsche Middle School would be given autonomy in exchange for results. Unlike charter schools outside the Milwaukee school system, in which new private-like public schools were started from scratch, the "instrumentality" charter was formed by an existing entrepreneurial school community that felt constrained even by Milwaukee's progressive attempts to decentralize power to schools during the 1990s. Fritsche was able to negotiate a deal with the school board in which the school became the client, and essentially "bought back" the services it needed to support its students and teachers from the central office. Money for each student started out at the school and flowed to the central office when necessary, rather than the other way around as was typically the case.

At a time when Milwaukee's schools were attempting to show they could compete with new publicly funded alternatives, Fritsche Middle School became the poster child for public schools trying to reinvent themselves. Andrekopoulos, who at the time was a student of a national performance management program, showed what could be done when sound decisions were made by entrepreneurial leaders at the school level rather than at the central office. (To further remind the bureaucrats in the Milwaukee Public Schools that they existed to serve his school, for example, the Fritsche team later developed a "report card" that it used to grade all of the various central office departments, based primarily on the "value added" each provided for Fritsche's teachers and students.)

The MPS central office busing operation, to cite one example, was a massive bureaucracy unto itself, transporting as many people over the course of a school day as the entire Milwaukee County Transit System. There was little incentive for anyone in the $60 million per year school transportation office to find new savings. But because every penny mattered to the team at Fritsche, they set their sights on every aspect of school spending, including the bus routes that served their students. With some slight tinkering of pick-up points and times, the school community was able to voluntarily eliminate two entire routes and make existing routes more efficient. Savings from these changes, and others like them in other areas of the school budget, were plowed toward additional instruction—including tutoring designed to help struggling eighth graders pass mandatory graduation tests. Because the staff had a vested interest in showing academic success (which would help maintain their charter agreement with the district), many teachers started showing up on Saturdays to work with students who needed extra help. "Ownership" of everything that happened in the building became the mantra.

This chapter examines the various forms of entrepreneurship, like the Fritsche Middle School example, that exist *within* modern public sector education systems. It defines "entrepreneurs" in the school sector as educators and school leaders who take risks to transform their classrooms, schools, and districts. They take ownership of the success or failure of everything that happens under their watch, often welcoming innovative ways of improving the delivery of education to students. In many cases, these public-sector school entrepreneurs have a keen ability to recognize opportunities that exist for improvements to (or abandonment of) the status quo in their schools and find imaginative ways to take advantage of those opportunities to benefit students. Unlike entrepreneurs who prod school systems from organizations built on the outside of the system, this chapter focuses on the "intrapreneurs" who accept the frustrations caused by bureaucratic inertia and willingly stick around to push for change from within. While their actions are often considered less risky than external entrepreneurs (since they continue to earn paychecks and benefits from the school system regardless of whether they succeed or fail), these entrepreneurs put their reputations and professional prospects on the line.

In many cases, opportunities for entrepreneurial change are caused by the sector's seeming inability to change on its own. Modern school systems have a poor track record when it comes to taking bold steps to solve clearly identified problems within the sector. Much of this chapter relies on case studies and examples from three cities: Milwaukee and New York, where the author has worked as a journalist, and San Diego, where the author participated in an in-depth analysis of the district reforms.

Schools like Fritsche in Milwaukee have historically been the exception within public education. The combination of strong leadership in the principal's office and in the classroom was realized at an opportune time in Milwaukee's history, as the city's schools underwent a radical shift in power as a result of pressure from private school vouchers and external charter schools. Michael Will, the teachers union's building representative at the time, described the huge commitment that the staff was required to make in order to have the freedom that comes from a charter school conversion:

"Every staff member needs to be on a committee, working extra hours and still maintaining lesson plans and grading papers. It's more work, but once you get to that point you say boy, this was worth it."[2]

Andrekopoulos, who went on to become the superintendent of the Milwaukee Public Schools in 2002, said, "It's a matter of schools self-actualizing and pushing the school community to take on a leadership role, to take ownership."[3]

Twelve months before the Milwaukee School Board voted to grant Fritsche's team its official autonomy, the Wisconsin Supreme Court ruled in favor of a private school voucher program, empowering entrepreneurial educators like Andrekopoulos who wanted to prove that the public school system could compete and win in the marketplace for city students.

Milwaukee faced a similar competitive threat just a few years earlier, when the state was contemplating a takeover of the school system and the school choice legislation was expanded to include religious schools. In his book *Revolution at the Margins*, Frederick M. Hess notes that there was a brief "explosion of innovative schools" in Milwaukee, as "energetic and atypical teachers" popped through the cracks to take advantage of the teachers union's desire to feed off more radical change.[4]

Former school board member John Gardner described the kind of bureaucratic paralysis that used to squash innovation and entrepreneurship prior to the onset of vouchers in Milwaukee:

> Reforms, including those with clear merit and without vigorous opposition, died because one of many parties—the board, Superintendent, central administration, teachers' or administrators' union, principals, or teachers— could effectively veto it. Lining up all internal vested interests for the same thing, at the same time, generally proved more than anyone could do.[5]

Andrekopoulos said the plethora of choices available to Milwaukee's parents forced the Milwaukee schools over time to be more responsive and enterprising. "Innovation is now part of our DNA," Andrekopoulos said.[6]

American school systems historically have been closed to entrepreneurs. Going along to get along has long been encouraged, and anything considered even close to rocking the boat has often been viewed as a good way to risk losing one of the best pensions the public sector has to offer. Administrators, many of whom have patiently worked their way up through the ranks of the school system by playing by the rules, have wondered why others shouldn't do the same and have been reluctant to surrender the power they hold. The end result is an education system in which creativity, innovation, and a desire to find better ways to do things often are blocked before they even make it out of the gate. The anecdotes are so rare that we devise monikers for those who take ownership for results and rock the boat. Those who find new and creative ways to do the job of educating children are often referred to in terms like "crackerjacks" by those who appreciate such entrepreneurship, or "renegades" or "opportunists" by those more inclined to following the rules and giving in to institutional inertia. In many schools and districts, entrepreneurial educators are considered not team players because walking a straight line—regardless of the results or the larger impact on students—is so strongly encouraged.

But while traditional public schools seldom see the kind of self-determined governance that Fritsche enjoyed, there *are* growing indications that entrepreneurial leaders are beginning to play a prominent role in reinventing public education across America. Pressure like the kind Milwaukee felt has become more familiar. The federal No Child Left Behind Act (NCLB), which took effect in 2002, has exerted pressure on struggling school districts to find ways to achieve better results for all categories of students. Additionally, a wave of "nontraditional" school leaders, often with some background in the business world, has attempted to take a crack at reforming long-failing urban school systems, opening the door for entrepreneurial educators.

I will attempt here to briefly categorize and describe six primary types of emerging school entrepreneurs, which I call "Fresh Bloods," "James Deans," "Johnny Appleseeds," "Destiny Grabbers," "Cooks Using All Their Burners," and the extremely rare "Bulls Managing the China Shop." At times, various school entrepreneurs may wear multiple labels. Each has its upsides and downsides, but all offer opportunities for antsy entrepreneurial types who would otherwise be forced to choose between settling for the status quo and leaving the world of public schooling. Often what distinguishes between the various types of entrepreneurs identified here is the degree to which they believe in following (or breaking) rules, and the extent to which their entrepreneurial efforts may be applied systemically.

"FRESH BLOODS"

Common sense dictates that the most important point in the delivery of education is at the classroom level, and that high-quality teachers are a crucial portion of any reform strategy. Efforts to attract, empower, and retain entrepreneurial teachers in the classroom are growing, through programs like Teach For America (TFA) and alternative certification programs like New York City's Teaching Fellows programs. Both efforts are designed to bring top-notch students from other specialties and professions into the classroom, and in the Teaching Fellows example, the city helps pay for teachers to earn a master's degree after school hours while they work toward certification.

The upside of these programs is that they often attract "risk takers" to the classroom—professionals who often are less inclined to settle for bureaucratic inertia and incompetence within their school systems and who similarly care little about what is said about them in the teachers lounge. They are often the kinds of teachers who are willing to go public in the press, at town hall meetings, or in Internet blogs about the real barriers that classroom teachers face within their school systems. They enter their schools with eyes wide open, and they feel it is important to share their experience with the world.

In New York, in addition to highly pedigreed Ivy Leaguers who enter the classroom through Fresh Blood programs like TFA, the Teaching Fellows program has attracted mid-career switchers, including lawyers, stockbrokers, and advertising executives. "I am determined to be a foot soldier in the movement to inject equity into our educational system," explained Mitch Kurz, 51, who left his job managing 8,000 employees in 250 offices in 77 countries for the advertising firm Young and Rubicam in 2002 to teach in a Bronx middle school.[7]

Created by former chancellor Harold Levy, who himself left his job as a corporate lawyer for Citigroup to take on the nation's largest school system, the Teaching Fellows program was designed to address a lack of quality in the teaching ranks and to appeal to the altruistic nature of many successful people who wished to somehow give back to their city. "To heed the call of social responsibility will make you a better person in your own eyes," Levy once said of the program.[8] The question, of course, remains whether these types of entrants to the teaching profession (and the worldly experiences and no-nonsense ethic they bring with them) will help better prepare students and/or stimulate the entrepreneurial spirit within schools and districts.

Beginning their work lacking formal pedagogical training in education schools, some Fresh Bloods are more open than traditional entrants to the profession to discovering and implementing teaching methods that they can see work with their students. (Upon leaving the advertising world, Kurz, for example, found classroom discipline to be the biggest challenge in his school, and he set out to find the best strategies to deal with disruptive students.) Critics have complained that Fresh Bloods tend to be so inexperienced and ill-prepared that it is unfair to subject needy children to the learning curve that their own teachers are facing. Other critics, such as Stanford's Linda Darling-Hammond, have argued that these Fresh Bloods are not as effective at the craft as traditionally trained and certified teachers and that they tend not to stick around in their jobs for more than just a few years.[9] Groups like Teach For America have disputed that concern, pointing to research it commissioned that found their corps members outperformed veteran and certified teachers in their schools.[10]

Aside from friction created by education school scholars like Darling-Hammond, however, Fresh Bloods face many other obstacles in school systems that, at their core, tend to be disdainful of those who take initiative or who rock the boat. Many NYC Teaching Fellows in the early years reported that they felt like second-class citizens in their schools and were even set up to fail by administrators who had little interest in seeing them succeed. As International Academy for Educational Entrepreneurship cofounder Chuck Lavaroni notes:

> While the "system" says it respects and wants creativity, more often than not, it does nothing to encourage or support it. The creative teacher often has to literally fight for time, money, resources, and/or equipment necessary to truly create and become involved in all aspects of the creative process. The "system" makes it difficult for teachers to share ideas, plan mutual activities, and build upon each other's strengths and interests.[11]

Thus, many cases of teacher entrepreneurship end up being isolated, even secretive. Sometimes teachers find themselves at odds with the school administration's generally low expectations for their students and staff. Zelman Bokser, a Teaching Fellow in New York City, came to the program as a Fulbright Scholar with a PhD in music and an extensive career in classical music, including teaching at the university level. He couldn't have been hired for the teaching job without the alternative certification program because he didn't have the required education school courses under his belt to become a traditionally licensed teacher. In 2000, Bokser landed a teaching job through the Fellows program at Public School 75 in Brooklyn and almost immediately encountered bureaucratic resistance when he began to develop a plan to teach violin to the students in his struggling school. It would be "too difficult" and a waste of time, he was told by administrators at the school. These kids had enough trouble getting through the school day, why throw more hurdles their way, the sentiment went. One administrator even advised him to forget the whole idea, suggesting she was doing him a favor by preventing the failure that was sure to follow.[12]

But as a Fresh Blood with an attitude, Bokser didn't let the naysayers stop him, and two years later, as his students tuned their violins inside Manhattan's Hammerstein Ballroom for a performance welcoming that year's crop of new fellows, Bokser reminded his peers what they were all up against. The story of the naysaying administrator incensed a deputy mayor who was in attendance at the time and who pledged to find the culprit and banish her from the system. But the system, as many Fresh Bloods quickly discover, is filled with so many naysayers that even entrepreneurial leaders at the top of the system are limited in what they can do.

"JAMES DEANS"

Some call them crackerjacks, others call them ball-busters. For our purposes, we'll refer to them here as education's James Deans, only these subversive entrepreneurial types tend to be rebels *with* a cause. Whether it's the principal in Queens, New York, who blatantly disregards the clear directions of her regional supervisors by throwing away the kindergarten curriculum because she has concluded that her kids haven't even come close to mastering the skills taught in the prekindergarten curriculum (instead using a preK curriculum that she has discovered produces better results), or the principal in Jersey City, New Jersey, who figures out it is easier and more efficient to get school supplies for her teachers by creating an illegal slush fund and an account at the local Staples store, we're talking about creative school leaders who generally believe that rules are for fools if they stand in the way of creating better schools. Note that we're not talking about ignoring rules that protect the welfare of the children under their charge, nor are we talking about breaking all the rules. James Deans use what they consider common sense when picking their battles.

Like some of the maverick school leaders in Milwaukee, these James Deans tend to become folk heroes of sorts and often have complicated power relationships with administrators and union leaders. They tend to have a healthy chip on their shoulder and some degree of confidence in their own ability to make things happen. Often times, the only thing that keeps them employed is the fact that they can point to measurable results and have used their entrepreneurial skills to forge political support among key stakeholders, like politicians, business leaders, and parents. They can be more effective at cultivating relationships with the media than their less entrepreneurial counterparts, enhancing both their power and the internal resentment within the school bureaucracy.

The underlying assumption guiding the James Deans is one of serving their students by any means necessary. That is, they see the problem in modern school systems as systemic in nature, and that effectively educating children requires creative measures and rule-breaking. So long as they are getting results, most school superintendents will allow them to quietly exist at the margins rather than tempt the political fates.

Anthony Lombardi, principal of Public School 49 in Middle Village, Queens, is a perfect example of a James Dean, but there are thousands of them quietly forging their way through dysfunctional school systems nationwide. In Lombardi's hallway office, which includes three portraits of Frank Sinatra, he keeps a copy of a manual called *Regulations and Procedures for Pedagogical Ratings*. He doesn't believe a word of it.[13] The directions contained in the manual for principals who want to rid their schools of incompetent teachers make disciplining bad teachers counterproductive, he believes. "It's impossible to prove incompetency," Lombardi told *New York Magazine* in 2003. By giving a teacher an unsatisfactory rating, a principal is preparing for a two-year process that may not even result in the teacher being removed from the school. More importantly, once a teacher gets an "unsatisfactory" rating, he or she is prevented from transferring elsewhere.

Lombardi is obviously not the first principal to figure this out, one of the primary reasons that of the city's eighty thousand schoolteachers, only a few hundred a year on average receive unsatisfactory ratings from their principals.[14] Lombardi's entrepreneurial skills, however, convinced him not to give up. Rather than avoiding paperwork, Lombardi bombarded his sub par teachers with memos based on his in-class evaluations. He drafted detailed plans for improvement for each teacher, set the bar high, and encouraged all of his teachers to work according to high professional standards. In short, he created a climate in which his weakest teachers found themselves asking whether they even wanted to stick around at the school to see whether or not they could rise to the occasion. "I've set a high expectation and when they haven't met it, they had to make a professional decision if they wanted to be a member of this staff," Lombardi said.[15] It becomes a sort of compact between the bad teacher and the principal: He won't give the unsatisfactory rating if they agree to take their act to some other school.

James Deans, like Lombardi, are good at bending and at exploiting the rules. Once Lombardi is able to get a bad teacher to transfer, he has been able to tap into exemptions in the teachers contract that allow for school-based hiring decisions, trusting that his teachers will continue to want to uphold the standards they have set together as a school community. "I used the system of rules to my advantage," Lombardi said.[16]

Lombardi has been able to survive through several regime changes in the city's school scene in large part because these schemes have paid off. In 2002, the school made it onto the list of the city's two hundred most-improved schools. Test scores in math and reading shot through the roof at the five hundred–student school under Lombardi's leadership.

The obvious downside of relying on James Deans like Lombardi to reform struggling school systems, however, is that there is nothing systemic at all about what is happening there. Lombardi, through his careful consideration of which rules are worth following and which are worth avoiding, has effectively taken care of business for his school. But even Lombardi admits that he has done so at the expense of the rest of the city schools, which have been forced to accept bad teachers that have been driven out of his building with "satisfactory" work evaluations in their files. "I've been unethical. I made my school better, but I made your system even worse," Lombardi told the City Council's Education Committee during 2003 hearings on the impact of contractual work rules.[17]

James Dean school entrepreneurs often work amid resistance from bureaucrats at the central office who don't appreciate their renegade styles. In the mid-1990s, a Milwaukee principal named Mary Beth Minkley got used to hearing about all the things she wasn't allowed to do at Congress Elementary School. After starting the city's first year-round school, she battled bureaucrats who refused to fix the air-conditioning in the summer months. When she needed more space to accommodate the swelling student population of kids who suddenly wanted to be a part of her popular school, the bureaucrats warned her to slow down. At a 1999 breakfast honoring her work in creating the year-round school, Minkley told the crowd, "I know there are people from the central office in the audience, but you made things extremely difficult for us when we were trying to make this happen."[18] For entrepreneurial school principals who work in real time, often one of the most frustrating experiences comes from dealing with foot-dragging administrators who seem incapable of making any decision other than, "I don't know about that. It's not how we normally do things."

"JOHNNY APPLESEEDS"

Like the legendary folk hero who traveled the countryside planting apple seeds so that they might someday blossom to feed American settlers, these entrepreneurial programs invest heavily in creating the kinds of school leaders who will someday lead transformations at the school level. Essentially, this is an investment in an army of change agents. These efforts are based on the notion that turning around whole systems requires turning around the sum of its school parts. Unlike our "James Deans," who tend to be smart leaders who find ways around stupid rules, the Appleseeds tend to be rule-followers, with strong allegiance to the leaders and the rules set at the top of the system. They often believe that if you do the job correctly, there are ways to bring change to schools within the existing school system framework.

Examples include programs like LAUNCH (Leadership Academy and Urban Network for Chicago), a joint effort to train new school leaders by the Chicago Public Schools, Northwestern University, and the union that represents principals in the Chicago schools. Aspiring principals in LAUNCH take part in hands-on lessons that emphasize leadership and management, in addition to education. Participants take summer courses at Northwestern's Kellogg Business School, and are then paired up with a principal mentor for five months of intense professional development. "The goal is to seize that opportunity by finding and training the best and brightest candidates, creating a critical mass of 'change agents' with the promise of transforming individual schools and—potentially—the entire system," said the University of Chicago's Albert Bertini when the project was announced in 1997.[19]

To date, one hundred LAUNCH fellows have become principals in the Chicago schools and many others assumed other leadership roles within schools and at the district office, according to the program's website. The district, not wanting to put all of its eggs in one basket, also partners with the University of Illinois–Chicago and the nonprofit group New Leaders for New Schools to help find and train promising change-agent Johnny Appleseed school leaders. Similar leadership programs have been run in districts like St. Paul (Leadership Institute); Columbus, Ohio; Norfolk, Virginia; and elsewhere.

In Chicago's case, it is noteworthy that the principals union participated in the creation and implementation of LAUNCH, essentially taking out one potential internal obstacle. In New York City, to name just one example, the union representing principals and assistant principals has been publicly skeptical of the city's nonprofit Leadership Academy. Insiders involved in the creation of the New York program noted that the lack of institutional buy-in from the traditional stakeholders within the system (primarily the school labor unions and the bureaucracy itself, including the state's education department) made it difficult at first to get clearance to certify graduates of the program as school administrators.

The New York case is peculiar in that while the aspiring principals program is run as a nonprofit appendage of the city's department of education (the city once gave the nonprofit a no-interest $10 million loan to help with start-up cash-flow problems),[20] the program has often thumbed its nose at traditional school leadership programs. Its founders believe they have good reasons for this nose-thumbing, namely, the status quo's inability to properly prepare the kinds of school leaders needed to turn around troubled schools. When the $75 million privately funded initiative was launched in January 2003, former General Electric CEO Jack Welch, an adviser to the project, boasted to reporters about how he used to deal with "jerk managers" and had set a high bar for what the city's newly trained school leaders would do. "This is no B.S.," Welch said. "We have a chance to take a swing at something and make it sensational."[21] It has been difficult to determine in New York whether some of the resistance the Leadership Academy faced was caused by Welch and Co.'s bravado or good-old fashioned institutional inertia. It also remains to be seen whether the donors who have supported the costly effort to create these school-level change agents will continue to do so.

As mentioned, these kinds of Johnny Appleseed programs, because they are aligned with and sanctioned by the official school leadership, tend not to produce the kind of rule-breaking James Deans who find creative, noncompliant ways to prosper in bureaucratic systems. Instead, Johnny Appleseeds tend to look for ways to do a better job leading schools within the existing rules and framework. On a visit to training sessions conducted at New York's Leadership Academy in 2004, I observed a session conducted by the Department of Education's legal department instructing principals how to build an airtight case against an incompetent teacher. The lawyers went over the common technical mistakes that often cause arbitrators to rule against management before they are able to even discuss the substance of the charges. Essentially, these budding school leaders were being taught how to dot their *i*'s and cross their *t*'s, so that they can level the playing field with labor. One long-time administrator who was present for the session remarked to me, "The way it used to work, you were lucky if someone pulled you aside and talked to you about these issues. The labor contracts were something nobody felt comfortable bringing up at meetings and training sessions."[22]

Other examples of the Johnny Appleseed approach include San Diego's efforts under chancellor Anthony Alvarado to conduct monthly meetings for principals through a district-sponsored training entity called the Institute for Learning. Part of the district's theory of change under superintendent Alan Bersin's "Blueprint for Student Success," the intense training sessions were designed to get every principal in the city on the same page to begin building an infrastructure for learning, starting with the principals at the school level. The principal conferences included field trips to successful schools and classrooms and discussions with experts about instructional techniques and peda-

Rule-Breakers

James Deans	*Bulls Managing the China Shop*
Fresh Bloods	

Targeted (School Level) | **Systemic**

Destiny Grabbers	*Johnny Appleseeds*

Rule-Followers

gogical philosophies. While designed to increase the professionalized nature of being a principal in San Diego, the Institute for Learning was an example of entrepreneurship at the district level, as all principals were expected to participate and follow the direction from the top instructional leaders in the district.

"DESTINY GRABBERS"

Of all of our categories of school entrepreneurs, this one is the least tapped to date, but it also represents the area of entrepreneurship most likely to take off in the current reform environment. These entrepreneurs tap into conditions created by the federal No Child Left Behind Act and other standards-based reform efforts to use accountability measures as a tool to turn around their own struggling schools. Rather than viewing sanctions for repeated failure as a punishment, these destiny grabbers view them as opportunities. In short, these entrepreneurs—typically teachers, administrators, and parents—are in the business of making lemons into lemonade.

Under California state law, for example, fourth-year failing schools (those that haven't made what NCLB considers adequate yearly progress for four straight years) can begin the process of developing plans to correct themselves. One of the options is that teachers and parents can vote to turn the school into a charter school as part of its turnaround plans. In San Diego, for example, three persistently struggling schools in 2005 voted to convert to charter school status and eventually won approval from a skeptical school board.

As charter schools, these learning communities become freed from many central office mandates and get considerably more wiggle-room within the teachers contract to change the structure of the school (teachers decide themselves what is fair game). At Gompers Middle School, for example, teachers voted to launch a turnaround plan that included an extended school day and school year, smaller classes, and afterschool and Saturday tutoring for struggling students. Parents voted to require that every parent at the school volunteer for a certain number of hours, and to send their kids to school in uniforms. Activists at the school spent six months working on the plans, including going door-to-door to get signatures of support from parents. A majority of teachers also signed on, despite the opposition of the San Diego Education Association. The University of California, San Diego, also signed on to supply tutors and mentors for Gompers students.

Former San Diego superintendent Alan Bersin credited the parents at those schools for organizing (with the help of district staffers) to take control of their own children's destinies. "For the first time we saw the authentic emergence of parents and teachers," said Bersin, who called the process a "magical six weeks in San Diego."[23]

The external hammer, obviously, is the system's ability to close these persistently failing schools entirely, a hammer that makes some teachers who normally are opponents of (or indifferent to) charter schools reconsider when faced with the option of doing something proactive to prevent it. As more and more persistently substandard schools face a day of reckoning that has been prompted by NCLB, the ranks of destiny grabbers may rapidly expand. As San Diego School Board trustee John de Beck noted, turning a failing school into a charter school is a beginning, not an end. "Be careful what you wish for because you might get it," de Beck said.[24]

Newsworthy in this context is the emergence of "teacher partnerships" in Minnesota and elsewhere, in which teachers literally own charter schools and are ultimately accountable for learning. These teachers help select the staff, decide teaching methods and curriculum, evaluate their performance, and decide their compensation. Similarly, the United Federation of Teachers, the union representing New York City teachers, took the unusually entrepreneurial step in 2005 of applying for and opening its own experimental charter school in an impoverished neighborhood in East New York, part of

Brooklyn. A high school is set to open in 2006, provided it is approved by the State University of New York, the charter authorizer. Neither school will operate with a principal (it will use a lead teacher) and teachers will sit on the schools' boards of directors. Union leaders have said they hope to show through increased student achievement that it is possible to run successful schools in the city within the confines of the teachers contract.

"COOKS USING ALL THEIR BURNERS"

These entrepreneurial school leaders (the cooks) are so committed to finding new ways to improve the delivery of education to students that they try every means imaginable to make it happen. They are betting that by placing so many pots on the stove at once, something remotely edible will surely emerge by the time the chow bell rings. Even more important, these entrepreneurial chefs understand that empowering principals and teachers to be change-agent entrepreneurial types themselves requires fundamental changes to the culture of school systems that have historically stifled and even frowned upon creativity and innovation. They understand that in order for change agents to succeed at their schools, a new culture needs to emerge that views supporting schools and learning as the system's top priority. These entrepreneurial school leaders find ways to embrace various entrepreneurial efforts even when their directions clash with one another or the stated mission of the school system.

Two prominent examples of modern-day multiburner cooks include New York City Chancellor Joel Klein and Philadelphia Schools CEO Paul Vallas. In both cases, these entrepreneurial leaders have come from nontraditional backgrounds. They have little invested in preserving the way things have been done in the past, and their own professional backgrounds have convinced them that radical change is not only necessary but will only occur with poking and prodding from multiple directions.

In both cases, word that these nontraditional school leaders were cooking on all burners spread quickly, sending a clear message to other entrepreneurial types in the hinterlands: "Your innovative spirit is welcome here, so let's talk." Business leaders, who for years sat on the sidelines because their efforts to assist the school systems were often squandered by ineffective school leaders and systems, suddenly found hope and became early partners in reform.

Vallas, who took over the helm of Philadelphia's schools in 2002, has engaged in the kinds of internal tinkering and engineering that are not particularly unique, like breaking up large campuses into smaller learning communities, virtually eliminating middle schools, and attempting to infuse schools with better technology that can be used in conjunction with the city's instructional programs. But he has also turned Philadelphia into a stomping ground for outside groups trying to push innovation. In that regard, his support from the highest levels of the school system has been unprecedented. Private companies, like Edison Schools, Inc., have found a welcome home under Vallas and are operating several schools. The University of Pennsylvania, Temple, and St. Joseph's universities also are now running schools for the system.

And while these types of privatization schemes are often extremely controversial, Vallas has managed to win some degree of support from teachers and from the larger community. Vallas from day one has unveiled a dizzying amount of reforms, programs, and partnerships—helping to keep up the public impression that things are moving at lightning speed toward improvement. One teachers union leader went so far as to note, "I don't remember a superintendent ever being on a honeymoon for three years."[25]

In addition to education-related businesses from outside Philadelphia who have found a home, outside businesses have been brought on board as well by Vallas's vision. Software giant Microsoft is even building an experimental new high school in the district. The end result is what Education Sector's Thomas Toch called "the early stages of a revolution in public education." Vallas, Toch noted, "has forced the Philadelphia education community to rethink the status quo and question the effectiveness for kids of a system built around rules and regulations designed to protect adults."[26]

Similarly, New York City's Klein made his fortune and reputation as a litigator, first in private practice and then as a deputy White House counsel and in the antitrust division of the U.S. Justice Department under President Bill Clinton. One of his crowning accomplishments since taking over the helm of New York's 1.1 million–student school system in 2002 is that he has turned the city's education landscape into one of the most desirable places in the country for other entrepreneurial types to relocate. Essentially, he turned New York City into a magnet for James Deans, Fresh Bloods, and Johnny Appleseeds.

After creating the nonprofit Leadership Academy, Klein sought additional help in recruiting dynamic new school leaders from nonprofit groups like New Leaders for New Schools, and has even been working with Teach For America to identify potential school principals from the ranks of their teaching corps and alumni. "I like competition," Klein has explained. Where the city's Teaching Fellows were the golden children under his predecessor Harold Levy, Klein's Leadership Academy graduates are the apple of his eye, and he has invested heavily in the notion that the school is the fundamental unit of change, and that the principal must be the change agent.

Klein's unprecedented support for charter schools from among the school establishment has attracted scores of battle-tested operators from other parts of the country to the city, and the city has worked with groups like Boston-based Building Excellent Schools to identify and train potential charter school operators. It remains to be seen whether these types of dynamic school leaders who were attracted to the system under Klein will outlast the chancellor and carve out enough turf within the overall system to provide long-term support on the inside for systemic reform.

One important aspect of entrepreneurial school leaders is their appreciation for the fact that radically altering the path of large school systems requires changes to nearly every piece of the system's puzzle. Functions like hiring and human resources are recognized as being crucial ingredients in terms of improving what happens in classrooms. Klein's labor relations team, to name just one example, has become a crucial part of the city's reform efforts. In addition to creating new lessons for principals about how to better handle teacher evaluations to make them more grievance-proof, the legal team has helped shape policy to usher in improvements within the existing framework. In the summer of 2004, for example, after New York Mayor Michael Bloomberg launched a program designed to end the practice of social-promotion in third grade, Klein created a new summer school program called the Summer Success Academy. The city had operated summer school programs for several years, but by calling it a "new" program, Klein was able to hire the best teachers rather than compete with standard practice—which called for hiring for summer school assignments based on seniority.[27] The city was even able to survive a grievance filed by the teachers union on behalf of senior teachers who didn't get summer school jobs that year, a rare victory for management.

It is worth noting that both Vallas and Klein came to lead their respective school systems after major changes in governance structures. Vallas was appointed by a school reform commission that formed after the Philadelphia schools were taken over by the state of Pennsylvania; Klein was appointed by New York mayor Michael Bloomberg after the state legislature stripped control of the city's schools from the former Board of Education (and thirty-two community school boards) and placed them under the mayor's control. Both school leaders have used these governance changes as a mandate. They recognize that not everything they try will be successful, but they are betting on the notion that significant change requires some degree of risk-taking.

"BULLS MANAGING THE CHINA SHOP"

One of the rarest forms of entrepreneurship within public education involves leaders of school systems who believe strongly that the normal rules of engagement actually contribute to the problems they are trying to solve. They charge forward, hoping that doing so will end a business-as-usual mentality within their systems. Because their theory of change often causes discomfort for entrenched interests within their systems, their features are typically controversial.

Former Milwaukee superintendent Howard Fuller took on the city's teachers union in the early 1990s by attempting to fire teachers who had been accused of misdeeds like getting caught goofing off on national television or flushing a students' head in the toilet. But Fuller really sent the union into a tailspin by supporting plans to allow outside groups—including the controversial Edison Project—to contract with the system to run underperforming schools. Fuller also was a strong proponent of decentralizing budgeting power and decisionmaking to the school level. Unlike most school superintendents, who come up through the ranks of the school system by following the rules, Fuller had been one of the most vocal critics of the school system before getting the top job. In fact, since Fuller was such a nontraditional school leader, a special waiver was required from the state in 1991 in order to allow him to serve as superintendent at all. But his desire to end the status quo as it existed by using means that his opponents labeled "privatization" ended up galvanizing the political efforts of the Milwaukee Teachers Education Association, which battled in 1995 to win control of Milwaukee's school board. Fuller resigned soon thereafter, saying he didn't want to die a "death of a thousand cuts."

Bulls who attempt to manage the china shop often grow extremely frustrated with the slow pace of change within systems, and in drawing the ire of entrenched adult interests within those systems they often see their terms in office cut short before meaningful systemic reform can be accomplished. At best, the changes that survive these bulls are usually considered incremental. That said, their efforts are not always entirely fruitless. By serving time at the top of the system, these reformers gain new insights into the precise nature of the problems they are trying to solve. They understand that knowledge is power and often use the lessons they learned in managing the china shop to continue pushing for reform from the outside of the system once they have left office. In Fuller's case, for example, he founded the Institute for the Transformation of Learning at Marquette University soon after leaving his job as superintendent. He went on to become one of the nation's most prominent proponents for charter schools and other market-based solutions for school reform.

CONCLUSION

Entrepreneurs within the public school system clearly play a role in improving conditions for learning in the schools under their charge, and in cases like Philadelphia's Vallas and New York's Klein, their efforts have the potential to go a long way toward transforming entire systems. It is still not clear whether it is possible for entrepreneurship alone, however, to change the overall culture of public-sector school systems that are as a rule disdainful of innovation and imagination, even when facing well-documented failure. As California's secretary of education and former San Diego superintendent Alan Bersin notes, "It's got to become institutional if we are to deliver on the promise of educating all of our children at high levels."[28]

Each kind of public school entrepreneur shares a common obstacle in their efforts to improve education. Each must overcome institutional resistance from the forces invested in the public-sector school monopoly: primarily the bureaucrats themselves, labor unions, education schools, and the state's tight control over entry to the teaching profession. In fact, there is strong evidence that public-sector school systems themselves are their own worst barriers to more entrepreneurial thinking and leadership. As Andrekopoulos, who is now superintendent in Milwaukee, puts it, "Creativity and problem-solving disappear in a bureaucratic structure."[29]

Policymakers who wish to unleash more entrepreneurial energy into struggling school systems should consider an approach that itself makes risk- taking more glamorous and rewarding than is currently the case. Pay scales for teachers and principals currently leave little room for incentives that reward putting one's neck on the line in order to find better ways to educate children. Awards are seldom given out to the school leaders who do the best job of sidestepping silly mandates from higher-ups. Rare are the occasions when top school leaders and policymakers try to find out exactly which rules many James Dean entrepreneurs must sidestep. This inevitably pushes off real discussions about why many of these rules exist in the first place, ensuring that they continue to hamstring less-entrepreneurial school leaders. School leaders like Klein and Vallas who roll out the welcome mat to entrepreneurial spirits provide a road map to get started, showing how to leverage private-sector support, attract a new talent pool, and foster innovation.

Two other areas remain ripe for support from policymakers. First, as more and more districts seek out ways to attract alternatively certified teachers and administrators, careful consideration should be given to the aspects of such plans that provide meaningful training and ongoing support for educators coming from other sectors to work in schools. It is one thing to attract well-educated, intelligent people to the classroom. But that is merely the starting point. The value of this human talent will be greatest only after considerable training and support. Finally, given the tremendous form of federal pressure presented by NCLB, policymakers should continue to consider actions that help more of the existing James Dean entrepreneurs become destiny grabbers. Specifically, converting existing struggling public schools into charter schools that would be run at the site level could unleash an unprecedented wave of entrepreneurship from school principals and teachers eager to be part of the solution.

CHAPTER 7

Markets, Bureaucracies, and Clans: The Role of Organizational Culture

Robert Maranto and April Gresham Maranto

What you don't realize is that we're a cult: people are married to KIPP. There's very little turnover among principals and very little burnout.
—A KIPP principal

One thing you're going to discover is the idiosyncrasies of a bottom up decentralized organization are such that I actually can't tell you the number of schools. . . . I can't give you a hard count, but there are over one thousand.
—Administrator in the Coalition of Essential Schools national office

The key to success for new, entrepreneurial education providers is creating strong organizational cultures that ensure uniformly good performance while adapting to local conditions. Successful providers combine centralized values with local management. Excluding highly individualized "mom-and-pop" microproviders, we outline in this chapter the key characteristics of four market-based models of schooling: market-movement schools, cooperatives, corporations, and clans. We argue that the policymakers and philanthropies assessing these alternatives face a paradox: The models that can expand most rapidly offer more incremental prospects for success, while those most assured of achieving educational breakthroughs can expand only gradually. This does not mean that policymakers should give up on alternative education providers, but rather that meaningful gains may take decades rather than years.

ORGANIZATIONAL APPROACHES TO EDUCATIONAL ENTREPRENEURSHIP

Political scientists John Chubb and Terry Moe argue that the very democratic control that makes public education public limits school-level autonomy, as organized groups impose ever greater numbers of rules on schools and ever larger bureaucracies to enforce those rules.[1] In contrast, private schools governed by market processes that serve niches rather than democratic processes attempting to serve everyone can maintain autonomy to serve students and parents. This is in accord with findings that less centralized public school systems have more success.[2] We draw upon notions of centralized, decentralized, and intermediate organizations; the typology of markets, bureaucracies, and clans; and theories of governing public institutions to make sense of the new, entrepreneurial public education providers.

Theory Z: Markets, Bureaucracies, and Clans

Researchers have examined how organizations minimize transactional costs and maximize efficiency through structures and via "softer" means, such as by managing culture.[3] Business scholar William Ouchi proposes three ideal types of coordination. In *market* networks and organizations, a series of contractual relationships determine the value of a product or service. Supply and demand determine value, and reciprocity governs relationships between parties. Near complete decentralization goes with easy passage in and out of the organization. In his bestselling book, *Theory Z*, Ouchi describes how some American corporations are essentially internal markets, with employees jumping ship as soon as they get better offers and companies laying off employees whenever possible. Networks linking public-sector organizations with private contractors can be considered either highly decentralized organizations or true markets, depending on the arrangements.[4] Market-based education providers stress branding, since they depend on consumer choice.

Unlike markets, hierarchical *corporations* (which Ouchi calls bureaucracies) are more centralized and more tightly coupled, with coordination by legitimate authority, formal rules, and standard procedures. They have more stability, less innovation, and their employees serve for long periods.[5]

Finally, *clans* are highly stable, disciplined organizations characterized by common values, having the highest informal centralization and the lowest formal centralization.[6] Here, decisionmaking reflects neither rules nor prices, but shared traditions and values. Clans carefully select, recruit, and indoctrinate their employees to control behavior "through an extreme form of the belief that individual interests are best served by a complete immersion of each individual in the interests of the whole."[7] They develop brand names to support their recruitment tactics and have highly uniform outcomes. Though centralized in practice, clans differ from bureaucracies in their reliance on informal centralization through common values to ensure adherence to policies. This permits the decentralization of day-to-day decisionmaking.

Clans achieve institutionalization by accepting only a small percentage of job applicants and forcing new recruits through long indoctrination and apprenticeship periods. After this process, at least symbolically, members belong for life. Ease of entry is lowest for clans, but so is turnover. This is particularly true for subunit-level managers, from whom considerable dedication and leadership skill are expected; in turn, these managers have considerable authority to make decisions. Such organizations as traditional Japanese companies, the U.S. Forest Service, and the U.S. Marine Corps are clans. Since the personnel policies developing clan-like dedication are costly, clans are most useful when organization values are stable and when work requires great dedication in the face of danger, temptations for corruption, or challenging work assignments with inadequate material compensation.[8] As we argue below, urban education requires clannish dedication.

Governance Approaches

Public administration scholars Karen Hult and Charles Walcott describe seven potential governance structures of public organizations, four of which are relevant here: markets, hierarchies, collegial-competitive organizations and networks, and collegial-consensual ones. Hult and Walcott's market model resembles Ouchi's; their hierarchical model replicates his bureaucracy, and their collegial-consensual organization suggests clans. They add a fourth model, however, the collegial-competitive organization, in which individual members advocate their own interests and views and decisions are based on bargaining or voting. This describes cooperatives owned or managed by their employees.

In summary, the four ideal types of organization relevant to analysis of educational entrepreneurship, from less to more centralized, are: markets, employee-managed cooperatives, moderately centralized bureaucracies (like most corporations), and clans. We use these models to examine seven relatively new education providers: the Coalition of Essential Schools, the Core

Knowledge Foundation, the EdVisions Cooperative, the Charter School of Sedona, Edison Schools, Knowledge Is Power Program (KIPP), and North Star Academy.

FROM MARKETS TO CLANS:
A BRIEF TOUR OF THE EDUCATION PROVIDERS

Movement-Markets

Two prominent associations attempting to reform American education, the Coalition of Essential Schools and the Core Knowledge Foundation, pursue their idealistic aims by employing the common model of a nonprofit that charges for its services. Yet these organizations are not like fast-food or housing markets, since products hold *idealistic* branding particularly attractive to some consumers; hence, we call them *movement-markets*.

Coalition of Essential Schools

History and mission. The former dean of the Harvard Graduate School of Education and Brown University professor Theodore Sizer, among others, founded the Coalition of Essential Schools (CES) in 1984. The Coalition aims to "create and sustain equitable, intellectually vibrant, personalized schools and to make such schools the norm of American public education" and works "to create a policy environment which is more conducive to the creation of equitable, personalized, intellectually vibrant schools."[9] In such books as *Horace's Compromise* and *Horace's Hope*, Sizer critiqued existing public schools as large, impersonal, hierarchical, bureaucratic, and more dedicated to schedules than learning. Sizer and his disciples hope to replace traditional public schools with small schools based on consensus rather than hierarchy, with student influence over discipline and individual courses of study. Students would learn through the project method, overseen by bright, caring teachers acting as coaches rather than taskmasters. Both students and teachers would have considerable power over their work. All school citizens would embrace the Coalition's *Common Principles* of depth rather than coverage; academic goals applying to all students without tracking; personalization; teacher-as-coach; demonstration of mastery through performance of real tasks; decency and trust; teachers taking on multiple obligations rather than narrowly dividing labor; resources dedicated to teaching and learning; and democracy and equity.

In practice, these may prove difficult. For example, Sizerite principal James Nehring details how his proudly nonhierarchical school struggled to develop a discipline code reconciling democracy and authority, and to adjust students and parents to a system with "no grades and no average."[10] Indeed, Nehring worries that traditional bureaucracy has killed progressive education.

Decentralization. Coalition of Essential Schools National has a small staff in Oakland, California, with thirteen employees and a roughly $5 million annual budget, with much of the budget used for grants to schools. Originally the Coalition was based at Brown University where Sizer taught, but as its initial Annenberg grant ran out, leaders moved headquarters closer to the CES schools. Some even questioned the need for a national organization. Later, No Child Left Behind (NCLB) convinced Coalition leaders, who eschew standardized testing, to support a stronger national organization capable of advocacy. Still, the CES remains so decentralized that it does not know how many schools are in the movement, since schools can affiliate with one of twenty-three regional centers, or with the national division, or both. Membership requirements are usually modest, providing easy entry. The national organization charges $500 annual dues, which allows attendance at its annual conference. Regional affiliates charge dues that range from nothing to $200. Some ask only that schools claim CES "Essential" status, although others offer an "affirmation process" culminating in portfolios demonstrating adherence to the CES Common Principles.[11] Based on informal reports and conference attendance, an administrator estimates that there are more than one thousand Coalition schools in thirty-seven states and the District of Columbia, but "I couldn't say how much it has grown . . . it has definitely fluctuated."

Expansion possibilities. The charter school and small school movements have helped the Coalition, which recently received a Gates Foundation grant to create ten small high schools and break up five large high schools into smaller ones. Traditionally, Coalition schools have had difficulty hiring teachers trained in the CES model. The Coalition is seeking to address this by influencing schools of education and claims fledgling relationships at UCLA, San Jose State, Rutgers, Ohio State, the University of Southern Maine, Antioch, and the University of New Hampshire.

In short, the Coalition of Essential Schools focuses both on school governance and on curricula, emphasizing democracy rather than hierarchy and multidisciplinary projects rather than content mastery. Yet it seems so decentralized that individual schools might not conform to the model. Fieldwork at a Coalition charter school found that a group of eight teachers on lunch break had never heard of an "Essential" school and certainly did not know that theirs was one.

Core Knowledge

Unlike the Coalition of Essential Schools, the Core Knowledge Foundation ignores school governance and learning processes to focus on *content*, since "knowledge builds on knowledge. Children learn new knowledge by building on what they already know."[12]

History and mission. Like the Coalition, the Core Knowledge Foundation was founded in the 1980s by a visionary leader—University of Virginia English professor E. D. "Don" Hirsch Jr. From a privileged Southern background, Hirsch sought to address racial and class inequities. While teaching at a community college in 1978, Hirsch found his low-income, predominantly minority students struggling over passages about Robert E. Lee's surrender to Ulysses S. Grant, not because they could not read but because they had never heard of Lee or Grant—even though the Civil War ended only a few miles from their homes. He came to believe that students could not comprehend what they read unless they had sufficient background "core knowledge." Accordingly, in a series of books, articles, and lectures, Hirsch campaigned for cultural literacy as a "civil right."

While the Essential Schools movement disdains state standards, Core Knowledge embraces such external accountability. Indeed administrators at the Core Knowledge national office in Charlottesville boast of having influenced state standards in Minnesota, Virginia, Massachusetts, Florida, and Arizona. Core Knowledge schools spread rapidly in the 1990s, in part helped by the standards movement and by the growth in charter schooling.

Decentralization. Despite their pronounced differences, the two movement-markets have key similarities. Neither has a powerful central office. While Core Knowledge Foundation revenues from Hirsch's writings, donations, and in-service training for schools have increased from $500,000 in 1992 to $5.9 million in 2004, it remains a marginal force. The foundation has about twenty full-time employees, with another fifty consultants as needed for in-service training. Furthermore, like the Coalition of Essential Schools, the Core Knowledge Foundation has variable admissions requirements for schools and is uncertain how many schools are affiliated. Official Core Knowledge schools must undergo a three-year process of staff training, including site visits, use suitable curricular materials, and agree to implement "80 percent or more of the *Core Knowledge Sequence* and have the eventual goal of implementing 100 percent." This process may cost up to $50,000, a high entry barrier. However, Friends of Core Knowledge schools "are schools that are implementing Core Knowledge at any level."[13] Not surprisingly, while the ranks of the officials are reasonably stable, the ranks of "Friends" are not. A Core Knowledge administrator admitted that

> it's harder for us to figure out how many we've actually lost because we send out surveys and sometimes we never get them back, so may assume a school is gone when it never left. Or we find out about schools we never knew existed which have adopted our curricula without any training and have gotten great results, and then we find out about it from a newspaper article.

For Friends of Core Knowledge, fidelity to the curricula varies. Fieldwork at one such school found that teachers and board members generally had little familiarity with Core Knowledge; rather, they identified small size and individualized instruction as key to their school's mission.

Expansion and impact. While the foundation staff believes that the charter school and standards movements have helped spread Core Knowledge, they also believe that NCLB has limited its growth. This is because many do not regard Core Knowledge as a "research-based curriculum." To counter such views, the foundation issued a report summarizing studies from nine states finding that their curriculum improves scores on standardized tests.[14] Hirsch has just published *The Knowledge Deficit,* which makes an empirical case that Core Knowledge improves reading.[15]

As of August 2005, the Core Knowledge website listed 186 Core Knowledge schools and 323 Friends schools in 43 states and the District of Columbia. Well under 1 percent of public schools use Core Knowledge at some level, with only Colorado reaching 4 percent penetration and only Arkansas, New Mexico, Hawaii, and Utah at 2 percent. Thirty-two percent of Core Knowledge schools are charter schools.

Core Knowledge faces at least three challenges. Perhaps most important, it lacks sufficient branding. One foundation official lamented that "a study done last year . . . validated for us that we are not a brand name." Accordingly the foundation hired a public relations firm and has developed a strategic plan. Second, Core Knowledge has curricula but lacks sufficient infrastructure to produce high numbers of teachers, though it is now negotiating with a school of education to begin to address this. Third, and relatedly, Core Knowledge faces opposition from progressive educators who see it as limiting teacher autonomy or oppose it on principle.

In short, movement-markets such as the Coalition of Essential Schools and the Core Knowledge Foundation can grow rapidly, but some of their incarnations show uncertain fidelity to the model, posing concerns for those intending to contract with them to bring school improvement. Still, with their ease of entry and potential branding, movement-markets reach more students than the other alternative providers chronicled here.

COOPERATIVES

Cooperatives are run by their members. The cooperatives profiled here feature process values of employee empowerment, as well as fidelity to child-centered curricula. In a society increasingly postbureaucratic and oriented to self-actualization, one might expect the number of educational coops to increase, though at present they remain insignificant. Ease of entry and turnover are moderate, while attention to personnel selection and emphasis on branding vary by school.

EdVisions

History and mission. Rural Minnesota has long had agricultural cooperatives. Within this context, in the early 1990s, when two small town school systems consolidated, the new combined board chartered the Minnesota New Country School (MNCS), in part to save a high school partnership with a local hi-tech firm. Influenced by educator and former journalist Ted Kolderie, the MNCS board developed EdVisions as a teacher coop and then contracted out management of the new school to the new coop, which developed curricula, hired and managed staff, and maintained the site. In short, the teacher-owners ran things as a collective, and parents chose to send children to the new high school. MNCS attracted an energetic staff with considerable experience in both education and business, and gradually grew. Parent and student surveys show the school is very popular. Test scores equal or better nearby schools, and two-thirds of graduates go on to higher education.[16]

To some degree, EdVisions reflects Sizerite values. MNCS has informally adopted the ten Essential Schools principles. MNCS uses the project method, and its website states that "MNCS is not interested in the number of minutes or hours a student spends at a desk," but rather in completion of individual learning plans. Yet MNCS also has more conservative elements, believing that students "are ultimately responsible for attaining standards higher than traditional public secondary schools."

Since its initial success at MNCS, EdVisions has grown to include eight more Minnesota charter schools. With the help of a Gates Foundation grant, EdVisions has developed or is now helping develop fifteen other schools in seven states, with the goal of adding twenty more.[17]

Peer governance and accountability. Key to EdVisions is the Teacher Professional Practice (TPP) in which teachers run their schools, as described by consultant Edward J. Dirkswager in *Teachers as Owners*. For many educators, "business" is a bad word, but Dirkswager argues that, as in most medical practices, a teacher practice would focus more on service than money: Teachers "need to understand that the most successful businesses are driven by a desire to provide excellent service." Doctors or lawyers "hire administrators, if necessary, to run the administrative aspects of their business . . . [so] they can spend their time using their expertise to its fullest extent." A TPP leader "is not the boss but first among equals, the *principal teacher*, who is also evaluated by his or her peers."[18] Furthermore, just as doctors would not want inept partners to harm a medical practice, so would teachers aim for competence in hiring and evaluating peers. EdVisions teachers are hired and fired not by administrators but by committees of their peers.

TPPs have significant advantages, empowering those who know the most about schools—teachers—and thus limiting transaction costs. Though no systematic analysis of test scores has been conducted, student surveys give the original eight EdVisions campuses high marks.[19] Despite the rapid expansion of charter schooling in Minnesota, most EdVisions sites reportedly have waiting lists. TPPs also bring efficiencies. One study finds that five EdVisions campuses were among the top ten schools in Minnesota in the percentage of spending devoted to instructional services.[20] A cofounder reports that its sites pay teachers above average salaries and avoid layoffs in hard times, since

> we have no bureaucracy, no superintendents, a few people designated as directors, but they are not paid more than the teachers so it is not a hierarchical situation. Certainly there's no union contract. In many cases they take care of their buildings themselves or do it by piecework.

Growth and branding. EdVisions operates as an umbrella cooperative, meaning that the central office does little more than provide training, payroll services, and advice on such legal matters as how to conduct hiring and firing. Other decisions are made at the building level, by the teacher-owners. A cofounder says that originally most teachers applying to EdVisions schools did so out of happenstance, though teachers increasingly seek the self-governance of the coop, particularly because it offers more security, at least for effective teachers.

EdVisions plans to grow, hoping to gain a regional presence in the manner of agricultural coops like Land of Lakes. Staff members and supporters frequently write books and articles extolling the virtues of their model. Yet EdVisions faces barriers. Because EdVisions has no collective bargaining, it faces union opposition. As a cofounder states, "There is no one to negotiate against except yourself, since you determine the salary and so forth." Furthermore, the novelty of the coop model makes it difficult to attract large numbers of teachers, at least in the short term. Cooperatives require that teachers learn the attitudes and people skills needed to participate in democratic governance. As a member acknowledges,

> it is not meant for everyone. It is not transferable to a traditional school structure. It is not intended to change or reform all public education. All it asks is that it not be harassed or derided, be allowed to go about its business of offering a genuine alternative, and be judged by its accomplishments and outcomes.[21]

Owing to its emphasis on face-to-face relationships, EdVisions cannot work in large schools, limiting near-term expansion prospects. An informant speculates that EdVisions will open fewer than fifty campuses over the next ten years.

The Sedona Charter School

History and mission. Among all the states, Arizona has the greatest penetration by charter schools due to its remarkably open charter law. The Sedona Charter School (SCS) received the second charter in the state and now serves about 198 K–8 students. A single Montessori campus, SCS was founded by a husband-and-wife team of education consultants in 1995. Like many reformers, the Bergers had long disdained traditional public education. Ed Berger found many educational administrators to be "politicians and opportunists" for whom "the bus schedule was more important than students' learning needs."[22] When he taught high school, Berger rebelled by developing learning contracts with each of his 150 students and their parents. He guided student projects in individual meetings, much as EdVisions teachers do with their much smaller numbers. This proved draining for Berger and unpopular among some parents and administrators, so Berger left classroom teaching to develop a much acclaimed archeology fieldwork program for high school students.[23]

Peer governance and accountability. The Bergers fashioned a school with uniquely "empowered" teachers. In each classroom a principal educator (PE) serves as instructional leader and resource leader. PEs adjust curricula, hire their "facilitator teachers," determine salaries (including their own), and budget for classroom materials within the constraints set by state funding and the building and insurance costs deducted by the SCS board. Typically, the board makes financial projections based on expected enrollments in June, and PEs then develop their annual budgets. They enjoy near complete control over classroom operations.

Individual PEs have somewhat more authority than EdVisions teachers, though they do not actually co-own the school. No one has tenure. Instead, PEs can terminate their facilitator teachers and are themselves held accountable, with annual contracts taking into account student test scores and parent satisfaction surveys. SCS conducts parent surveys every spring, as required by its charter, and asks PEs and teachers to address any issues in the coming year. SCS has no paid administration, save a parent/business manager who gets occasional assistance from parent/volunteers.

Goal controversy and effectiveness. The iconoclastic Bergers left SCS in its third year, complaining that PEs spent insufficient time fostering parental involvement. The SCS charter calls for nine individual meetings with parents, meaning that for a Montessori classroom of fifty, a PE (perhaps assisted by other teachers) might have 450 meetings annually—far more parental involvement than either PEs or parents wanted. In addition, the founders were displeased when PEs balked at spending up to ten hours a week in meetings with stakeholders, preferring to run their own classrooms with little schoolwide coordination.

Despite the Bergers' concerns, SCS had the highest test scores in Sedona in eight of its first ten years, despite demographics similar to nearby schools. Value-added measures show SCS to be highly successful, and the school spends about 20 percent less than district schools do for operating costs. Similarly, parent surveys conducted by external researchers show SCS among the top 15 percent of Arizona charters in parental satisfaction.

Growth and branding. Unlike the previous cases, SCS does not seek expansion. No one has written books or articles about it, nor do PEs seek consulting contracts to spread their model, which remains unknown outside Sedona. Indeed, insiders doubt that their model can spread, since, as the school's business manager complained, "the whole district model is about administrators telling people what they can and cannot do. . . . I mean, can you see a district where the teacher can hire their staff?" Secondly, while PEs enjoy the ability to fashion the educational program as needed without prior approval, they suspect that few regular teachers are ready to do the same. As one PE remarked, "At other schools, if a kid acts up, you send them to the principal, but here it's your problem—you *are* the principal." Others complained about having to spend summers planning, budgeting, and hiring. Successful PEs often have nontraditional backgrounds. One formerly ran a private school, a second managed a battered women's shelter in Mexico, and a third worked in arts administration.

CORPORATIONS

Successful corporations combine centralized hierarchy to assure accountability and reasonable uniformity of practices for branding, coupled with the decentralization of day-to-day operations through highly empowered subunit managers (principals), who can choose staff and adapt to local conditions. In the world of public education, the role of profit-seeking corporations (education management organizations, EMOs) is highly controversial. In theory, EMOs can nimbly adapt to changing environments to fashion mission-driven organizations, unencumbered by political interference and employee tenure. EMOs can train and reward staff as needed, and can use capital markets or stock offerings to gain capital for rapid expansion or to replicate proven models.

Yet in practice, EMOs may have difficulty keeping contracts over the long term. New superintendents or school boards may have little commitment to their predecessors' contracting decisions. Moreover, one Edison executive muses that "there are just whole departments of the AFT and NEA devoted to trying to extinguish us. Our own political budget is pretty trivial." Politics aside, EMOs face high marketing costs, more regulation than most industries, relatively low profit margins, short-term contracts that make long-term planning and capital investments difficult, nonexistent economies of scale, teachers' needs for idealistic rather than profit motives, and pressures to plough profits back into the business to please consumers and teachers. Indeed elite private schools rarely make profits, even though many could do so.[24]

Edison Schools

History and mission. Of the estimated 59 EMOs managing 535 schools with 240,000 children in 2004–05, Edison Schools is by far the largest, with over one-fifth of the campuses (116) and over one-fourth of the students (70,000).[25] As with Core Knowledge, the Coalition of Essential Schools, and the Sedona Charter School, Edison began with a visionary leader. After building a successful media conglomerate and the first news network for middle and high school students, Chris Whittle recruited leading figures, including the president of Yale University, to develop a national education system capable of bringing economies of scale to improve what had been a cottage industry. The political climate seemed right, in part since President George H. W. Bush and U.S. Secretary of Education Lamar Alexander favored education markets. Furthermore, Whittle understood that "one share point—that is, 1 percent of American public education—equaled a Fortune 500 company."[26] In 1992, Whittle began a three-year, $40 million dollar research and development effort. Whittle intended Edison Schools to be a learning organization that emphasizes the importance of research up front and continues through the life of the company, which employs several prominent academics in executive positions.[27]

Training and governance. Edison standardized as much as it could to provide clear guidance to schools to replicate a uniform brand, *The Edison School Design.* Frequent assessment of student learning was key. Edison invested heavily in teacher training, leadership development, technology, and assessment instruments. Ease of entry was moderate, easier than a clan, but much more difficult than in a movement-market. Designers reasoned that well-trained teachers and principals could use assessment data to improve performance. Within the constraints of local contracts, Edison principals have considerable autonomy to hire and fire teachers. Within schools leadership is further decentralized, with "academies" for different grades led by lead teachers. In short, Edison is a moderately decentralized corporation.

Where contracts permit, Edison uses individual and site-based bonuses based on meeting academic performance and financial goals, with amounts often exceeding $6,000 per teacher and $20,000 per principal. Employees also get stock options. But incentives are not enough. Edison makes significant use of professional development to improve skills and integrate the organization. One principal recalls of her first off-site training session, "At first I wondered if I was getting into some kind of cult." Fieldwork at two Edison campuses suggests that administrators and faculty understood and supported the model.

An Edison executive reports that principal turnover has declined over time, perhaps in part because the company increasingly trains its own lead teachers to become principals. Teacher turnover, which averaged in the 20 percent range in the first years of the company, fell by 2004 to about 14 percent. The same executive reports that "finding teachers has generally not been a huge problem, because of the reputation that it's as supportive an environment as you're going to find in the inner city."

Systematic comparisons of Edison campuses to nearby district school campuses find that Edison does not short-shrift instructional spending, but does spend relatively more on professional development and principals and vice principals, and less on teachers' aides and teacher salaries. Edison principals make about the same base salary as comparable district school principals, but 20–30 percent more with merit pay. Edison schools are relatively new and so have less experienced teachers, who both cost less and are easier to "Edisonize."[28]

Performance and growth. Edison took fourteen years to make its first profit, in 2004, and that largely reflected tutoring services, a growth market under No Child Left Behind. The company faced financial woes as early as 1994, when investors first questioned its viability and Chris Whittle had to temporarily step down as CEO. From 1995 to 2001, Edison expanded at annual rates of 50 percent, in part to please investors. Overexpansion, combined with a disappointing offer from the Philadelphia public schools, led to contraction: Edison surrendered 15 percent of its campuses between fall 2002 and fall 2004. Company stock plunged from $38.00 a share to less than $1.00. Moreover, in contrast to EdVisions and the Sedona Charter School, Edison has failed to educate children for less than traditional public schools. Though Edison has not proven lucrative, data suggest that it and other EMOs do seek profits, locating where laws allow significant numbers of charter campuses and where states spend more on education.

Despite its financial woes, research on student achievement by RAND Education finds that while schools in their first year managed by Edison do not do well, Edison schools steadily improve over time and by year four show substantially greater test-score gains than nearby district schools.[29] Edison's internal calculations show nearly 90 percent of Edison parents giving their schools As or Bs on customer satisfaction surveys, compared to about 70 percent for traditional public schools.[30] Finally, there is some evidence that the threat of Edison spurs improvement in traditional public schools.[31] A smaller entity would exert less competitive pressure. District school personnel simply may see Edison as more threatening than, say, EdVisions. In this sense Edison has achieved branding; indeed, a Google search results in 177,000 hits for Edison Schools, compared to only 91,900 for the Coalition of Essential Schools, 42,700 for the Core Knowledge Foundation, 30,300 for KIPP, 15,400 for EdVisions and MNCS combined, and 769 for the Sedona Charter School.

Edison has not approached its founder's goal of one thousand schools in ten years. Certainly, there seems little reason to fear that for-profits may drive out nonprofits in the education sector. Yet Edison has survived, and its school design improves parent satisfaction and student achievement. Over the long term traditional public schools might be expected to purchase or otherwise adopt parts of the Edison model, now field tested by the early adopting company.

CLANS: THE MOST EFFECTIVE MODEL

Inner-city schools are often compared to war zones, where teachers need almost clan-like talent and dedication to succeed. As noted above, clans are highly stable, elite organizations characterized by common values and traditions that are ensured by careful recruiting, selection, and indoctrination of members. This makes entry difficult, but also limits turnover. Clans have low formal centralization with empowered principals and teachers, but high informal centralization through their unique personnel policies. This assures quality, but also slows expansion since it takes time and money to find, recruit, and indoctrinate members willing to give as much as clans require.

Knowledge Is Power Program

History and mission. Teach For America teachers David Levin and Michael Feinberg opened the first Knowledge Is Power Program (KIPP) in Houston in 1994 and a second in New York the following year. From the start, KIPP focused on the most difficult students: low-income, minority middle school children. KIPP features a longer school year and longer school day to make rapid progress with its students, who typically began middle school two years or more behind. KIPP's "five pillars" call for high expectations of students and staff, choice and commitment to ensure student and parent "buy-in," more time for instruction, principals who have the power to lead their schools by having near total control over money and personnel, and an uncompromising focus on results as measured by standardized tests.

KIPP creates a strong academic culture to rival the gang culture of inner cities, through chanting slogans, t-shirts, wall charts advertising where KIPP alumni attend college, strict attention to discipline and teamwork, and incentives, such as earning KIPP dollars redeemable for trips and prizes for perfect attendance and behavior. Those who fail to complete assignments face "Wall Street hours"—staying late to finish. Acting-up meets symbolic punishments, such as wearing KIPP shirts inside out.

Clannish personnel policies. The KIPP website declares, "Teaching the hardest working students requires the hardest working teachers"—not a pitch aimed at traditional teachers—and follows up with online application materials. Teachers are issued cell phones so they can help students with homework after hours, a practice that eliminates excuses and sends the message that *everyone* at KIPP works hard. A volume published by the KIPP Foundation estimates that KIPP pays teachers 20 percent more than comparable district school teachers, but demands 60 percent more work hours.[32] A KIPP official states that for both students and staff, KIPP pays "a lot of attention to creating that effective organization culture. . . . We don't want people to think these are miracle schools. We try to be the Southwest Airlines of the educational world and the cell phone is the symbol of that because it keeps us in touch with our customers."

KIPP chooses only 6 percent of teaching applicants. About half of those come from Teach For America and about two-thirds have prior teaching experience. Teachers are selected by principals and typically receive four weeks of KIPP training before school starts. Those who don't work out are fired.

KIPP is principal-centered, with new campuses appearing where new principals choose to open them. KIPP's appeal to principal recruits does not mention material benefits, but rather asks people to "join the movement" of those with "entrepreneurial spirit to open and run great public schools in educationally underserved communities." KIPP chooses only 4 percent of those who apply to become principals.

In 1999, the television show *60 Minutes* profiled KIPP, attracting notice from the San Francisco–based Pisces Foundation, which committed to funding its expansion. Three new campuses opened in fall 2001. Since 2001, seven to sixteen new schools have opened each year. Those accepted as KIPP principals receive a year's salary to prepare for opening. Training includes a six-week course at the University of California's Haas School of Business and a month-long residency at a KIPP school, where a new recruit is matched with an effective principal with a different management style, followed by eight months of charter writing, budgeting, facilities planning, and student and teacher recruitment, all with the help of KIPP staff. It costs Pisces about $400,000 to open a new KIPP campus, with a remarkable $250,000 of that going to train new principals.

All this ensures clannish dedication. As one principal explained, "What you don't realize is that we're a cult: people are married to KIPP." Of the forty-seven schools that have opened as KIPPs, forty-four remain in the network.

Impact. Despite a student body roughly 90 percent minority and three-quarters eligible for free and reduced-price lunch, KIPP's academic success is largely unquestioned. Data suggest that a typical KIPP student improves performance by roughly one standard deviation on a normal curve in three years' attendance. KIPP campuses typically spend somewhat less than nearby public schools, in part saving resources through large class size. This enables KIPP to pay teachers more and be more selective.

Despite its impact on individual students, KIPP is slow to expand because of the very staff selectivity that makes it successful in the first place. Furthermore, traditional district schools have seemingly ignored KIPP. Cofounder David Levin laments that officials at an unsuccessful New York public school will not visit his site to seek ideas—even though it is located in the same building.[33] Still, a KIPP official notes that under pressure from NCLB to perform, superintendents increasingly embrace KIPP campuses: "We really think this is going to be a long-term revolution, and we are starting it. . . . Our challenge is finding enough principals."

North Star Academy: A KIPP-Like School

A number of KIPP-like charter schools exist, including Amistad Academy (New Haven), Green Dot Public Schools (Los Angeles), and North Star Academy (Newark). Following a script similar to KIPP, North Star Academy runs two middle schools and a high school, and is slowly expanding. Like KIPP, North Star has produced very good scores on standardized tests and reportedly sends 95 percent of graduates on to four-year colleges, compared to 26 percent in the home district. It also spends less than district schools.[34]

Cofounders Norm Atkins and James Verrilli founded North Star in 1997 to copy the small, mission-driven private schools that serve inner-city New York children. Verrilli had been principal of one such school, while Atkins had managed a community foundation. Like KIPP, North Star features a longer school year, longer school day, attention to measurement, and attention to organization culture, with Core Values resembling KIPP's Five Pillars. A cofounder suggests that both KIPP and North Star "have extremely high expectations for poor kids. Both schools are expecting all kids to go to college." Indeed, to the researcher, the differences between the two seem superficial. A cofounder admits that

> when you're at 50,000 feet above, North Star and KIPP look identical, but when you are standing right next to them there are differences. KIPP has larger class sizes. KIPP has an even longer school year. KIPP relies more on absolute all-star teachers. . . . North Star has a high school, KIPP doesn't. North Star kids dress better; KIPP does more of a dress code. North Star students are probably a little bit more low income. North Star has more daily rituals about culture.

Like KIPP, North Star has powerful principals who hire the staff. At its founding, Atkins and Verrilli recruited widely and sifted through four hundred applications to staff their small school. They watched the finalists teach, and spent the summer before opening working with their teachers to iron out problems before school opened. Today, North Star receives thousands of applications for perhaps ten jobs annually. New teachers are trained the July before they start work, while school is in session. North Star teachers work a much longer school year and school day (typically 7:15 a.m. to 6:00 p.m.), but earn salaries comparable to those of district teachers, with modest merit bonuses. North Star's leadership team has stable "long-distance runners," but 20 percent annual teacher turnover is common.

THE PARADOXICAL PROMISE OF ALTERNATIVE EDUCATION PROVIDERS

The structural differences of the new alternative education providers can produce varied outcomes. The movement-markets, Coalition of Essential Schools and Core Knowledge Foundation, seemingly have such limited control of school quality as to make generalizations difficult. While some parents and teachers in the movement-market schools find their curricula appealing, others know little about them. Yet limited control does allow rapid expansion. There are an estimated one thousand Essential schools and five hundred Core Knowledge schools. Over the long term, significant numbers of market-movement schools penetrating a given state could influence its traditional schools. Movement-markets might alter education in other ways—by influencing state standards and standardized testing in the case of the Core Knowledge Foundation, or opposing them, in the case of the Coalition.

Cooperatives such as EdVisions and the Sedona Charter School can differ in scale, origins, models of teacher empowerment, and growth plans; the former calls for regional expansion, while the latter stays put in Sedona. Yet each has teacher-run schools, with Sedona teachers held accountable by a board using objective measures, while EdVisions teachers hold themselves accountable, again using data. Each model of teacher empowerment seemingly succeeds: The coops have high test scores and parental satisfaction, even while spending 10 to 20 percent less than nearby district schools. Teachers in the two coops regard test scores, parental satisfaction, and basic economy as authoritative criteria of success.

Yet neither coop seems likely to expand enough to have a national impact. It is not clear that schools of education produce large numbers of teachers who can handle empowerment, or indeed want it. The more successful coop teachers have substantial business or administrative experience, preparing them for resource allocation roles. Furthermore, the very novelty of the coop models makes them difficult for traditional public schools to copy. When the Sedona-Oak Creek School district lost large numbers of students to the Sedona Charter School, it reacted by changing curricula and leadership, not by empowering teachers.

In theory, of the four models considered, corporations should have the greatest impact. Corporations accept the legitimacy of standardized testing, customer satisfaction, and financial efficiency as criteria of success, and have sufficient insulation from civil service rules to ensure that their employees do too. Corporations can borrow capital to develop coherent models and expand them quickly, making them more threatening (or catalytic) to traditional public school bureaucracies. Yet the controversial nature of EMOs makes it difficult for them to expand; the largest for-profit provider, Edison, serves as a lightning rod for privatization opponents. Yet Edison's school model may prove more influential to traditional public schools, not only because of the company's relative fame (or infamy), but also because the Edison design is less novel than those of cooperatives and clans, making it easier for traditional public schools to adopt parts of it. Indeed, public schools often buy services from Edison.

Finally, clans have the strongest organizational cultures and best quality control. They accept only a small percentage of those applying for principal and teaching positions, spend considerable resources training those leaders, and then hold employees accountable. With lower operating costs than nearby district schools, clans produce far greater test-score gains and seemingly please parents (though customer service in that sense seems less of a clan motive). This illustrates the great irony of alternative education providers: Those most likely to produce outstanding student outcomes, clans like KIPP and North Star, are also those most difficult to expand in the short term because of their careful attention to quality control. In the short term, no large community will be able to find sufficient numbers of outstanding principals or teachers to make the models work. A small community could use clan-like alternative education providers, though there seems little evidence that any wish to try. Furthermore, the very novelty of the clan model makes traditional public schools less likely to copy it.

Over the long term, incrementally, any of these four models might have a substantial impact on traditional public schools. In the medium term, a big-city superintendent seeking the greatest impact might use various new education providers, employing the comparative advantages of each. By encouraging clans and cooperatives to enter the market, the superintendent could provide superior education to a small number of students. Indeed, KIPP and

North Star officials report getting support at the superintendent level in their various communities. KIPP opens campuses where its new principals want to open, not necessarily where school systems demand. Yet there is nothing to prevent city- or state-level education officials from creating their own principal-training academies along KIPP lines to increase the supply of clan-like schools. Given the tiny percentage of KIPP and North Star applicants accepted for principal and teaching posts, it seems likely that there is a sufficient talent pool to open far more clan-like providers. KIPP and North Star results suggest that over the long term, such an undertaking would improve education without costing more.

Second, the superintendent could encourage traditional schools to adopt Core Knowledge or a comparable market-movement curricular design with a good track record, thus having at least a limited positive impact on a large number of schools. Finally, the very threat of corporations could push traditional schools to reform, particularly since they could buy or copy corporate curricula and assessment tools. In effect, corporations could become a stalking horse for reform. They could also serve niche markets that traditional public schools do not care to serve, such as the severely disadvantaged.

The short-term impact of new education providers is limited by factors inherent to the different models, particularly the trade-offs between quality and expansion and the controversy over for-profit education. Yet over the next few decades, the impact of new education providers may prove revolutionary, depending on the strategic decisions that policymakers make.

CHAPTER 8

Why Is This So Difficult?

Henry M. Levin

The term "entrepreneurship" has been used commonly in recent years to describe strategies to improve education.[1] Because the term has been associated generically with the development of new alternatives in the marketplace, its educational variant has typically referred to a system of school choice, especially charter schools and vouchers. The general view is that the rewards of the marketplace provide incentives for undertaking the risk of innovation that is required to develop better educational alternatives. Even in the public school districts it is not unusual to hear of a quest for entrepreneurship through the establishment of new schools, especially small high schools, or to hear of "intrapreneurship"—the quest to transform an existing school.

What is clear from the literature on entrepreneurship is that the term is used to describe a wide range of phenomena. To some it is the establishment of a new enterprise under risky conditions and with a high potential financial return for taking that risk. Others see entrepreneurship as closer to the act of invention, also with great risk and great potential payoffs. Still others attribute entrepreneurship to any act that is likely to add considerable value to a product or service.

Perhaps the most important two voices on entrepreneurship are those of economist Joseph Schumpeter and management icon Peter Drucker. Schumpeter emphasized that entrepreneurship was much broader than the act of invention. To him it entailed the processes of harnessing inventions to create new products, new means of production, and new forms of organization—all adding value to society. Drucker also tended to equate entrepreneurship with innovation, but particularly in the role of management:

Management is the new technology (rather than any specific new science or invention) that is making the American economy into an entrepreneurial economy. It is also about to make America into an entrepreneurial *society*.[2]

These broad definitions of entrepreneurship suggest a potentially key role for entrepreneurship in education, through innovation and managerial breakthroughs, providing the spark needed to improve the productivity, quality, and equity of American education. The focus of this chapter is to ask whether it is a shortage of entrepreneurialism or obstacles to entrepreneurial success that have accounted for the inertia of the educational industry.

Schools are the focus of great expectations, but are habitually charged with producing disappointing results and being unable to meet expectations. Education is widely believed to be the solution to major social challenges, including those of workplace productivity, economic competition, social equity, civic behavior, technology, cultural knowledge, and effective democracy. In response to these persistent issues, schools are under constant pressure to change, often in conflicting directions, not only in the United States, but in most countries.

One of the most common complaints about education is its resistance to change. Historically, there have been many attempts to shift the direction of education through new ideas, new leadership, national campaigns for excellence, and by instilling fears of losing status or economic and military superiority to competitors because of an underperforming educational system. In some cases these concerns have been addressed by bold declarations, such as those embodied in federal legislation in the 1994 law, the Goals 2000: Educate America Act, which declared:

By the Year 2000—

1. All children in America will start school ready to learn.
2. The high school graduation rate will increase to at least 90 percent.
3. All students will leave grades 4, 8, and 12 having demonstrated competency over challenging subject matter, including English, mathematics, science, foreign languages, civics and government, economics, the arts, history, and geography, and every school in America will ensure that all students learn to use their minds well, so they may be prepared for responsible citizenship, further learning, and productive employment in our nation's modern economy.
4. U.S. students will be first in the world in mathematics and science achievement.

5. Every adult American will be literate and will possess the knowledge and skills necessary to compete in a global economy and exercise the rights and responsibilities of citizenship.
6. Every school in the United States will be free of drugs, violence, and the unauthorized presence of firearms and alcohol and will offer a disciplined environment conducive to learning.
7. The nation's teaching force will have access to programs for the continued improvement of their professional skills and the opportunity to acquire the knowledge and skills needed to instruct and prepare all American students for the next century.
8. Every school will promote partnerships that will increase parental involvement and participation in promoting the social, emotional, and academic growth of children.[3]

Six years after the target year of 2000 and more than a decade after the law was enacted, progress toward these goals has been minimal.

The question arises, is this lack of progress due to a shortage of entrepreneurship or opportunities for entrepreneurship? Or are there larger obstacles to change that overwhelm the entrepreneurial explanation? In what follows, I explore a number of explanations for the resistance to educational change and try to relate those to the possibilities for entrepreneurship. I suggest that there are much larger barriers to change that presently undermine the possibilities for entrepreneurial innovations in education. Moreover, I suggest that major departures from existing practices in the short run are often equated with an assumption of long-run sustainability. In fact, it is the challenge of gaining such sustainability over the long run that is the greatest obstacle, not the establishment of initial departures.

OPPORTUNITIES FOR INNOVATION AND ENTREPRENEURSHIP IN EDUCATION

Given the wide range of interpretations of entrepreneurship, it is important to focus on a specific one. As Drucker and Schumpeter have done, I emphasize the process of innovation as a measure of entrepreneurship, particularly innovation that has promise for improving the quality of education. Of course, not all educational change is necessarily innovative or an improvement. In general, the entrepreneurial view assumes that if a change in a product, process, or application produces advantages in the marketplace, it is an innovation. In education there are very few pure markets, because there is considerable regulation at every level and the vast majority of schools are sponsored by public authorities. This difference is an important facet of educational debates today—that is, the notion of how to free up schools so that they can become more entrepreneurial and innovative.

The dominant traditional approach to educational change is that of public school reform. Historically, schools have been criticized for their perceived deficiencies. These criticisms have varied from concerns about pedagogies, achievement results, inequitable practices and outcomes, funding patterns, and the quality of the labor force produced by the schools. School reform is the general term given to attempts to dramatically change some of the operational premises and practices of both individual schools and entire groups of schools. Many school reforms have been national in scope in response to major events. Thus, when the Russians were able to put a satellite in space in 1957, "Sputnik" became the impetus for a massive call and subsequent actions to improve U.S. schools in science, mathematics, and foreign languages. When the report *A Nation at Risk* was issued in 1983, blaming the schools for deterioration in the U.S. competitive position in the world economy, the schools were again charged with great urgency to improve their performance. In these cases, federal, state, and local governments pressed a variety of reforms to change and improve the schools.

Education historian Larry Cuban has suggested that these calls for change have often resembled a recycling of the same reforms, again, and again, and again.[4] Specific reforms included changes in curriculum, textbooks, teacher training, teacher certification, leadership preparation, school governance, educational technology, and educational funding. These proposed interventions have been dedicated to improving educational quality and equity. Although many reform attempts have been locally inspired, most have been responses to externally imposed national and regional movements and state initiatives, with the heaviest concentration of reform attempts aimed at urban areas. The most ambitious of these, so-called whole-school or comprehensive school reforms, have represented attempts to transform schools in their entirety in terms of goals, organization, curriculum content, and pedagogy. These have been promoted in the largest school districts, such as New York City, where a major expansion in numbers of small schools with highly differentiated themes and sponsorship is at the heart of educational reform.

Many commentators believe that the possibilities for school improvement and reform will not be possible without a greater role for parental choice in school selection for their children. Since about 1980, attempts to change and improve schools have focused heavily on public choice options, the provision of public school alternatives for parents. Initially the strategies were based on increasing choice within school districts by reducing dependence on residential location in determining which school a child could attend. Thus, parents could choose to send their children to another school within a district if they preferred it to their neighborhood school. In some cases, magnet schools with different educational themes (e.g., science, art, career) were established to attract students with particular interests from throughout a district. In many states students were also given the choice of attending schools in other school districts or enrolling in courses in higher educational institutions when such courses were not available in local high schools. These options were based on the view that parents' incentives to choose good schools for their children and schools' incentives to compete for students would enhance the overall quality of all schools.

However, the fruition of the public choice movement did not arrive until the early 1990s with charter schools, as discussed by Patrick McGuinn in chapter 3. Presumably such schools have incentives to be innovative and to incubate new ideas that will be attractive to conventional public schools. Many charter schools enlist private firms to manage their schools, providing further competition and possibilities for innovation.

The most complete approach to seeking educational change and innovation is promoting a marketplace of private alternatives to existing public schools through educational vouchers or tuition tax credits. Both of these are premised on the belief that government operation of schools must always be more rigid, restrictive, and less risk-taking than private institutions that rely on competition in the marketplace. Thus, the most dynamic strategy to gain long-term educational improvement through innovation is the funding of private schools in a competitive market. Under a voucher plan, any school meeting certain minimum standards is permitted to compete for students and is reimbursed through public funds. Parents are given a tuition voucher for each child that can be redeemed by the school. Tuition tax credits represent a different form of public subsidy by providing reductions in the tax burden for families who pay tuition to private schools. Although the use of educational vouchers is not widespread, voucher systems are found in Milwaukee, Cleveland, and Washington, D.C., and have been proposed recently for the devastated Gulf Coast, where many existing public schools have been destroyed. Parental tuition tax credits or deductions are sponsored by several states, including Minnesota, Arizona, Iowa, and Illinois.

Even in the absence of formal choice mechanisms to promote innovation and change in schools, parents tend to locate their residences in proximity to communities and neighborhoods with better schools. Although a large portion of the population has used the housing option to choose schools, this alternative is less available to the poor or to those whose choices are restricted by segregated neighborhoods. Studies of educational choice suggest that about 60 percent of the population has choice options in schooling, based on such mechanisms as residential choice, interdistrict and intradistrict choice, private schools, charter schools, vouchers, and tuition tax credits. Most of this choice is due to residential choice and options within or among districts.[5]

Change Is Not Easy

But, the overall finding from studies of public school reform, charter schools, and the limited experience with vouchers and market reform is that educational change does not come easily under any circumstances. Particularly telling in this regard is Cuban's study, which documents how schools functioned over an entire century, from 1890 to 1990.[6] Cuban draws from extensive historical materials on schools, including photographs, teachers' accounts, journalists' accounts, principals' reports, evaluations, and thousands of records from four different cities and rural areas. He compares schools, classrooms, and the teaching process at the turn of the century, in the 1920s, and in more recent times. He concludes that constancy is a far more accurate description of these core elements of education than substantial change. Seymour Sarason, a longtime observer of schools, arrives at a similar conclusion in examining the educational reforms in the latter part of the twentieth century.[7] History does not suggest that massive changes in education are in the offing, even if we could harness a new wave of entrepreneurship.

RAISING PRODUCTIVITY

There are two ways to raise productivity: lower costs for a given outcome, or improve results for a given cost. In acknowledging the strong rise in the cost of education over recent decades, one might first ask about entrepreneurial efforts to reduce costs or increase productivity. Three prime candidates that are often discussed for educational service delivery organizations are achieving adequate economies of scale, raising the productivity of labor, and using cost-saving technologies.[8]

Cost Disease

On the issue of educational productivity, it is important to note the work of eminent economist William Baumol in his analysis of the "cost disease."[9] Baumol has argued that some industries are able to raise worker productivity by substituting capital for labor or less-skilled workers for higher-skilled ones, and using newer and more productive technologies, thus offsetting higher labor costs. In contrast, he argues, other industries, including education, are labor intensive with limited ability to change production through investments that reduce the need for skilled labor.

Education and the performing arts are the poster children of industries that simply absorb increased labor costs because they are limited in their ability to substitute capital or less costly labor for teachers and other professionals as labor costs rise. Baumol views education as more akin to a string quartet or orchestra than a steel factory. Replacing two musicians in a string quartet with electronic music is not a feasible response as labor costs rise. There are similarly few options for replacing teachers. Some proof of this production rigidity is found in the fact that private schools and charter schools with fewer legal restrictions and union contracts produce education in largely the same way as public schools.[10] I suggest reasons for this behavior below.

Economies of Scale

A second area for a potential increase in productivity is to seek economies of scale. Although economies of scale can be sought for very small educational units, schools, or districts, the vast majority of students are in educational organizations that are large enough to neutralize or undermine scale economies. Education is characterized mainly by variable costs (especially labor) that increase with enrollments, rather than by fixed costs that can be divided over more and more students. Decades of study of economies of scale in education have shown this result.[11] Unfortunately, some of the pioneering educational management organizations such as Edison Schools lost hundreds of millions of dollars pursuing expansion to gain the elusive economies of scale by managing more and more schools.[12]

New Practices

The evidence on the use of new practices to raise productivity or reduce costs is also discouraging. For example, for-profit educational management organizations (EMOs) expected to improve productivity by improving selectivity, training, performance incentives, and supervision of personnel; by adopting better curriculum and teaching practices; and by reallocating funding from administrative overhead to classrooms. In fact, studies of EMOs have found greater administrative costs than comparable publicly operated schools.[13] EMO contracts have also been more costly than funding received by similar public school sites. For example, EMOs in Philadelphia have received about $22,000 more per classroom than comparable public schools, and schools in Baltimore received even greater additional resources.[14] Moreover, there is little evidence that EMO-run schools outperform public schools with similar students.[15] For example, the most comprehensive evaluation of Edison Schools, undertaken by the RAND Corporation, found that its schools fared no better in reading after five years than comparable public schools. Although Edison showed higher achievement in mathematics, the results were not statistically significant.[16] Educational technologies have not served to replace teachers, and while every new technology is associated with claims that it will reduce costs and increase learning, the various promises have not been realized in evidence from public, private, or EMO-run schools.

Reports of Cost Savings: Higher Test Scores?

No rigorous evidence of cost savings for comparable students and comparable services is found in the literature. Schools seek to control costs by seeking students who are less costly to educate or by providing fewer services. An example of the first case is found in the division between market-oriented and mission-oriented schools, where the former group of schools tends to "shed" high-cost students and try to attract those who are more easily educable.[17] Many charter schools set stringent requirements on student behavior, parental responsibilities, and daily and Saturday schedules that only the most dedicated parents and students will aspire to. The nationally renowned KIPP Academies are one example of this. Although these requirements may be educationally defensible, they represent a sorting device that makes the school appear to be more productive in achievement than schools with students who are not required to meet these standards. KIPP Academies also have a large reservoir of philanthropic support for their operations beyond the public funding they receive, something that needs to be factored in.

Virtual charter schools provide an example of an area where fewer services are provided. Such schools are designed to enroll homeschoolers and use the Internet to deliver instruction. Given their considerably lower personnel and facility requirements, these schools can deliver a limited set of services at a highly reduced cost. What evidence does exist on their performance suggests that they hardly provide a challenge to Baumol's cost dilemma.[18] However, their public funding levels relative to their limited services hints at enormous profits for their private sponsors.

The challenge remains to find schools that have lower costs for delivering similar services to similar students or superior results for the same amount. Sadly, a review of the literature on school productivity for this effort does not show consistent, sustained, radically different results for the new entrepreneurial endeavors, despite the claims. When favorable differences are found, they tend to be small (for example, closing a tenth of the black-white achievement gap), and it is not clear that all of these can be replicated or sustained over a long period.[19]

LIMITS TO ENTREPRENEURIAL SUCCESS

If one were to ask public school authorities what limits their ability to innovate and change, their answer would almost invariably be "the regulations." Schools are highly regulated at all levels of government, and especially by the states. The schools are the constitutional responsibility of the states, and most state constitutions generally delegate to the state legislatures the responsibilities to establish and maintain schools. Legislatures in turn have created a huge accumulation of laws and rules that pertain to school operations, often in behalf of the educational professionals and lobbies who benefit from them. The legislatures have charged the interpretation and enforcement of the laws and rules to their state school boards and education departments, thus promulgating additional administrative regulations that schools must follow. To these we can add federal laws and requirements and the policies set by local school boards. From the perspectives of school leaders, professionals, and parents, the ability to pursue innovation and change is largely blocked, due to the proliferation of such regulations.

This issue came to a head in California in the 1980s, when even the state's superintendent of public instruction supported legislation that would allow school districts to apply for waivers of existing laws and regulations if they could demonstrate that such waivers were needed to undertake educational improvements. The California legislature passed the education waiver law with broad authority "to provide flexibility in a school district or county office of education without undermining the basic intent of the law."[20] At that time I asked the official in the California State Board of Education who began to monitor the waiver requests to keep a record of the number of requests and the specific rules or regulations that schools wanted to be waived. This scrutiny resulted in two surprises. The first was that in spite of the high visibility of the law and the existence of almost 1,100 school districts and county education offices, relatively few formal requests for waivers were made. My recollection was that fewer than one hundred were made in the first year of the legislation. But even more surprising was that, with the exception of requests to waive special education provisions, the vast majority of all requests for waivers were unnecessary. A review by legal counsel found that the educational improvements that were proposed could be undertaken without waivers because they did not violate laws or regulations. That is, to a large degree, educational changes that were fully permissible under existing laws were not being undertaken because of local officials' belief that there were restrictions that required appeal to the state for waivers. It appeared that in an overall regulatory climate, the laws and regulations were being used as a scapegoat by local authorities to justify maintaining existing practices.

In discussions with the former superintendent in Memphis, Tennessee, Gerry House, a parallel story emerged.[21] House encouraged schools to try new approaches where old ones were not working. She emphasized that if district regulations and policies were barriers to new practices, the individual schools should request waivers of those regulations and policies. She found that almost all requests for such waivers were unnecessary. That is, the schools would be permitted to establish the proposed new practices under existing district policies.

However, a much better test of the role of laws, rules, and regulations to limit opportunities for innovation and change is found in the thirteen-year history of the charter school movement. One of the most basic tenets of charter schools is that they are granted considerable autonomy from most rules and regulations in order to have the power to be innovative. By being immune from most of the rules, they are free to be incubators of new ideas and practices that will eventually be adopted by and improve more conventional public schools. This is what economists refer to as an external benefit because, beyond the improvement of education for their own students, their autonomy enables charter schools to create innovative practices that can be emulated by other schools to the benefit of all students. And, since charter schools compete with public schools for enrollees, there is a putative incentive on the part of both groups of competitors to innovate to gain advantage.

Christopher Lubienski, a professor at the College of Education at the University of Illinois at Urbana-Champaign, has done considerable research on innovation in charter schools, comparing their instructional practices with those in conventional public schools, as well as among states with a high degree versus a moderate degree of charter school autonomy. Lubienski finds that at an administrative level, charter schools are engaging in a number of distinctive practices relative to public schools, such as merit pay, marketing, parental incentive contracts, and use of private financing arrangements. But a specific comparison of core instructional practices (pedagogy, curriculum, and school organization) reveals that almost all instructional "innovations" reported by schools in their charters and reports are practices already found in many conventional public schools.[22]

Over the long run, the main innovative impact of charter schools may be their record in taking advantage of online learning to incorporate homeschoolers into an official schooling experience. However, as hinted previously, this movement has been characterized by a quick quest for profit in its ability to obtain high reimbursements under the charter school provisions, without providing either the facilities or personnel costs that are consistent with those levels of reimbursement.[23] Evidence on effectiveness is also lacking, with large numbers of virtual charter students failing to take the required state tests used for evaluation.[24]

The lack of core pedagogical innovations in charter schools is predictive of an absence of comparative gains in student achievement. Summaries of studies comparing student achievement in charter schools with that in conventional public schools enrolling similar students show no distinct advantage for charter schools.[25] Even when individual studies show an advantage of one type of school over the other, the differences are very small—not close to the revolutionary differences claimed by each side.

One additional test of the "regulatory" obstacles to innovation is found in the independent school sector. Although the states are authorized to regulate independent schools in almost all of their instructional dimensions, they have been reluctant to do so for political reasons. The result is that regulations surrounding private or independent schools have been minimal in virtually every state. At the same time, there is a high demand in most urban areas for independent schools because of middle class families' perceptions of low standards and safety issues in public schools, and possible racism, particularly in large cities. It is not uncommon for applicants to face long waiting lists and vigorous competition for a limited number of spaces in the most desirable schools, despite tuition levels of $20,000 a year or more.

Under these conditions, one might expect to see new schools enter the market and compete for students in what appears to be a lucrative market. In fact, few competitors have arisen to take advantage of the regulatory freedoms and potentially high tuition that can be charged by an attractive private school. Paradoxically, the schools facing the highest student demand for available spaces are those known for such traditional and costly instructional features as small class sizes and numerous elective courses.

CAN SCHOOLS BE ENTREPRENEURIAL?

We know from reports of innovative charter schools, conventional public schools, and EMO schools that efforts have been made to be entrepreneurial and innovative. Site visits to many such schools suggest that they are at least partially successful in effecting some innovative changes. Yet, we cannot ignore Larry Cuban's conclusion that the preponderance of evidence suggests that constancy rather than change has characterized schools over the past century, and that new technologies that have arisen over this period have had little impact on the core activity of schools.[26] Beyond the textbook and chalkboard, we saw the emergence of slides, film, radio, closed-circuit television, video tapes and cassettes, computers, interactive and multimedia approaches, and the rich possibilities of the Internet.

Different instructional trends from multiage grading to year-round schooling to new configurations of facilities to immersion with electronic technologies to whole-school reforms have characterized educational reform during the post–World War II period. After the Sputnik launch some fifty years ago, new curricula were spawned in the sciences and mathematics, new teachers were trained in these subjects and foreign languages, and existing teachers were retrained. Yet over the long term there has been little "residue" from these reforms. Schools tend to mount a frenzy of reform and innovation with little to show for it. Thus, we are confronted with a paradox of new ideas and new schools but little evidence that they are sustainable over the long run.

One of the best examples is Central Park East Secondary School (CPESS) in New York City. CPESS was essentially an expansion of innovative elementary and middle schools started in East Harlem by noted educator Deborah Meier in the 1970s. The establishment of the high school in 1985 was a response to students', parents', and teachers' frustration with the poor quality of the high schools CPESS students were relegated to, along with the influence of Theodore Sizer's ideas and his newly formed Coalition of Essential Schools (CES) (see McGuinn's discussion of this in chapter 3). CES is a comprehensive school approach that commits to a set of ten core principles, including an emphasis on personalization, depth in studies, learning to use one's mind well, and demonstration of mastery. The latter means that assessment requires the ability to ensure the mastery of a body of knowledge or technique that can be demonstrated before experts and others, rather than simply meeting a requirement by taking a course. Under Deborah Meier, CPESS focused on five major intellectual habits that were expected to be applied to all studies. These included concern for evidence (how do you know that?), viewpoint (who said it and why?), cause and effect (what led to it and what else happened?), hypothesizing (what if?), and who cares (what difference does it make and to whom?).

The results reported for Central Park East were outstanding. With a student population that was predominantly poor and minority, fewer than 5 percent dropped out before graduation. More than that, observers found both students and teachers deeply engaged in school activities. Apathy was nonexistent, as the students worked assiduously to gain mastery in the areas that they were studying and their teachers served as coaches to make it happen. CPESS was heralded in both the professional literature and in the press for showing that a new kind of high school could be established and succeed. Debbie Meier was able to attract talented personnel and provide the inspiration and leadership they needed. Others on her staff were able to follow her example by providing leadership and role models for students and staff. Assiduous fundraising and the attractions of supporting a successful school led to substantial extra funding from both government and philanthropic foundations, as well as considerable autonomy.[27]

In 1995, a decade after CPESS was launched, Debbie Meier left to establish a new school in Boston. Finding her successor as principal was not a problem, since her codirector, for whom she had high regard, was in place to continue the CPESS tradition. After Meier left, however, the school began to look more and more like other high schools educating a similar population, but with far poorer academic results. In an interview in 2005, Meier explained what happened after she left. She cited increased enrollment, the departure of experienced teachers, and the watering-down of special programs in reaction to a greater emphasis on standardized testing. "I stopped visiting. It was too painful,"[28] she said.

SUSTAINING INNOVATION

The problem does not seem to be a lack of initiatives to innovate or reform, but schools' ability to effect and sustain change. There is something about schools that seems to excise or modify change, eventually returning them largely to their former way of functioning. Even new schools that start out with strong departures from existing practice seem to move back toward the norm. At least three related explanations for this phenomenon can be found in the organizational literature on schooling: school culture, schools as mutating agents, and the school as a conserving organization. Although the literature on each of the first two explanations is vast, I will provide just brief descriptions.

School Culture

School culture refers to the widely shared understanding, behaviors, and attitudes of school participants that are accepted as the norms for how schools should function. These are dimensions of schools that are usually not acknowledged directly because they are so widely inculcated that they are taken for granted. We are so immersed in them that we do not question them. School operations depend on a stable and shared understanding or culture that provides a framework that integrates and defines school activities and roles. That culture is built on traditions, habits, expectations, and images of what schools should do and be. To suggest that schools should change or that new schools should be different is to suggest that traditions, habits, expectations, and images be immediately abandoned, modified, or replaced by others—a virtual impossibility when dealing with human agents.[29] So, school reform usually tends to focus on the illusion that it is only trainability and skills for innovation that must be improved and ignores the more deeply rooted aspects of school culture. But it is attitudes and routinized modes of operation, according to this theory, that are the greatest obstacles to change, not a lack of skills. Skills can be acquired by school staff if they are sufficiently convinced that they need those skills and have access to appropriate resources for professional development.

School culture has many dimensions that give meaning to the daily lives of participants, including students, staff, parents, and members of the larger community. These dimensions include expectations about children in terms of behavior and what they should learn, including the possibility of different expectations according to class, race, and gender; students' own expectations about appropriate school experiences and their self-images of proficiencies; expectations about the roles of adults in the school; opinions about acceptable educational practices; and basic beliefs about the desirability for change. It is the tacit agreement around these dimensions that enables schools to function as purposive institutions. If each were a source of contestation, schools would have difficulty carrying out their missions, for the missions themselves would be undermined.

Because schools have their own cultures, they resist changes that are premised on a very different set of beliefs. For example, a school that believes that students must be tracked into ability groups will not be enthusiastic about a reform that is premised on mixed-ability grouping. A school that views writing as highly stylized will resist a new curriculum where writing is viewed primarily as a creative and expressive skill. Every school reform is embedded in specific assumptions about school culture, assumptions that may not be compatible with the actual culture that exists in a given school or that is represented by the staff recruited for a new school. According to those who study school culture, this lack of congruence is primarily responsible for the failure of school reforms to take hold in new settings.[30]

Mutating Reforms

In many cases, school culture is incompatible with proposed reforms or innovations. In those cases, it is rare that the reform is implemented more than superficially. In fact, when reforms are forced on schools, the school often has more influence in modifying the reform than the reform has in modifying the school.[31] Although those who push innovations on schools view them as "interventions" that will modify school behavior, schools respond to such interventions by remolding them in ways that disarm the threat to existing practices.[32] Education can do this simply by ignoring them or "going through the motions." Schools are not inert entities that can be fashioned easily into the shapes desired by reformers. Schools are active communities of members united by a deeply etched culture that will resist the invasion of alien ideas and practices. This reality has been ignored by most educational reformers, yet, much of the attempt to effect educational change and innovation has failed because of the ill fit between the reform and the extant culture of the school, inducing the school to defuse the change attempt.

This challenge is even true for new schools, although their founders often believe they are immune from old patterns. Despite selective recruitment, students and staff do not enter such schools with pristine views on what is possible or desirable or how schools should function. The ability of a school to modify innovative intentions may not be the result of a deliberate attempt or conspiracy, so much as of staff members attending to deeply held beliefs and expectations about school operations and ignoring the innovation. When pressed to comport with the reform, many staff members may leave to go to a more conventional school or may leave teaching altogether. A hint of this phenomenon is suggested by the departure of charter school teachers in Ohio. Almost half of all teachers in Ohio's charter schools quit over a four-year period (2000–04), compared to about 8 percent in conventional public schools and 12 percent in high-poverty urban public schools.[33]

Schools as Conserving Institutions

In stable democratic societies, schools are not revolutionary institutions designed to transform social outcomes. Schools are conservative institutions charged with the primary goal of preparing the young to acclimate to and participate in the cultural, social, economic, and political life of an existing social entity. That is, schools are conserving institutions with responsibility for inculcating the values, attitudes, and skills that reproduce existing social, economic, and political structures. As parents, teachers, students, taxpayers, and citizens, we expect our schools to fulfill this role. But fulfillment of this role means suspicion of and resistance to change by parents, teachers, students, and school administrators, exactly what we find in school culture and in the tendency of schools to modify external attempts to reform them. In fact, parents may be looking for schools that have not attempted to innovate but that represent the image of education that they believe was emblematic of the past, "when schools worked." Today most charter schools are using their autonomy to emphasize the "basics" or teach a traditional curriculum.[34]

Although it may appear in retrospect that schools and schooling have changed society, eminent educational historian David Tyack has argued precisely the opposite: that school change was a response to major turning points in U.S. history.[35] Thus, schools have largely served as conserving institutions rather than as institutions of change and innovation, and this reality is well understood by parents, students, and school staff in their behaviors. The demand for schools to excel in the 3 Rs reflects this conservatism.

INSTITUTIONAL INERTIA

In my view, new institutional theory represents the best overall explanation of schools' resistance to innovation. In their seminal article "The Iron Cage Revisited," sociologists Paul DiMaggio and Walter Powell ask at the outset

> why there is such startling homogeneity of organizational forms and practices . . . not variation. In the initial stages of their life cycle, organizational fields display considerable diversity in approach and form. Once a field becomes well established, however, there is an inexorable push towards homogenization.[36]

They conclude that organizations that are highly dependent upon other organizations, such as mainstream economic, political, and social institutions, will become isomorphic with those institutions. In other words, they will come to mimic their form and appearance. They hypothesize that the greater the dependence of an organization on another organization, the more it will become similar to that organization; the less certain the relation between means and ends, the greater it will model itself after those organizations that appear to be successful; and the more ambiguous its goals, the more it will model itself after organizations that appear successful.

Schools tend to mirror all of these dependencies. For example, schools have many goals rather than a single one, and the relationships between their inputs and outputs (means and ends) are uncertain and unpredictable. All schools, even charter schools, are heavily dependent upon largely centralized sources of finance and other resources. And, finally, schools' dependence on other educational institutions such as colleges and universities that enroll their students later, economic institutions that support them through tax levies and hire their graduates, and civic institutions through which they will express themselves politically must recognize their legitimacy and the value of their credentials. Based on these dependencies, schools will tend to gravitate to and become isomorphic to other institutions, rather than maintaining independence.

In their groundbreaking work, organizational sociologists John Meyer and Brian Rowan argued that traditional theories of coordination and control of formal organizations often fall by the wayside in education.[37] Normally, innovation is introduced to educational organizations by managers responding to external pressures. It is assumed that innovations will be implemented in a straightforward manner under the monitoring of managers. But since schools have been shown to be only loosely coupled, command and control is almost futile.[38] Under such circumstances, myths, rituals, and symbols validate the organization and legitimate its claim for resources and for the honoring of its operations.

These criteria are often in conflict with the dictates of efficiency. For example, American schools once provided specific training for jobs in which the educational efficacy of schools and student prowess could be evaluated according to specific criteria. However, over time this has shifted to more ambiguous measures, such as credits or certificates that may or may not promote efficient operations. At the end of the day, however, it is precisely these features that one expects of schools that gives them their legitimacy and stability.

The institutionalist perspective provides a general framework that is able to integrate much of the previous analysis. The importance of isomorphic behavior requires that schools regulate themselves through their dominant rituals, symbols, and images, irrespective of the degree of external regulation. Ethnographers label this behavior "school culture." Such institutions operate inexorably to modify and neuter attempts to impose change and innovation, as the school has more power to alter the reform than the reform has to change the school. Finally, this institutionalist umbrella tends to explain why schools serve largely as conserving forces rather than forces of change.

Can educational innovation succeed over the long run? According to institutional theory, the answer would seem to be, only if there are major changes in those institutions on which schools are dependent, for changes in those organizations will create pressures for a new isomorphism.

As noted, one of the foremost educational historians asserted this some forty years ago in his interpretation of how educational change took place historically.[39] Tyack suggested that major changes in schools coincided with significant changes in social, political, and economic institutions, what he called turning points in educational history. Even those with more activist interpretations of school change accept the limits imposed by institutional theory.[40] All of them acknowledge that this dependency is the main challenge to innovation in education and the success of the educational entrepreneur.

Should we give up the quest for beneficial change through spirited entrepreneurialism? Of course not. While Central Park East Secondary School flourished, it provided important benefits for its students and inspiration for many other entrepreneurial efforts. But to ignore the forces that undermine long-term change in education is to repeat the futility that has characterized virtually thousands of well-intentioned attempts to alter education. These forces need to be taken seriously if there is any chance of overcoming them. Most important, it seems to me, is to understand the role of social movements in education and other parts of society for opening windows of opportunity for change. Finally, we should acknowledge that the resistance to change that is so often deprecated by policymakers can also be a valuable safeguard or firewall that protects us from bad policy initiatives.

CHAPTER 9

Opportunities,
but a Resistant Culture

Steven F. Wilson

Why has entrepreneurial initiative succeeded brilliantly in some sectors of the education industry and—at least as yet—proved a disappointment in others? The runaway success of for-profit higher education, including such behemoths as the Apollo Group, stands in stark contrast to the history of for-profit K–12 education providers (education management organizations, or EMOs), which have generally struggled to gain profitability. The largest EMO, Edison Schools, just posted its first profitable year, but only after expanding into the tutoring market spawned by the No Child Left Behind Act (NCLB). Both the K–12 management and higher education sectors have received considerable attention from journalists and investment analysts, but rarely have their dramatically different fates been examined. Other initiatives in K–12, many of which are new, have been largely overlooked. A wide range of companies offer products and services to students, including test preparation, tutoring, and college admission counseling, and to schools, such as formative assessment software, Web-delivered educational technology, and data management and warehousing. How have these ventures fared to date and what are their likely prospects?

In higher education, entrepreneurship is flourishing. While traditional institutions remain focused on full-time students who have not yet entered the workforce, a number of for-profit education conglomerates target a vast, underserved population of working adults seeking out new professional skills. Well over one million adults, many of whom are minorities, are now enrolled in for-profit career schools, attending classes at convenient local campuses at night, on weekends, or via the Internet.[1] Some twenty-two publicly traded companies, including Apollo Group, Career Education, Laureate Education, Strayer, and DeVry, Inc., compete in this burgeoning education sector, with a combined market capitalization of over $24 billion.[2] Each of several companies, including Apollo Group, Career Education, Education Management, Laureate Education, ITT Educational, Strayer, DeVry, and Corinthian Colleges, has a stock value of over $1 billion.[3] From 2000 to 2003, the industry posted the strongest gains on Wall Street of any sector: publicly traded postsecondary education stocks climbed 460 percent over the period, while the Standard & Poor's 500-stock index fell 24 percent.[4]

Education entrepreneurs have also carved out a successful, if far less spectacular, niche in a second market: child care. Once again, entrepreneurs capitalized on a profound societal trend. While only 19 percent of young women were employed in 1960 and only 10 percent of three- to five-year-old children were enrolled in child-care programs, some 70 percent of young mothers are in the workforce today and 65 percent of young children attend day-care centers and preschool programs. Many centers offer private kindergarten and afterschool programs for elementary school–age children along with infant care and preschool. One-fifth of the more than a half-million child-care centers are run by for-profit companies. Among the publicly traded companies are Bright Horizons Family Solutions and Learning Care Group (formerly Childtime Learning Centers). Privately held companies include KinderCare Learning Centers, Knowledge Learning Corp., and La Petite Academy.

Operating alongside K–12 education are a number of companies that offer select services; some have gained solid footing and others but a toehold. With the emergence of the accountability movement and NCLB, test-preparation companies have seen an explosion in opportunities as families confront high-stakes high school exams. NCLB's supplemental educational services (SES) provision is driving growth in the tutoring industry, with its mandate that schools that fail to meet adequate yearly progress (AYP) two years in a row use Title I dollars to offer free tutoring to low-income students. Together, the revenues of the test-preparation and tutoring industries are likely to exceed $1 billion in 2006.[5]

But the $400 billion market segment these sectors bracket, the provision of public primary and secondary education, remains only weakly penetrated by private entrepreneurship. A 2005 report lists fifty-nine for-profit EMOs serving 240,000 students; only thirteen operated ten or more schools.[6] Edison Schools is among the leading providers, along with National Heritage Academies, the Leona Group, Mosaica Education, and Imagine Schools. More than three-quarters of the schools are charter schools, and industry analysts predict that growth in the industry will be driven by continued growth in charter schools. Total revenues for the 2003–04 school year were estimated at just $1.07 billion.[7]

Why has entrepreneurial initiative in the last decade met with such striking success in some sectors of the education industry but not—at least as yet—in K–12 education management? In what measure can the limited results of for-profit companies and nonprofit organizations in K–12 be attributed to political and regulatory obstacles, to defects in the organizations' business models, to poor execution, or to still other factors that have been largely overlooked?

INDUSTRY SECTORS

Higher Education

Entrepreneurial initiatives in higher education have taken off over the last decade. There are some 2,500 for-profit postsecondary institutions eligible for federal Title IV (of the Higher Education Act of 1965, or HEA) funding, which are operated by 1,400 different corporate entities. Roughly one-fifth of these schools are operated by publicly traded companies. Overall revenues for the for-profit postsecondary market were estimated to be $15.4 billion in 2004.[8]

The largest of the postsecondary companies, Apollo Group, which includes the industry behemoth University of Phoenix, is remarkably profitable: For 2004 it reported net income of $277 million, a remarkable 15 percent of sales. The stock market values the company at nearly $12 billion, or more than six times its 2004 revenues of $1.8 billion.[9] The University of Phoenix is now the largest private university in the country, and considered separately, the online campus would be the second largest. Many of this for-profit company's students receive financial aid from the federal government, including guaranteed student loans and direct grants under Title IV. For-profit higher education is the most dynamic and influential segment of higher education today.

Economic trends would seem to ensure a virtually unlimited demand for career-oriented education programs aimed at adults looking to advance their careers and remain competitive in the job marketplace. But the industry faces important risks. Allegations of impropriety dogged several companies in 2004, and investors, fearful that fraud might prove endemic to the industry, punished higher education stocks. Maintaining quality and complying with regulatory requirements may be difficult for some already large companies that, like Career Education Corporation, are growing at a rate of 15 percent a year.

Child Care

The child-care industry is a rich mix of nonprofit and for-profit providers. One category of for-profit operators, employer-sponsored day-care providers, grew rapidly in the 1990s by following an innovative business model: Large employers would offer their employees an increasingly important amenity, on-site child care, by contracting with a for-profit provider. The largest provider of employer-sponsored child care, Bright Horizons Family Solutions, posted revenues of $552 million in 2004, up 90 percent from $291 million in 2000.[10] Contractual arrangements vary across the company's 552 locations, but typically the client employer provides the capital for construction of the facility in accordance with Bright Horizons specifications (as well as for pre-opening expenses, start-up costs, and initial supplies) and contracts with the company to operate the center and provide child care and education, giving priority to the children of its employees. In some cases, the employer may subsidize employee tuition or guarantee minimum levels of enrollment.

K–12 Select Services

Alongside K–12 education are many firms that exploit the failures of the public school franchise. The ballooning test-preparation sector helps families who can afford its services to raise their children's scores on high school exit and college admissions exams, most notably the SAT. Test-preparation companies and mainline educational publishers spot a large market in school districts under increasing pressure from NCLB to raise scores on state-mandated tests and meet the increasingly challenging requirement of posting AYP.

The tutoring industry also thrives proportionately to the failures of public schooling. One business model targets middle-class parents concerned with their child's school performance; Kaplan's Score! Education Centers division (now part of the Washington Post Company), founded in 1992, operates 160 tutoring centers in 12 states, often in suburban retail locations, that lure students with sports themes.[11] New York-based Platform Learning, which was founded in 2003 to meet the SES demand, has grown from one thousand SES students in 2003 to fifty thousand in 2005, according to the company. Another such company, Catapult Learning, a division of Educate, Inc., grew in one year from five thousand students in 2003 to twenty-five thousand in 2004.[12]

Because the SES provision forcibly shunts public funds away from school districts, it has been aggressively opposed by public education interest groups, creating some uncertainty within the tutoring industry. The U.S. Department of Education continues to refine and clarify the regulations regarding the use of Title I funds. In 2005, the department granted a waiver to school districts, including Chicago and Boston, permitting them to continue to operate their own tutoring programs, even though the districts had failed to meet state academic expectations. But the industry is also vulnerable for a far more interesting reason: To cater to prevailing pedagogical fashions, many SES providers offer an activities-based curriculum that promises to make learning fun. Some companies deploy curricula that have not been developed by experts in instructional design, let alone proven effective in raising student achievement levels. If industry opponents call for providers to demonstrate the efficacy of their interventions, as is inevitable, it is likely that many will be hard pressed to show evidence of material gains in student achievement.

Online tutoring is another category of select services likely to experience rapid growth. The best-known such company, Tutor.com, was founded in 1998. Although the company today has annual revenues of only $10 million, it claims to be growing 40 to 50 percent a year. Students can access homework help over the Web and be instantly connected with one of Tutor.com's twelve hundred trained tutors in a virtual chat session; six hundred thousand tutoring sessions are administered annually. Each tutoring session is followed by an online satisfaction survey; the company claims a satisfaction rate of 94 percent.[13] Another such company is Growing Stars, which provides one-on-one tutoring via the Internet by remote tutors, many of which are based in India. Students interact with their teachers via an electronic whiteboard, electronic pen, and two-way audio connection, emulating a face-to-face exchange. With offshore instructors, Growing Stars can tap a highly educated but relatively inexpensive workforce.[14]

As NCLB's requirements for demonstrating AYP prove ever more difficult to meet—and the consequences for falling short more severe—school systems are rushing to buy "formative assessment" software that permits teachers and administrators to gauge students' progress toward state learning goals. Formative assessment is a rapidly growing component of the larger and booming assessment market, which grew to over $1 billion in revenues in 2004, up 22 percent from just the year before.[15]

E-learning. Within the educational software market, so-called e-learning (also virtual learning and distance learning) products exploit the Internet to enable students to learn online. During the Internet boom of the late 1990s,

Wall Street analysts feverishly promoted the promise of e-learning start-ups to transform teaching and learning. In time, most of these companies went belly up. There are some exceptions. Leading educational software company Riverdeep, founded in 1995, reports that its products, which directly instruct students in core subjects like reading and math, are in use in forty thousand schools worldwide.[16]

Many of the survivors make products that do not teach children, but instead affect teaching and learning indirectly. The publicly traded Blackboard.com, which was founded in 1997 and now posts revenues of $111 million, provides course management software that is widely used by universities; the company reports twelve million users at two thousand institutions worldwide.[17] The system manages curriculum content provided by users, administers assessments, and electronically networks participants, including students and professors, but does not itself instruct or deliver content.

One of the fastest growing companies that sells to school districts, Wireless Generation, markets hand-held devices for administering reading assessments like DIBELS and TPRI. Teachers administer the reading exam on a Palm Pilot and then upload the results to a Web-based system where teachers and administrators can easily analyze the results. Wireless Generation claims its products cut the time to administer assessments in half. Founded in 2000, the company today posts revenues of $20 million, generates positive cash flow, and expects to post its first profit soon.[18]

The "killer application" for schools—the equivalent of word processing, spreadsheets, and databases in the office—remains to be invented, and no one can persuasively claim to have demonstrated at scale that computers can be deployed to dramatically boost student achievement. But the potential for technology to boost K–12 educational productivity remains. Recent advances in underlying technology, including orders-of-magnitude gains in connection bandwidth, new compression algorithms, and tools for delivering high-quality streaming video, may give rise to new instructional products that demonstrably accelerate learning—and, for the first time, boost educational productivity. A new wave of start-up companies is offering products that may enable students to learn independently, thereby fundamentally altering student/adult ratios, and in turn lowering the cost of achievement. One such start-up, Academy 123, offers a surprisingly engaging and simple electronic whiteboard system that permits exemplary lessons to be captured at almost no content development cost and be delivered interactively to students anywhere via the Internet. Another product with considerable potential for self-learning is HeyMath, in use in schools in top-achieving Singapore. HeyMath was developed by teams of Indian, British, and Chinese education specialists in partnership with the Millennium Mathematics Project at Cambridge University. The founders aimed to create nothing less than the Google of math instruction, with a product that brings exemplary instruction in every individual math concept to students anywhere.[19] Animated lessons unlock math abstractions by rendering them as familiar physical representations.[20] Rigorously designed early reading software from Headsprout, beta-tested with more than one thousand children, is another new program of great promise. Headsprout announced in March 2005 that it would partner with Kaplan to provide the online, interactive online program at SCORE! Centers nationwide.[21]

Virtual schooling. One rare break-the-mold innovation in K–12 education is virtual schools, where children learn at home and are linked to a teacher and/or classmates electronically. The first such schools opened in 1998; by 2004, more than thirty-one thousand students were enrolled in eighty-six online charter schools. Sixty-two of these schools have opened their doors since 2000.[22] K12, the largest contractor of virtual charter schools, reports that more than seventy thousand students use its learning program in traditional public classrooms, virtual schools, and home schools.[23] Founded in 1999 by former U.S. Secretary of Education William Bennett, K12 offers schools and families a combination of textbooks and online learning tools that spans the complete curriculum from kindergarten through grade 12. The company has encountered political resistance in several states to public funding of its online schools.

District-management systems. To comply with NCLB's myriad requirements, districts must track not only their students' performance districtwide, but also that of specific subpopulations at each individual school and a broad range of process measures, including the credentials of their teaching forces. These requirements are driving demand for newly sophisticated information technology products. Data-warehousing systems and instructional-management systems that aggregate information make up one growing product category. Companies including SchoolNet provide districtwide software that integrates academic standards, formative assessment data, lesson-planning tools, and remedial education resources. Integration gives teachers and administrators insight into the effectiveness of the education function so that districts can better direct instructional activities and improve student achievement. For instance, "dashboard" displays aim to show administrators at a glance the condition of their schools and their progress toward meeting NCLB requirements, including AYP, and permit users to "drill down" into increasing levels of detail to pinpoint problems and intervene early.

A still more ambitious product category, enterprise software, aims to integrate the currently disparate databases present in school systems. Rather than maintain isolated systems for tracking student information (student information systems), special education enrollment and individual education plans, human resources, accounting and finance, supply management, food services, transportation, library management, parent communication, and instruction and assessment, enterprise products integrate these disparate software applications and map cause-and-effect relationships across processes.

My Learning Plan offers a Web-based system for managing teacher professional development compliance and licensure. The product enables teachers and districts to track professional development hours or points accumulated toward recertification or licensure, to manage teachers' choice of and enrollment in qualified professional development activities, and to track districtwide compliance with NCLB's highly qualified teacher and high-quality professional development requirements. Demand for such professional development management systems is likely to grow rapidly in coming years, as districts struggle to track and ensure compliance with NCLB and state requirements for teacher qualifications, professional development plans, and certification records. As with other districtwide products, the sales cycle is long and challenging and market penetration is as yet weak.[24]

Student services. Entrepreneurs are also building businesses that offer services traditionally provided by school districts. For instance, College Coach, founded in 1998, identified the weakness in high school guidance counseling, where the ratio of students to counselors is five hundred to one nationally.[25] Large corporations like Goldman Sachs and the New York Stock Exchange contract with College Coach to counsel and educate employees trying to navigate the process of enrolling their children in college. The typical client corporation pays the company $100,000 a year for its services.[26] Notably, College Coach's customer is the parent's employer and not the local school district.

Education Management Organizations

Companies that do not challenge the institutional structure of K–12 public education and education interests by offering such services as data management, special education, and the education of delinquent students have run into limited resistance and experienced some level of success. But most companies that compete directly with the public system for management of schools have struggled for survival. Only one major EMO has consistently made money and faces solid prospects for growth: National Heritage Academies. Many others benefited from tens of millions of dollars in venture capital but continue to lose money. The only two publicly traded K–12 management companies have both fared poorly on the public market. Nobel Learning Communities runs 147 nonsectarian private schools in thirteen states, including preschools, elementary schools, and middle schools. Last year it posted only $164 million in revenues and, after years of losing money, was just barely profitable. The market values the company at $70 million, substantially less than its annual revenues.[27] Edison Schools, with over $400 million in revenues in 2005, withdrew from the public market after its shares plummeted from a high of more than $35 a share to under a dollar in 2002. Nonprofit EMOs have also struggled to reach financial stability. Why has school management proven such a difficult business?

INDUSTRY ENVIRONMENTS

To attribute the extraordinary success of one sector or the persistent struggles of another solely to differences in business models or quality of execution would belie the importance of external factors, including but not limited to the regulatory environments in which they operate. Entrepreneurship in education appears to succeed where favorable conditions attend: there are uniform, manageable, and supportive regulatory structures; public funding is sufficient to provide a high-quality product or service and generate a return on private capital; private operators have sufficient governance authority to ensure that their products or services reliably generate the claimed benefits for customers; the political environment is not dominated by powerful employee interests, especially the teachers unions, which may be threatened by entrepreneurial competition; educational outcomes are either fairly and accurately measured or unexamined by public authorities; and the culture is compatible, that is, private involvement in the provision of education does not violate deeply held—if often unexamined—normative conceptions among Americans about public education. Many of these environmental conditions are familiar and their importance self-evident, but the effects of others—especially the last—have received little scrutiny yet may powerfully affect entrepreneurial outcomes.

Higher Education

The for-profit postsecondary industry has benefited from a number of supportive environmental conditions. As in K–12, state government owns and operates public institutions of higher education—community colleges and state colleges and universities—which it subsidizes through direct appropriations. At the same time, the regulatory environment has long fostered an extraordinarily rich array of high-quality private institutions that compete successfully with the public sector. Beginning with the GI Bill, the federal government has built a complex system of direct and indirect financial subsidies and support for private sector institutions, including both tax programs (which assist families in saving for their children's higher education) and spending programs (which offer students Pell Grants and other grants, loans, and loan guarantees). Postsecondary education companies have been able to participate in many Title IV subsidies; the regulations require only that for-profit institutions receive at least 10 percent of their tuition revenues from nonfederal sources. Even this constraint may be relaxed in the near future. For-profit providers benefit from a nearly ideal funding environment: Their customers can access public grants or loans (or private loans made possible by public guarantees) and, better still, providers are often the direct recipient of the loan proceeds, while the student remains responsible for repaying the loan. Because the proceeds are collected prior to the service being provided, the companies have exceptional cash flow. As they are competing with high-priced traditional providers with high labor costs and costly infrastructure, they have ample opportunity to make substantial profits.

The sector benefits from many other attractive regulatory characteristics. Rather than cope with a dizzying complexity of federal, state, and local regulations, as in elementary and secondary public education, companies operate in a sector where the federal government has delegated its regulatory function in large measure to private accreditation agencies. So long as providers are accredited by national agencies and comply with basic regulatory requirements, they are eligible for participation in federal funding programs.[28] In large measure, then, they operate primarily under a single set of rules across all domestic jurisdictions.

Their adult customers—unlike the clients of K–12 and, often, traditional college students—have elected to return to school and complete coursework or obtain a degree. Befitting this transactional environment, postsecondary providers promote outcome measures like the percentage of students employed in their chosen field by a certain time. The industry is not subject to direct measures of students' academic outcomes, as in primary and secondary education under state and federal accountability programs. Higher education has never been afflicted by the pedagogical faddism that curses K–12 (and contributes to high costs, including for decreased class size, and to poor outcomes), and customers embrace traditional delivery styles, most notably, lecture-style instruction. Companies "own and operate" their sites directly; they lease or own their own facilities; they contract with their own instructors, whom they are free to hire, reward, promote, and fire as they judge; and their authority is not subordinated to a public governing board. They face little opposition from organized interest groups, including labor, except for relatively weak efforts by traditional nonprofit providers to arrest their growth.

Child Care

The for-profit day-care industry must engage a more complex yet still manageable environment. Funding levels are relatively low, and individual receivables must typically be collected from client parents. The industry is highly regulated by both state and local governments. But the underlying concerns of rule-makers are predictable and consistent across jurisdictions— for instance, the ratio of adults to children and the adequacy and safety of facilities—and therefore, from the perspective of business owners, relatively easy to accommodate. Political and cultural resistance is virtually nonexistent; indeed, child care is considered to be a scarcity, and responsible private providers are embraced by the public and politicians. Operators have governance control; they are free to devise their programs, hire and fire staff, and otherwise control their operations—often in a facility that is built to the provider's specifications and, in the case of employer-sponsored providers, typically funded by the client company. Best of all, there is essentially no accountability to government officials for educational outcomes; companies are unfettered in catering to prevailing progressive orthodoxies of early childhood education, regardless of whether the methods are measurably effective.

K–12 Select Services

Compared to these market segments, K–12 select services companies face conditions that are less uniformly hospitable. The burgeoning SES tutoring industry enjoys favorable conditions, but these may not last. NCLB's requirement that tutoring services be provided to students from low-income families in schools that fail to meet AYP for two consecutive years was a political compromise lacking deep bipartisan consensus.

The enabling legislation effectively diverted public dollars to private providers, rather than requiring them to compete against school districts in the marketplace for students. Providers have been able to reap substantial profits from generous levels of funding while operating in an environment of minimal regulation. As private entities, SES providers have been free to hire and fire staff and operate without union involvement. With little or no scrutiny or even measurement of remedial outcomes, some companies have felt free to deploy educational programs that suit the vogue for "discovery learning," "differentiated instruction," "interdisciplinary learning," and the like, without having to worry whether they are academically effective. Many programs are more recreational than educational, and their curricula are not based on sound principles of instructional design.

There are indications that the climate is changing. The recent waivers granted by the U.S. Department of Education to some urban school systems underscore the fragility of the enabling regulatory structure of the SES industry. If the federal government continues recent steps toward relaxing certain of NCLB's provisions and private companies come under fire to demonstrate their programs' remedial effects, growth in this sector may slow and profit margins contract. If subjected to rigorous evaluation, few programs are likely to show significant academic gains.

Other providers of select services in the K–12 space that are experiencing modest success are also benefiting from federal legislation that, indirectly, mandates their use by school districts; are selling to a customer other than the school district; or are selling products that are so narrow in their scope that they do not threaten the districts' hegemony. For instance, many of Wireless Generation's customers are states, not districts; the company benefits from the unusual provisions of the new federal Reading First K–3 reading initiative (a component of NCLB). Unlike many federal programs for K–12 education, Reading First permits state education agencies (SEAs) to retain a significant part of federal program funds and requires that SEAs prescribe a reading assessment for all the state's Reading First schools. By February 2006, eighteen states had chosen to contract with Wireless Generation for Reading First assessments. Because the company's products fulfill a narrow and obscure function, it suffers little from commercial competition. These rare circumstances created "the perfect storm," Wireless's CEO Larry Berger explains—"a large opportunity that is rarely created" in K–12 education.[29]

Similarly, Tutor.com's natural customer is the local school system, but the company found in early telephone surveys that districts had little interest in buying the product and, by 2006, the company counted only a handful of districts as customers. The company instead sells almost exclusively to municipal public libraries and youth-service programs. After purchasing Tutor's "Live Homework Help" product and witnessing its popularity with students from the local school district, many libraries have called on the district to subsidize the program's cost. In turn, the state agency that oversees local libraries and distributes state support to them has become a natural ally. While the agencies themselves are minimally funded, they can press their counterpart SEAs to fund a statewide program of "Live Homework Help"—at a cost to the behemoth SEAs that is a "rounding error in their budgets," in the words of Tutor's CEO George Cigale.[30]

Education Management Organizations

Of all the education industry sectors, K–12 management represents the largest entrepreneurial opportunity, and the most challenging by far. The ambition and scope of EMO efforts make them a useful and illustrative tool for exploring the barriers confronting entrepreneurs of all stripes.

Regulatory structure. Consider, first, the sector's regulatory structure. Unlike in higher education, the states have all chosen to fund and operate district schools while providing almost no subsidies to private elementary and secondary schools. State laws, with few exceptions, do not permit private companies to open and operate charter schools that compete for students and public funding. Where they do, spending levels have been too low to open new schools profitably. Arizona's unusually liberal charter school law permits private companies to hold charters directly, but per-student spending is among the lowest in the country.

Governance. Given statutory constraints, K–12 EMOs have had to settle for acting as the agents of school boards—whether traditional district school boards or charter school boards—by entering into a term "management agreement." This highly compromised structure has often proved unworkable in practice. EMOs have had difficulty protecting their investments in schools and lacked the authority to implement their school designs accurately and consistently. Management contracts have often been breached or terminated capriciously by unsophisticated (or, occasionally, unethical) boards of trustees, and authorizers and regulators have generally chosen not to enforce them. When millions of dollars in facility improvements, technology, and instructional materials had to be written off, sometimes for just one school, capital requirements for the company skyrocketed and investors' confidence was shaken.

As important, the indirect governance structure—where the company's authority was subordinated to the license-holding board—undermined program implementation, and therefore academic results. A few schools benefited from extraordinarily supportive and able boards. The Edison Friendship School in Washington, D.C., a collaboration of an established community organization and Edison, is one example. But Friendship was the exception. Time and again, to satisfy the charter law requirements for community control, EMOs hastily cobbled together weak boards. For that, EMOs are rightly criticized. But the greater fault lies with a policy that requires boards in the first place.

Funding levels and capital. The absence of capital funding for charter school facilities has long been identified as the greatest flaw in charter school legislation, and progress in remedying it through legislative change has been painfully slow. A variety of patchwork programs have sprung up across the states, but only a few jurisdictions have successfully leveled the financial playing field between district schools and charters. The economic implications for the K–12 management industry of the absence of capital funding are self-evident. The playing field was sharply tilted toward district schools, as charter schools had to pay for facility costs (whether in rent or borrowing costs) out of operating revenues. Opening and operating schools profitably under these adverse economics proved immensely challenging, and few companies succeeded.

Idiosyncratic regulations and reporting requirements. As charter school legislation was debated, teachers unions generally succeeded in imposing limits on the number of charter schools that could be established. In Massachusetts, for example, the law initially only permitted twenty-five schools statewide. In order to grow, education companies were forced to seek charters in many and distant states, enormously increasing the cost and complexity of their operations. Each state and authorizer had its own education laws and regulations; mandated reporting formats; central computerized data collection system; special and bilingual education policies; discipline policies governing suspension and expulsion; and emerging academic standards and criterion-referenced testing regimens. Simply understanding the requirements of compliance in each state was a challenge. In truth, each market requires a new reporting and compliance product—even if for only one school. Organizations that were able to operate primarily in one high-revenue jurisdiction— like National Heritage Academies, whose first thirteen schools, opened from 1995 to 1998, were all in western Michigan—were able to reach profitability sooner.

Outcome scrutiny. The lack of governance control made for highly inconsistent implementation of the companies' academic programs. In schools with supportive trustees and competent principals committed to the school design, schools orchestrated the programs with fidelity and posted strong achievement gains. But in many other schools, boards and EMOs tangled over staff and programs, and the quality of implementation of the design suffered. Whether or not EMOs made specific promises, the expectation was that they would post results on state tests superior to the districts in which they were located. They faced intense scrutiny of their educational outcomes, often well before their programs could reasonably be expected to have affected the achievement levels of their students.

Low funding levels, lack of governance control, complex and idiosyncratic regulatory regimes, and intense scrutiny of academic outcomes are by now well-known challenges to the education management industry and are documented elsewhere.[31] But an additional factor, no less important, has thwarted entrepreneurial success in school management: the culture of public schooling.

THE CULTURE OF PUBLIC SCHOOLING

Any entrepreneur proposing to operate public primary and secondary schools must confront the ideology of American schooling—an array of deeply held but often unexamined normative beliefs embedded in American culture. EMOs had no choice but to tackle the first of these beliefs head on: that it is wrong to make a profit running schools. Perhaps because this fight alone was so taxing, they often elected to accommodate a range of standard schooling practices where to do otherwise would have required violating another tenet of the ideology. But their adherence to conventions compromised both their educational and financial results.

Localism

The two hundred-year tradition of localism in primary and secondary education contained two distinct expectations that hinder nationally minded entrepreneurs, and especially EMOs: local control and differentiation. Opponents of private operators invoked the public's commitment to both local control and school differentiation when they argued that charter school legislation was intended to spawn community-based schools, each with its own lay board, each tailored to the unique needs of its students, and each a laboratory for an innovative model—not to foster a system of schools that implemented a common design and was operated by an out-of-state corporation.

The EMOs' responses to both expectations often bordered on the disingenuous. To open schools, EMOs frequently assembled boards to meet statutory requirements. Trustees with little substantive knowledge of schools or experience as fiduciaries presided over schools with multi-million-dollar budgets. When they inevitably asserted their authority over the EMO, bitter conflict often ensued. Similarly, rather than dispute the premise that each school need be unique, many EMOs publicly embraced it while attempting to do as little actual customization as possible. Frequently, EMOs agreed to implement special programs in individual schools—a performing arts curriculum, for example—to satisfy school founders and improve their position with charter authorizers. But EMOs later regretted committing to these "one-off" modifications, as they lacked the resources and expertise to make them work.

One reason National Heritage Academies (NHA) has performed well financially is that it avoided such one-offs; it advanced an ideological message of its own that appealed to both target parents and authorizers. The company's promise of a "moral education" resonated with its primarily middle-class parents, especially evangelical Christians disaffected with the public schools. NHA's founder J. C. Huizenga doesn't flinch at the charge of operating "cookie cutter" schools and sees the company's mission as making quality broadly available. "If you're going to do something, it has to be replicable," he says.[32]

Class Size and Structure

EMOs also rarely confronted the ideology of class-size reduction, even though reducing staffing costs was essential to improving productivity and realizing a profit. Throughout the 1990s, when the EMOs were launched, and continuing today, the national teachers union pressed for smaller classes. Smaller classes made intuitive sense to the public: Teachers, with fewer children to handle, could devote more attention to individual students. Entrepreneurs knew that the research support for achievement gains from reduced class size was weak at best. They also knew that many of the nations with the strongest results in rigorous comparisons of academic achievement made use of much larger classes—not smaller—than American norms, and that increasing class size (and thereby lowering staffing costs) was among the few obvious levers for reducing costs.[33] Yet few EMOs made use of larger classes, and several actively promoted *smaller* classes as a primary value to their customers. Chancellor Beacon Academies (now Imagine Schools), for instance, capitalized on widespread concerns about school overcrowding in its home state of Florida by promising classes of twenty-five students or fewer. "Your child won't get lost here," CEO Octavio Visiedo promised parents.[34] But, burdened with low revenues and high staffing costs, the company has struggled to become profitable, and its institutional investors sold the company at a substantial loss.[35]

Two organizations took a different course. The Knowledge Is Power Program (KIPP) believes its orderly environment permits large classes (occasionally with as many as forty-five students) to be effective. David Levin explains, "Class size is not an issue if teachers know how to manage kids."[36] SABIS chief executive Ralph Bistany would agree; the company rejected the American orthodoxy of aiming toward smaller classes and insisted on the efficacy of larger classes. In higher education, no one would think it practical—let alone normative—to educate in one classroom students with widely diverse preparation and precursor skills. Students would be expected to master fundamental skills before being instructed in more advanced ones. But as applied to American K–12 education, Bistany's plan seems radical, even repellent. SABIS's approach may encounter resistance from parents but seems capable of achieving high performance at affordable cost.

Teacher Invention

Generations of American teachers have been schooled in an ideology in which prestige is often accorded those who exercise creativity in the classroom, rather than those whose students obtain academic results. But leaving teachers to develop their own lesson plans in critical elementary subjects, as did most U.S. schools, makes for a kind of institutionalized chaos. The consequences are predictable; a few lessons are exceptional, the majority mediocre.

Even though instruction is their business, most education companies have adhered to the norms of the education culture and have been disinclined to manage teacher practice closely. EMOs did invest more heavily in professional development than districts, and a few companies, most notably Edison, sought to implement instructional programs exactingly in elementary reading and math. But in general, EMOs failed to develop an effective system of instructional oversight. Good teaching was not codified, and teacher observations and evaluations were, as in most district schools, infrequent, undiscerning, and without consequence.

Teacher Qualifications

Few work environments are as people intensive as schools. EMO founders knew that selecting and retaining the strongest teachers, and letting go of the weakest, was critical to realizing exceptional academic results. They were willing to confront the teachers unions on the dismissal of plainly incompetent teachers, sensing that pubic opinion was squarely on their side. Yet they did surprisingly little to challenge other components of the orthodoxy, in particular teacher selection and compensation. Unions contend that teachers are largely interchangeable and of equal ability, and what matters is their formal preparation and working conditions. But research finds otherwise;

as measured by value-added testing, switching from an average teacher to a strong one has approximately twice the effect on achievement gains as a 10 percent reduction in class size.[37] Research also suggests that teachers who have graduated from selective-admission colleges and who have strong intellectual skills, verbal aptitudes, and subject-matter knowledge are the most effective.[38] Yet EMOs failed to publicly challenge the prevailing assumption that teacher preparation—certification and advanced degrees in teaching—drove teacher quality. Nor did they systematically organize to recruit teachers with these characteristics. Given the culture of K–12 schooling, to do so would have been to invite charges of elitism.

The school network KIPP took a different approach. KIPP recruits heavily from Teach For America, which draws corps members from elite colleges and universities. KIPP and many of the emerging nonprofit charter management organizations (CMOs), which often seek to replicate a successful individual charter school, are following a common strategy in teacher recruiting; that is, looking for teachers who succeeded in top colleges, possess broad knowledge of their subjects, are highly articulate, and have a strong drive to work with urban children from disadvantaged families.

Pedagogy

A final component of the culture of American schooling is pedagogical faddism—the adherence to a constantly repackaged set of progressive notions that often are neither proven practicable and effective in the classroom nor based on science. Whether to inquiry learning, multiple intelligences, the disparagement of "facts" and "right answers," or to the insistence that writing skills are best fostered by withholding corrections, EMOs showed a surprising obeisance. As in district-run schools, teachers were often discouraged from lecturing in favor of small group or independent activities where students "discovered" knowledge. These activities proved exceptionally difficult to orchestrate so that real learning occurred, and much time was wasted that could have been applied to traditional instruction. As with other areas of practice, the new "no-excuses" CMOs have broken rank, unabashedly favoring whole-class, teacher-led, interactive instruction by engaging and demanding teachers.

The poor quality of much of what passes as education research has contributed to the challenges of entrepreneurial innovation. The absence of a strong evidence base has made consumers susceptible to the American public school ideology and its many dubious propositions, which the EMOs might otherwise have challenged more vigorously. For instance, the claim that an EMO's class size of twenty-eight or thirty is educationally unsound compared to a district's class size of twenty-two or twenty-five is not supported by rigorous empirical research, but education interests succeeded in persuading the public that this was true by invoking "research findings," so that EMOs either accepted it or chose to capitulate to it. Entrepreneurs who were not advised by experts in the education sciences accepted these claims unquestioningly; others just decided to fight other battles. To reject such propositions might be educationally sound *and* reduce costs, but it would clash with both the expectations of most parents and the beliefs of its educator workforce.

MOVING FORWARD

In surveying the broad landscape of entrepreneurship in education, one is struck by the seeming ease with which a large and growing number of postsecondary education companies penetrated what was once the nearly exclusive preserve of nonprofit and public institutions. At the other end of the industry, day-care entrepreneurs over the last decade have also built large, if not as profitable, national organizations.

The success of such entrepreneurs in building valuable companies stands in sharp contrast to the ongoing struggles of companies in the K–12 sector, where profitability, after more than a decade, has generally proven elusive. Vast differences in the regulatory environments of these sectors are the primary cause; postsecondary entrepreneurs can own and operate their own schools, which their students attend, thanks to public grants, loans, and guarantees, whereas K–12 entrepreneurs must settle for serving as mere consultants to charter school trustees who retain control over the school yet expect the companies to provide all the investment and shoulder all the risk.

But these fundamental differences in the legal and governance structures only partly explain the differences in business outcomes. K–12 operators, their schools concentrated in inner-city neighborhoods blighted by decades of poverty, took on one of the most intractable problems in American society—the education of the disadvantaged. The test results of the schools they ran were closely scrutinized, and expectations for immediate gains were unrealistic from the start. All the while they faced relentless opposition from the strongest organized interest, the teachers unions, which sought to discredit their purpose and block their progress in legislatures and the courts.

Yet K–12 education remains the largest business opportunity for education entrepreneurs and their investors, and the sector most in need of entrepreneurial transformation. A growing number of promising ventures are targeting discrete opportunities within the sector, using innovative products and services that have the potential to increase educational productivity. Holding public schools accountable for achievement results is creating a market for such products, whether to better assess students' progress toward year-end learning goals, collect and act on instructional data, or tap into technology to supplement or improve classroom teaching.

Meanwhile, the private nonprofit sector has taken the lead on school management, and its early history has much to teach future K–12 entrepreneurs. Not only did CMOs and school networks often devise ways to mitigate regulatory defects—most notably, governance problems—but they were bolder in challenging, whether directly or implicitly, the norms of the public school culture. EMO founders, by contrast, were remarkably acquiescent to that culture, even when it stood between them and productivity gains.

Policymakers should learn from the first decade of private education management and devise regulatory structures that support entrepreneurs and investors as they launch new for-profit schooling companies that compete with district-run schools. Privately managed public schools should have access to the same resources, in both operating and capital dollars, as district schools. Authorizers should award charters directly to management organizations wherever permissible. Accountability for school performance would be clarified, investment risk and control would be in the same hands, and the long-term stability that is essential for the implementation of any comprehensive school design would be assured. Private managers and their schools would be directly accountable through choice to parents and to state authorizers. Perhaps most significantly, we must devise ways to reduce barriers unrelated to performance so that entrepreneurs can focus their energies on producing impressive results and avoid the trimming and compromise engendered by the need to define political opposition.

Entrepreneurs should adopt a universal standard for reporting the longitudinal value-added achievement gains of their students and permit outside researchers to access achievement data in a fully transparent database. They should also boldly confront aspects of the K–12 establishment culture—localism, teacher quality, class size, pedagogy, and others—that impair their ability to post superior academic results and operate profitably.

CHAPTER 10

The Bias against Scale and Profit

John E. Chubb

Entrepreneurship is not new to public education. Schools spend $10 billion every year on textbooks, instructional programs, and educational software so diverse and abundant that they fill the convention floors of every national meeting of public educators. Schools spend another $5 billion annually on computer hardware, including innovations such as laptop carts that bring computer labs to every classroom and hand-held devices that put high-powered assessment at teachers' fingertips. As Newman and Wilson have discussed, school districts have long turned to the private sector for noninstructional services such as transportation, food service, and construction, but even here innovation is on the rise: consider the spate of new small high school facilities conceived by creative architects to realize a radically new approach to secondary education. In all of these areas, public education has served as a catalyst and consumer for ideas and entrepreneurship—for individuals, organizations, and businesses to inject change and improvement into public education, for the mutual benefit of educators, providers, and, ultimately, students.

But as common and indeed integral as entrepreneurship has been to public education, entrepreneurship has recently taken a radical and therefore controversial turn. Heretofore, the private sector—not-for-profit as well as for-profit—provided public education with essential products and services to *support* the schools' core mission. Now entrepreneurs are aiming not to support this mission but to carry it out themselves. Entrepreneurs are offering to provide public education directly, through charter schools, district contract schools, and state or federally inspired takeover schools. Entrepreneurs are also providing publicly funded tutoring services, traditionally an exclusive province of public schools.

Entrepreneurs have entered these spaces because public policy has provided encouragement to do so. Charter school legislation allows entities other than public school districts to run public schools, while state accountability systems often provide for chronically failing schools to be reconstituted under new management, such as a private provider. The landmark federal No Child Left Behind (NCLB) legislation, enacted in 2002, requires schools to be "restructured" after six years of failing to make adequate yearly progress (AYP) and lists private management as one of a small number of restructuring options. NCLB also authorizes free tutoring for low-income students in schools that fail to make AYP three years running, and provides that parents may select any state-approved tutor, including for-profit companies.

As McGuinn discusses in chapter 3, these legislative developments are part of larger movements in public education to bring more choice, competition, and accountability to the traditional system. Since the mid-1990s, the nation has moved swiftly to establish academic standards that all students must meet, standardized tests to measure achievement, and sanctions to enforce progress. At the same time, states and the federal government have become persuaded that schools and students will make more progress if the provision of education is not limited to traditional school districts but opened to other providers—teachers and principals, community groups, universities, and entrepreneurs. Policymakers have tried to give families the opportunity to choose among new providers and traditional schools, and to foster competition among all providers of public schooling.

The merits of these ideas—choice, competition, and accountability—have been the subject of analysis and debate for nearly two decades. Yet for all the ink that has been spilled over these reforms, very little has been written about one of the potentially key elements of all of them—what difference the entry of new entrepreneurs might make to public education.

What is it about entrepreneurs getting involved directly in the provision of education that is promising—or concerning? Entrepreneurs have been welcome supporting players in public education for a long time. Now that they are assuming leading roles and sometimes competing with traditional educators for those roles, should entrepreneurs be welcome still—or resisted? The answer is, we do not know. Opinions, clearly motivated by politics, abound. But the consequences of the new entrepreneurship have not been considered systematically.

BENEFITS, RISKS, AND CONTROVERSY

Entrepreneurs have the potential to introduce new factors into the public education equation. *Ideas:* Innovations that have not been possible or welcome within conventional public schools may be introduced by entrepreneurs. For example, the Knowledge Is Power Program (KIPP) has been able to bring dramatically higher expectations into middle schools by launching dozens of charter schools. *People:* Individuals who may have the energy, intelligence, and skills to help public schools may be more attracted to the work if they can join entrepreneurial organizations than if they must enlist in the traditional public education bureaucracy. Teach For America, most notably, draws thousands of students every year from America's best colleges and universities to teach in inner-city public schools—students who would rarely have pursued public school teaching otherwise. *Money:* Investors and philanthropists anxious to help public education but lacking a promising vehicle may be excited by new entrepreneurs to contribute. Consider the hundreds of millions of dollars investors have poured into education management organizations (EMOs) like Edison Schools, National Heritage, and Victory Schools, or charter management organizations (CMOs) such as Aspire or Amistad—dollars that would otherwise not have reached public schools.

These are not unambiguous benefits, to be sure. Bad ideas can certainly be introduced into public education by entrepreneurs, and the 10 percent of charter schools that fail are a glaring example. Ivy League graduates frequently fail as inner-city teachers, causing Teach For America to attract its fair share of critics. And, neither philanthropic nor pecuniary investments have provided clear educational or financial returns to investors. Is new money just being wasted, as some detractors would have it? Well, benefits usually come with risks, and the new educational entrepreneurship is no exception.

But these issues do not get to the heart of what is exciting—and unsettling—about the new entrepreneurship. Ideas, people, money: these are major byproducts of entrepreneurship. But they are not the driving forces of entrepreneurship, nor the elements of entrepreneurship that most distinguish it from public education as we know it. What is most important about the new entrepreneurship is that it brings to the very heart of public education—at least potentially—the twin engines that drive innovation, quality, and value in the private sector: profit and scale. Virtually all of the goods and services that Americans enjoy are produced by for-profit companies. A large percentage of those goods and services owe their various virtues to the large-scale organizations that produce them. Public education is distinctively not-for-profit and small scale, several large urban school systems notwithstanding. If the new entrepreneurship is allowed free rein, it will ultimately test a most important proposition: that profit and scale can bring the same kinds of benefits to public education that they bring to so many other services throughout the private sector.

The benefits of profit and scale, however, come with risks. And those risks have generated controversy. Will the pursuit of profits somehow compromise what private businesses are willing to do or spend to help children learn? Will private businesses try to avoid serving students who are difficult—and expensive—to educate? Will large-scale organizations, whether for-profit or not-for-profit (think of the Gates Foundation), become too distant from children and their families to serve them effectively? How will communities, taxpayers, and parents retain control over public education if big firms and organizations are doing the educating? Such questions have led policymakers to place limits on the roles of the new entrepreneurs, especially on the roles of for-profit and scale providers. Are these limits appropriate and prudent, or are they stifling the very forces that give entrepreneurship its greatest potential?

Perhaps the best way to answer this question is to look at the arena where the new entrepreneurship could make the greatest difference for public education: charter schooling. Here the United States has a vehicle for bringing new providers from the periphery and into the core of public education—teaching students and operating schools. Charter schools offer an opportunity for entrepreneurs to demonstrate everything that they might be able to bring to public education—new forms of school organization, curriculum, instruction, assessment, technology applications, and more. Charter schools compete with regular public schools, permitting competition between traditional approaches to education and the new entrepreneurship.

A COTTAGE INDUSTRY

Although not by conscious design, charter schools have become a cottage industry. Charter schools are small, serving fewer than two hundred students on average—about a third the size of the typical public school. Charter schools number over 3,600 nationwide, with concentrations of nearly a hundred or more schools in ten states.[1] But few of these sizable numbers have joined forces in larger entities to exploit economies of scale. No more than 15 percent of all charter schools are run or supported by management organizations, which work with multiple charter schools. Contrast this with regular public schools, where the average school is part of a system of six schools and a quarter of all schools are part of systems twice to many times that size.[2]

In the fifteen years since the first one was authorized, charter schools have shown a powerful tendency toward small size and total independence.

Is this a good thing? Curiously, the topic has received little serious attention. Advocates of charter schools have sometimes painted a picture of a proverbial "thousand flowers blooming." And charter schools were certainly intended to give rise to a range of innovative and alternative schools. But charter schools were also founded on the premises of the free market—choice for families and competition among providers generating a new and improved supply of public schools. No economic analysis ever suggested that the market would or should generate mostly small schools, operating independently and without economies of scale. The debates over charter schools—political and academic alike—never addressed the ideal organization of charter schools. Nobody ever argued that charter schools should become a cottage industry.

Why a Cottage Industry?

The cottage status of the charter industry is, nevertheless, not an accident. Charters are a cottage industry largely because opponents of charter schools want them to be. Since 1991, some forty states and the District of Columbia have authorized charter schools. Charter legislation has been fiercely debated, with opposition coming from the traditional public school world, concerned about the loss of students and revenue, and support coming from uneasy coalitions of business interests and community groups frustrated with the quality of regular public schools. Every charter law is a compromise. Few laws—fewer than ten, most would agree—give charter schools the opportunity to compete on a level playing field with traditional schools.[3] Opponents limit the funding for charters to less than the funding for regular public schools. They cap the number of charters that can operate statewide or in a district, and they are often able to give traditional public schools control over the granting of charters. These restrictions discourage the growth of charter schools to a substantial scale.[4]

But two additional limitations that have become nearly ubiquitous may best explain the scale of charter schooling. One is the ban on for-profit operators of charter schools. Charter opponents have long viewed private business as both an inappropriate participant in public education—except as a provider of books, computers, and the like—and a potential threat to traditional public schools. That opposition has successfully limited the role of for-profit companies in running charter schools. At most, three states permit for-profit companies to hold charters directly. Several states also prohibit for-profit companies from contracting with not-for-profit charter holders to provide comprehensive management services. Because for-profit entities generally pursue scale in seeking to maximize profits, the restrictions on for-profit companies reduce the potential for scale to emerge in individual charter schools and systems of charter schools.

Scale has also been limited by the widespread prohibition on charter holders of operating more than a single school under one charter. Few states explicitly allow charter holders to operate more than a single school. Even those that do often require each school to have its own board, though boards can occasionally share some members—a "daisy chain" of boards—to facilitate common policies and integrated operations. Most states, however, limit each charter to a single school, overseen by a unique board. Such governance requirements ensure that charters cannot become systems; they can only be individual schools. Again, opponents of charters, concerned about the proliferation of well-resourced systems of schools, prefer governance this way—and have successfully lobbied for it in most places. The argument is not that charters will perform best if their scale is limited. The argument is that charters should not threaten the traditional public school system.

Charter schools, then, are a cottage industry not because anyone thought they would do a better job educationally if they were organized this way, but due to political opposition and compromise. But does it matter? Would charter schools work better if they could benefit from the direct involvement of business or from economies of scale? More modestly, is there evidence that business involvement and scale operations are a detriment to charter schools, and deserving of the restrictions now on the books?

ECONOMIES OF SCALE

Although the term "cottage industry" is often used pejoratively to refer to an enterprise that is exceptionally fragmented and inefficient—though perhaps also quite entrepreneurial—there is nothing inherently wrong with small-scale organization. The appropriate scale of an organization depends on what the organization is trying to do. Five-star restaurants, for example, are almost always small, independent operations. The extraordinary quality found in such establishments depends largely on the individual chef, and gifted chefs do not scale. Grocery stores, by contrast, which also sell food, scale very nicely. Grocery stores with hundreds of sites can offer consumers far lower prices and far more choices than a single mom-and-pop grocery store, including a wide range of quality prepared foods—not unlike a respectable restaurant. National grocery chains have superior purchasing power to the independents, and they bring scale economies to all of their operations—

from the design of their stores, to the perfection of their operations, to the training and development of their staff.

Whether an enterprise should be small scale, as with five-star restaurants, or large scale, as with grocery stores, depends on many factors. Can the core competence of the enterprise be replicated through strong systems and processes? Do the marginal costs of producing more of the good or service generally decrease with larger and larger volumes? Is the mission of the organization to serve large numbers? *Private* enterprises regularly ask these questions and then try out their answers in the marketplace. If scale is beneficial, consumers flock to the larger enterprises, for their lower prices, their higher quality, their greater convenience—or whatever mix of benefits consumers value. If scale does not offer benefits that consumers value, smaller-scale enterprises prevail. Over the last century, consumers have clearly chosen large scale over small for a wide range of goods and services: food, clothing, finance, transportation, communication, and more. Yet small businesses remain an integral part of today's economy. The free market values enterprises large and small.

The Politics of Scale

What about schools? First and foremost, we do not have the benefit of the market to evaluate the ideal scale of schooling. Public schools are products not of market forces but of public policy. Public education is provided as a public good in the United States and in most countries. It is in the public interest to ensure that every child receive an education sufficient to prepare him or her to be a responsible citizen and a productive adult. Education is therefore provided freely and universally in most countries. As a public good, education can be provided in various ways, and countries do differ in this respect. Education can be provided exclusively through schools run by the government. It can also be provided by funding private, parochial, and other types of schools with tax dollars. Until very recently, all public education in the United States was provided through government-run schools.

The scale of public schooling in the United States has therefore been largely a matter of public policy. To be specific, state policy establishes the fiscal and educational requirements for local school districts, and district policy determines the size of schools. A century ago, public schooling was generally small scale. With the exception of major city school systems, public schooling was community based, every community having democratic control over its own schools. Some one hundred thousand school systems dotted the national landscape, many containing but a single school. One-room schoolhouses with a single teacher serving students at multiple grades were very common. The average public school system had barely two schools; the average school served a little more than two hundred students.

Over the last century, however, the scale of public schooling changed decisively. In the early 1900s, education authorities, from leading universities, the business community, and the governing elite, began calling for a more "scientific" organization of schools.[5] They wanted schools less influenced by the political prerogatives of amateur school boards, less dependent on the wiles of the individual classroom teacher, and more driven by planning, systems, and specialization. Students needed differentiated programs, teachers needed prescribed curricula and formal training, and schools needed the support of sophisticated professionals, including a superintendent and expert staff.[6]

To be organized scientifically, schools and school systems needed greater scale. Over the course of the twentieth century, school systems were consolidated, creating fewer than fifteen thousand systems from the original one hundred thousand. Schools grew, more than doubling to over five hundred students on average. High schools were especially affected, with most adopting the postwar "comprehensive" model providing students with programs tailored to their post–high school aspirations, whether vocational or collegiate.

The impact of all of this consolidation on school performance is an unsettled issue. The comprehensive high school has certainly come in for strong criticism in recent years for being too large and impersonal. The biggest school systems in America, serving mostly major cities, have long been criticized as being too politicized, too bureaucratized, and largely unsuccessful. The effects of district consolidation on rural education have not been clearly positive. One might say that while the question is unresolved, it is not clear that scale is an answer for what ails America's schools.[7]

Yet that would be jumping to a conclusion, for scale has been put to a very different kind of test in public education than in private enterprises. Scale has not been put to a market test; it has passed a political test. Schools and school systems are the scale that state and local politics, through time and compromise, have caused them to be. Schooling is not organized to maximize what consumers—be they students, families, or taxpayers—value. The closest we have to a market test of educational scale is private schools, which tend to be small and independent. But the private market is widely dispersed, serving only 10 percent of all students and only families with the ability to pay. There is no telling what scale public schooling might assume if market forces, driven by all families and students, determined its organization.

This is the crucial point: With charter schools, the nation has a potential vehicle for exploring the ideal scale for public schooling. The organization of public schooling heretofore has been determined entirely by politics. This is appropriate to a degree; public schools must ultimately be accountable to democratic authority. But politics need not be the only determinant of how education is organized and delivered. For education to remain the only important enterprise in American society for which we have so little idea how scale or alternative forms of organization might benefit its delivery is a high price to pay for democratic control. Charter schools could provide a test of how scale might or might not benefit education. But the test has been hampered by the limitations on scale imposed by charter laws—by politics.

The Potential of Scale

Consider the budget of a typical charter school with, say, two hundred students. Assume (see table 1) the school is funded with roughly the national average per-pupil revenue of $9,000, which gives the school total funding of $1.8 million. If the typical class size in the school is twenty, the school will need ten core teachers, plus another three teachers of noncore subjects (e.g., art, music, physical education) to provide the core teachers—and themselves—one or two planning periods per day. The school will inevitably serve special education students; if we assume that 12 percent of the students—the national average—require special education services, the school will need two special education teachers, each with a case load of twelve students. The total teaching staff therefore will number fifteen. If each is paid the national average salary of about $47,000 with typical benefits of 25 percent of base, each teacher costs approximately $60,000. Total cost of teaching staff: $900,000.

The school will require additional personnel. A principal will cost $100,000, including benefits. The school will almost certainly want a counselor—another $75,000. A part-time nurse is usually necessary—at least $25,000. If the school employs technology, it will want the hardware and software maintained—another $75,000. The front office needs student information recorded, reports produced, phones answered, and parents greeted: two administrative assistants, $100,000. Total "noninstructional" staff: $375,000. Total personnel costs for the small charter school: $1.275 million.

On the nonpersonnel side, the biggest cost is rent or mortgage. Students on average require at least one hundred square feet per pupil—and that would be tight by most new public school standards. Minimum school size then would be 20,000 square feet. A new facility would cost at least $2 million to construct, plus land, which could be assumed valued at 25 percent of construction costs, or $500,000. A $2.5 million new facility could be financed, but at rather high interest rates, say 10 percent, because charter schools are only authorized for five years at a time. Even an interest-only loan imposes a

$250,000 burden on the budget. Market rents would be in the same ballpark, based on replacement costs.

Students need books, equipment, and computers. The average cost of new durable curricula, equipment, and materials is $750 per student for grades K–8. The total cost of $150,000 can be spread over five years, for an annual cost of $30,000. A computer lab with server runs another $50,000, which also can be spread over five years, for a yearly hit of $10,000. Schools must be furnished with desks, chairs, bookcases, etc. Average cost for a school this size is $100,000, which amortized comes to $20,000 annually. Nondurable materials, like workbooks, paper, and art supplies, cost about $100 per student, or $20,000 per year. Instructional materials, furniture, and equipment total $80,000. Office supplies, photocopier rentals, and the like add another $20,000 per year to a typical small school. Total supply bill: $100,000.

Psychologists, speech pathologists, and other specialists required for special education services not provided by school staff demand that $25,000 be set aside for contracted services. Charter schools inevitably face legal fees, especially those associated with special education; $25,000 is a conservative estimate. Schools have utility bills, which for a 20,000-square-foot school could easily cost $50,000 per year. Maintenance, assuming one full-time custodian and night-time cleaning under contract to a school maintenance firm, costs at least $75,000. The total cost of contract services, legal, utilities, and maintenance: $175,000.

The total annual expenses of this typical charter are $1.8 million. This sum assumes that the school does not provide transportation or food. It also assumes it is not a high school, which would be even more expensive. What remains, if the school does a superb job of watching its expenses, is a surplus of $100,000. With this the school must do everything else necessary to meet state and federal academic standards, fulfill all other commitments of its charter, and compete successfully with traditional public schools. But what can a school do on its own for $100,000 to improve its performance? The answer is, not very much.

Teachers and principals need help with a range of issues vital to their success. How should a curriculum be constructed to maximize student success on the standards of a particular state? What should be done about the achievement of disadvantaged students who are not responding to published reading programs? How shall students be assessed on an ongoing basis? How should standardized test data be interpreted? How shall student management be handled? As students get older and the subjects more demanding, where do teachers turn for advice in the sciences, the branches of mathematics, and different fields of literature? What if managing data and instructional infor-

TABLE 1   Annual Budget of Typical Charter School

Revenue: 200 Students @ $9,000 per student	$1,800,000
Personnel Expenses (including benefits)	
Teachers: 15 @ $60,000 per	$900,000
Principal	$100,000
Counselor	$75,000
Nurse (part time)	$25,000
Technology Manager	$75,000
Administrative Assistants: 2 @ $50,000 per	$100,000
Total Personnel Expenses	$1,275,000
Nonpersonnel Expenses	
Rent or mortgage	$250,000
Furniture (amortized over five years)	$20,000
Durable books, materials, equipment (amortized over five years)	$30,000
Computers and lab technology (amortized over five years)	$10,000
Nondurable instructional supplies	$20,000
Office supplies, copier rental	$20,000
Contracted professional services (e.g., psychologist)	$25,000
Legal fees	$25,000
Utilities	$50,000
Maintenance	$75,000
Total Nonpersonnel Expenses	$525,000
Total Expenses	$1,800,000
Surplus	$100,000

mation requires technology; who is going to handle the necessary technology systems and their integration? If we want to assume that the teachers and other professionals in the schools will bring some of these skills with them, how do we assume that the school will recruit and hire the best education staff when great educators are very hard to find?

Addressing these questions, the school will find that its $100,000 surplus will not go very far. The school could hire a curriculum, instruction, and assessment specialist for the whole sum, hoping to find a brilliant jack of all trades. The school could send the entire staff to two professional meetings a year. The school could buy professional development and consulting, which might meet a need or two annually. The $100,000 surplus will not allow the school to do the research and develop the solutions and systems it needs to address the challenges it confronts. The school will be left to depend, much like schools a century ago, almost entirely on the wiles of its own staff.

But schools do not have to suffer for lack of crucial support services. If schools are banded together or are larger, economies of scale are possible. Larger schools are not proportionately expensive. Almost every cost except teachers declines on a per-student basis. The "surplus" of a five hundred–student school could easily be $500,000. More dramatically, the sum of the surpluses of multiple schools could fund a serious support organization, with the specialists necessary to meet key school instructional needs. A support organization paid a fee of $500,000 per five hundred–student school would be a $25 million operation if it served only fifty schools. That kind of scale is still small by the standards of corporate America, but it is great by the standards of public education. The average public school is part of a system of only six schools. Three-fourths of all public schools are served by systems with fewer than fifteen schools.[8] Even the larger school systems do not devote anything like $25 million to support services focused on curriculum, instruction, and assessment.

Comprehensive support organizations should be able to offer charter schools a range of education services at a much lower total price and a much higher quality level than schools would find if they tried to provide the services themselves or tried to purchase them individually from multiple vendors. Schools do not have the resources to develop serious expertise in any of the specialized areas of knowledge crucial to school success, nor the systems to ensure consistent and effective execution. Scale organizations do. And when scale organizations offer comprehensive services, they enjoy additional economies. Field staff can be trained to provide multiple forms of support to their schools. Training conferences can address a wide range of needs. Schools are therefore likely to find it more efficient to purchase support—assuming they need multiple forms of support—from comprehensive organizations than from specialized ones. Educational support organizations have traditionally been set up on a specialized basis, offering discrete services such as curriculum alignment, data analysis, student assessment, special education, classroom management, leadership development, and a long list of other training needs. With the advent of charter schools, however, the comprehensive model of service provision has become increasingly popular.

Charter schools and charter advocates are beginning to recognize the potential of comprehensive service providers—and scale. In California, a leading charter state with more than five hundred charter schools, serious organizations have sprouted up to support multiple charter schools. The NewSchools Venture Fund, an investment philanthropy capitalized with some $15 million, is funding the start-up of charter management organizations. These not-for-profit entities, which include Aspire Schools, Green Dot Schools, and KIPP, among others, aim to provide bundles of well-researched and highly developed educational services that charter schools could never provide themselves and could never buy effectively unbundled or a la carte. KIPP, for example, offers among other services an exceptional leadership-development program. Other philanthropies such as the Pisces Foundation (funded by the Fisher family, founders of Gap) and The Walton Family Foundation are funding the leading extant CMOs and cultivating new ones. These prominent philanthropies, like growing numbers of charter advocates, believe that charter schools will perform better if each school does not have to solve every problem on its own—if each school can benefit from scale educational services organizations.

The Benefits of For-Profit Scale Organizations

The CMO movement represents one form of scale organization—the not-for-profit form. But scale can obviously come from organizations with the same mission as CMOs but organized on a for-profit basis. For-profits have come to be known by the similar title of education management organizations. What might they add to the potential benefits of scale organizations?

In most cases, for-profit organizations have a natural tendency to push scale economies to their limit. As long as the mission of a for-profit organization is to provide its services as widely as possible—as in the case of a grocery chain, for example, and not a five-star restaurant—a for-profit organization wants to reach scale. With scale come operating efficiencies, additional revenue, and greater profits—in absolute terms and as a percentage of revenues. For-profit organizations seek to maximize profit, and thereby scale. But they don't do so without limits. In a proper market they must compete with other organizations for customers—a process that rewards quality and drives profit down. As consumers of for-profit services, charter schools would be the ultimate beneficiaries of a market for service providers. Schools would receive the best service that scale can offer and at the lowest price. If a for-profit operator tried to skimp on quality to increase profits, it would lose business to operators who did not reduce quality and kept the same price.

This all assumes, of course, a free market for for-profit charter support organizations—which does not fully exist.

For-profits have another potential advantage over not-for-profits. For-profits tend to have much greater access to the capital needed to achieve scale. Launching and building an organization requires investment or philanthropy. No business of any scale pays for its own operations from opening day. The advantage of for-profits is that they can raise capital in the private market, where vastly more funds are available than through philanthropy. Investors put money into for-profit organizations to help them get started, or to grow, or to develop the next great innovation because they hope to get a return on their investments. Donors put money in philanthropies because they want to help a cause, usually one that the market does not support, and donors, unlike investors, do not expect anything in return. Organizations that can promise investors a return on their money usually have a far easier time attracting funds than organizations looking for gifts.

For-profits, then, should have more motive and better means than not-for-profits to get to scale. But not-for-profits have their own advantages, particularly in the support of charter schools. Not-for-profits may be able to beat for-profits on price. The not-for-profit needs about 8 percent less revenue because it is not seeking to make money. The not-for-profit can also subsidize its services with philanthropy. For example, with generous philanthropic support, schools supported by KIPP have budgets that sometimes exceed per pupil public revenue. The schools pay KIPP, but KIPP tops off the paid services with offerings paid for by philanthropy. Not-for-profits also have advantages under current charter law: They can hold charters directly, while for-profits generally cannot.

The Evidence: Scaling Up

Although scale organizations, both for-profit and not-for-profit, have been limited by existing charter law, they have not been thwarted altogether. Over the nearly fifteen-year history of charter schools, scale organizations have accumulated enough of a track record to suggest what their contributions may ultimately be. Many organizations have been in existence since the mid-1990s. Organizations are working with charter schools in over half of the states that authorize charters. In 2004–05, roughly six hundred schools were supported by organizations that can be labeled EMOs or CMOs by virtue of their scale and the comprehensive services they provide charter schools. In a study including data through the 2004–05 school year, I examined their performance.[9] Several important patterns emerged.

Geographic coverage. There is a strong tendency among EMOs and CMOs not toward the national scope that sometimes concerns educators, but toward geographic concentration. Over half of the management organizations studied—eighteen out of thirty-two—work in only a single state. Only seven organizations work in more than five states. Why no rush toward national operations? Some of the not-for-profits, especially universities, have no mission to work beyond their local community. They might some day work in a significant number of local schools and develop true scale operations, but they would never work beyond their immediate borders. Another explanation is time. Most of these organizations have less than ten years experience offering comprehensive services; they may not have had time to expand beyond a state or two, though they will eventually. The truth of this is unknowable.

A final reason for geographic specialization may be the nature of public education itself. Controlled by the states, public education differs a great deal from state to state, as gauged by academic standards, high-stakes assessments, school law, program regulations, and school culture. Support organizations need to master the details of each state's education system, which takes major resources. An organization would seem more likely to grow to scale and succeed if it focused on a small number of states it could perform in exceedingly well. For the most part, management organizations have concentrated on certain geographic areas. This is probably a good thing for improving schools, since expertise matters.

Yet, some organizations have chosen to set up shop in many states. Seven CMOs or EMOs are working in seven or more states. Two organizations, Edison and KIPP, are in eighteen and sixteen states respectively. What can we say about the tendency to try to serve multiple states? It is clearly a tendency of for-profit firms. Six of the seven organizations working in seven or more states are trying to make a profit. Only one of the fourteen organizations operating in more than one state—KIPP—is a not-for-profit.[10] What the data unmistakably show is that while there is a preference among all organizations for geographic specialization, the for-profit firms have frequently chosen or been driven to expand their operations beyond single states. To be sure, KIPP provides evidence that a not-for-profit can approach national scope; it is second to Edison in state penetration. But KIPP notwithstanding, for-profits and not-for-profits seem to prefer somewhat different geographic playing fields. Indeed, the average for-profit is working in nearly twice as many states (4.08 vs. 2.67) as the average not-for-profit.

Growth rates. Another question about for-profits and not-for-profits is their relative ability to get to scale. We know the theoretical advantages and disadvantages of each, but what does actual experience suggest? First, EMOs and CMOs have been around for the same amount of time on average, both sectors with modal operations commencing in the mid 1990s. Despite the same amounts of time on the scene, for-profit firms have achieved more scale than not-for-profit organizations. The average EMO works with 20.1 schools; the average CMO works with less than half that number, or 10.1 schools. The average EMO serves 9,232 students; the average CMO serves less than a quarter of that, or 2,051 students. EMOs are reaching the scale of midsize public school systems, while CMOs are currently more like small public school systems. The EMOs also include several firms that have reached the scale of moderate to major school systems. It is too early to tell what scale for-profit and not-for-profit support organizations will ultimately reach, because none has been operating long enough to have established a growth plateau. But it seems safe to say that for-profits are moving toward achieving scale more rapidly than not-for profits.

School size. The average sizes of schools supported by for-profits and not-for-profits do not show great differences. The average school served by for-profits enrolls 373 students; the average school served by not-for-profits enrolls 300. This difference is in the expected direction. Larger schools are more efficient and generate more of a surplus than smaller schools. Because they lack philanthropic support, for-profit firms have more need to work with schools that can pay their own way. And several of the larger EMOs tend to work in significantly bigger schools than the EMO average, which serves as many as five hundred to seven hundred students.[11] But these numbers are not all that large when compared to the national average of all public schools, which approaches six hundred.

The more striking deviations from sector averages are two prominent CMOs, KIPP and Aspire. Their schools are absolutely tiny, averaging only 91 and 86 students respectively. KIPP and Aspire want them this way. They build their schools slowly but surely, grade by grade, over a period of years, and reach capacities well below national averages. This approach requires substantial external support, as tiny schools are not efficient. But with philanthropy, it has certainly proven workable: KIPP in particular is second only to Edison in the number of states served and fifth in the number of schools operated. KIPP served fewer than four thousand students in 2004–05, but its footprint was all over the nation. Time will tell whether the gradual rollout of small schools, with philanthropic support, is a viable strategy for helping large numbers of charter schools succeed.

Students served. Both sectors tend to serve students who are more diverse and more disadvantaged than public school students generally. Most obviously, African Americans make up 35 percent of the for-profit enrollment and 53 percent of the not-for-profit enrollment, versus a national average enrollment for African Americans of 13 percent. Poverty has a similar tendency. Students eligible for free or reduced-price lunch represent 54 percent of the for-profit enrollment and 71 percent of the not-for-profit enrollment; the national public school average is only 38 percent. The not-for-profit sector is enrolling a more diverse and needier group of students than the for-profits on average, but the differences between the sectors are considerably smaller than the differences between schools run by management organizations and public schools generally.

It is also the case that some of the largest providers in each sector tend disproportionately to serve students who have traditionally not been served well by public schools. Among CMOs, KIPP students are 82 percent eligible for free or reduced-price lunch; Green Dot students are 85 percent eligible; Universal students are 81 percent eligible. Among EMOs, Charter Schools USA students are 100 percent eligible; Victory students are 89 percent eligible; Edison students are 69 percent eligible. Critics of business participation in charter schooling have argued that firms might exploit the poor, who are the most desperate for alternatives to their traditional public schools and least able to evaluate the quality of what a new provider might offer. But the data do not show such a pattern. For-profits, like not-for-profits, serve needier students than the national average by far. This indicates that both groups are reaching the students that charter schools were supposed to reach. But there is no evidence that for-profits are somehow trying to capture a niche of the poorest of the poor. Not-for-profits on average serve the students who are most in need.

Student achievement. Any policy that stands to affect the operation of charter schools ought to be evaluated on how it affects students. Unfortunately, policies concerning scale organizations have historically been based on the arguments of political opponents and not on hard evidence of effects. Arguing that scale organizations will weaken public control over charter schools and that for-profit organizations will put profits ahead of students, opponents have persuaded policymakers that large entities will behave in ways that are likely to compromise educational quality. Yet, it is also clear that economies of scale may permit an organization supporting many schools to provide more and better services than any school could secure on its own.

The key questions, then, are really empirical: How do scale organizations actually behave and what difference do they make for students?

To begin, the data indicate that management organizations have not generally committed the sins that opponents feared they would commit—going national, driving up school size, serving the easy-to-serve. The data also indicate that for-profits are achieving scale more rapidly than not-for-profits. If it turns out that scale organizations are helping charter schools, understanding how organizations get to scale may prove helpful. But the decisive data for making good policy regarding charter schools are data on student achievement.

Under NCLB, all states are required to administer reading and math assessments to all students in grades 3–8 and to one grade of high school every year beginning in 2005–06. Before that, states were permitted to test fewer grade levels each year, but all states had begun annual testing during the 1990s. State tests measured achievement of academic standards and gauged student progress toward "proficiency"—providing increasingly common metrics for analyzing student achievement. State standards and tests differ in difficulty, to be sure, but they bring a singular perspective to assessment: annual measurement of achievement in reading and math at consecutive grade levels calibrated against an objective standard of proficiency.

The study summarized here considers average reading and math scores on state tests measured as gains against proficiency. The focus is on gains rather than on absolute scores because we want to know whether the charter school or its manager is adding any value. If a school in its first year of operation posts a score of, say, 50 percent proficient, there is no easy way to evaluate the score. If the students were very bright upon arrival, a 50 percent success rate would be terrible. If the students had historically been very weak, a 50 percent success rate would be very good. To know whether the school is making a difference for students, the simplest test is to see if the school helps more kids achieve proficiency each year. Comparing scores from year to year—calculating gains—gives a rough measure of the effect that the school is having on student achievement.

Gains alone do not tell the whole story, however. For many reasons—from student experience with tests to adjustments in state proficiency standards to the state release of information to help schools prepare for tests—scores can move upward without students really learning anything more. If a school, for example, posted a five-percentage-point gain in its proficiency score but every school in the state did the same thing, the gain would hardly be an indicator that the school was doing anything special. Accordingly, it is useful to look not only at gains, but gains relative to average gains by the whole state. The study included data for the period 2002–05 and examined one-, two-, and three-year gains.

What do the data reveal? First, charter schools operated by all managers are making academic gains against their state proficiency standards. Over a three-year span, many of the gains are in double digits, which is close to what NCLB demands in lower-performing schools. No manager has test scores showing no progress. Given all of the failure in public education, it is striking that not a single manager is failing on average to make academic progress.

But how impressive is the progress? All of the states in which the managers work have also been making gains. Typical gains are two percentage points a year, though higher in some states. When the average state gains are subtracted from the respective manager gains, the manger gains are less impressive than in their absolute form. In relative terms, the results are generally positive. With only a few exceptions, managers are posting one-, two-, and three-year gains greater than state averages. Since the positive findings are not only evident in one-year data, it is clear that the relative gains are not short-term flukes. The long-term data are pretty clear evidence that management organizations can help charter schools perform better than state norms.

Does it matter whether the management organization is for-profit or not-for-profit? The evidence on this point is insufficient to draw any firm conclusions. The data on the not-for-profits in particular are rather scant because few of those organizations have had sufficient history with their schools under current state testing regimes. Yet, the evidence hardly points to any concerns with for-profits, relative to the not-for-profits, on student achievement. The average gains for the for-profit managers relative to state gains are virtually indistinguishable over the three years examined.

Generally speaking, the academic track records of for-profits and not-for-profits are similar to each other and superior to state averages. The concern that for-profit managers would trade short-term profits for achievement gains is not supported by the data. The idea that not-for-profits will be academically superior scale operators is also not supported. Both types of scale operators are making gains in excess of state averages. Scale seems to benefit student achievement.

The New Entrepreneurship: Implications

The basic idea behind public policies facilitating a new entrepreneurship in education is to try to bring the benefits of the private sector to the very heart of education—to teaching students and running schools. After years of watching the private sector successfully support public education, policymakers have recently encouraged the private sector to offer education directly. Policymakers have also been cautious. They recognize that public education is not a private good and that regulation of providers and markets is necessary. But policymaking is not an analytical process, it is political, which means that regulations may or may not ensure a role for entrepreneurship that is in the interests of students, families, taxpayers—or what might be called the public interest.

The experience of charter schools is a frustrating one for entrepreneurship, and for the improvement of public education. Charter schools in America have become a cottage industry, with thousands of small schools struggling alone in far too many cases to develop the wherewithal to function effectively. Yet, their ability to join forces in larger entities that could support them effectively and efficiently is limited by policies that discourage or prevent organizations of scale—for-profit and not-for-profit—from running multiple charters.

The evidence suggests that the biases of charter laws against scale and profit are inappropriate if the purpose of charter school law is to promote quality alternatives to traditional public schools. Charter schools that are part of for-profit or not-for-profit scale organizations are improving student achievement at rates consistently in excess of state averages. These schools also show no evidence of the sins that policymakers are afraid scale operators will commit: failing to serve disadvantaged or minority students, building schools that are overly large and therefore impersonal, or turning schooling into a province of national behemoths.

But inappropriate though the restrictions on charter entrepreneurship may be, they are part of the reality that drives public education more generally. Education policy is a political product shaped by a range of interests, including most prominently those of the education establishment, which is threatened by the new entrepreneurship. If the evidence adduced here is correct, charter policy ought to be relaxed to allow charter holders, who are subject to strict performance accountability to authorizers, to operate multiple schools. Policy should also permit for-profit authorizers to hold charters directly. With these restrictions lifted, the United States would have the opportunity to learn a truly fundamental lesson: what difference choice, competition, and entrepreneurship can make for public education. Without such basic changes in charter law, however, the new entrepreneurship will never get to the heart of what ails public education.

Educational Entrepreneurs Redux

Larry Cuban

> *Entrepreneurs are change agents who combine business acumen with education expertise to create lasting change. They are both mavericks and institution builders. They excel at both identifying opportunities and building solutions. By their very nature, entrepreneurs are problem solvers focused on results—they won't survive if they don't deliver the outcomes they promise. Because of this, entrepreneurs will act with a sense of urgency that is critical if we are to buck the inertia of the current public school system and give today's students the educational opportunities they need to succeed in life.*
>
> —NewSchools Venture Fund[1]

In this chapter, I make four claims regarding the promise of educational entrepreneurship.[2] These claims are anchored in my work on educational reform, my reading of the literature by entrepreneurs, conversations with some of them, visits to start-up schools, and my five decades of experience in urban schools as an administrator, researcher, and teacher. For "educational entrepreneur" I use the definition offered in the prospectus for this volume of "risk-taking behavior intended to enhance productivity or offer new services in a manner that yields lasting change."[3]

I recognize that this definition covers many individuals, schools, intermediary organizations, and hybrids of all of these. Neither I (nor anyone else) can squeeze all entrepreneurs, past and present, into a one-size-fits-all category (see the chapters by Maranto and Maranto or by Williams). Yet to make these claims I have had to compress the rich variation that exists among entrepreneurial ventures into brief statements. As is true of my fellow authors, I can be accused of being reductionist, since there are obvious exceptions. Even with the exceptions, however, I believe that I am on safe ground in making these statements because they are rooted in a solid body of direct experience, my analysis of earlier school reforms, and the work of other researchers. This is no apology; I want readers to know what I am doing.

Trained as a historian, I will dip into the treasure trove of entrepreneurial ventures between the early 1900s and the present to offer some cautions to current entrepreneurs. Although historians are notorious for pouring cold water on those who parade their favorite reforms by recalling similar circumstances when so-called agents of change stumbled over themselves, I prefer not to be seen as a spoiler. I do understand, however, why those readers who are true believers about contemporary entrepreneurs being unlike any previous generation may consider skipping this chapter.

FOUR ASSERTIONS

1. Since the early twentieth century, educational entrepreneurs have made major changes in U.S. public school goals, governance, organization, and curriculum.
2. With all of these major changes in schools, educational entrepreneurs, past or present, have seldom altered substantially or permanently classroom regularities and low-income students' academic achievement.
3. Current educational entrepreneurs' efforts toward making radical changes in the governance and preparation of school leaders have ended up preserving present organizational structures and school practices in urban schools.
4. Current educational entrepreneurs' commitment to a narrow economic purpose for schooling has seriously neglected civic and social purposes that have historically integrated schools into community life.

After elaborating each of these claims, I offer some reflections and advice, informed by the history of school reform and the checkered past of entrepreneurial work in schools.

Assertion #1: Since the early twentieth century, educational entrepreneurs have made major changes in U.S. public school goals, governance, organization, and curriculum.

Over a hundred years ago, a cohort of entrepreneurs similar to the present generation in its use of business approaches to improve school efficiency succeeded in reinventing a system that established the very conditions that the current generation of adventurous risk-takers has labeled a serious problem in need of innovative solutions. How did this cadre of reformers of a century ago transform schools?[4]

In the years prior to World War I, the United States competed with world powers Great Britain and Germany. Both nations had staked out global markets that American manufacturers envied. The shortage of skilled workers and the breakdown of the traditional apprenticeship system in the United States turned industrialists' attention to public schools as the solution for the growing lack of machinists, welders, electricians, and engineers to meet employer needs in a changing economy.

Top industrial leaders became convinced that Germany had surged ahead of the United States because its government had recognized the connection between national economic growth and school-based vocational training. Driven by both altruism and self-interest, U.S. manufacturers and business, civic, and philanthropic leaders soon plunged into the emerging progressive movement aimed at transforming U.S. schools.

Progressive reformers drawn from the ranks of corporate, civic, religious, and union leaders argued that schools should do more than teach literacy. From Jane Addams, who founded a Chicago settlement house to serve poor immigrants, to Indiana school superintendent William Wirt, who invented the Platoon School for educating students from working-class families in arts, crafts, and academics, to social reformers Maria Montessori, who created schools for very young orphans, and Jacob Riis, the muckraking photographer and writer who revealed the human face of city slum dwellers, progressives worked to have schools reduce poverty, Americanize immigrant families and, of course, turn out graduates who not only prized labor and had skills readily usable in industries, but also contributed to their communities.[5]

These reformers scolded schools for hewing to their traditional academic curriculum and rigid teaching practices, ignoring the workplace, and persisting in inefficient governance while doing nothing about the obvious problems of urban slums, crime, and turning immigrants into Americans. Reformers started private kindergartens and afterschool programs for immigrant parents, hired doctors and dentists to care for children, built playgrounds next to schools, and provided food for hungry children. A few founded private schools to do what public schools couldn't or wouldn't do. J. P. Morgan, for example, endowed the New York Trades School with $500,000 at the turn of the twentieth century.[6]

By the first decade of the twentieth century, an extraordinary reform coalition included top corporate leaders, social workers, labor leaders, university presidents, academics, superintendents, and a sprinkling of teachers. They generally agreed that the problem was a tradition-bound wasteful system of schooling, vulnerable to corrupt local politicians, and staffed by mediocre teachers teaching a curriculum dreadfully out of touch with a rapidly changing economy and society. They believed in a science of education that could yield solutions to problems, particularly inefficient school organization, operation, and governance. Many progressive educators borrowed industrial leaders' language and managerial techniques and grasped the mantle of expert and the title of educational engineer. They had, in the words of one progressive, the "largeness of vision, and the courage to do and dare." Today, we call them entrepreneurs.[7]

In the decades bracketing World War I, progressive reformers reorganized urban district governance by establishing small, nonpartisan, corporate-like school boards. They invented junior high schools and created large comprehensive high schools. In these secondary schools, they installed newly developed vocational curricula that offered occupational training. They used scientifically constructed ability tests to place students in classes with those of similar aptitude. They designed tests and compiled test scores that compared students from one district to another so that taxpayers would know that their monies were being spent efficiently. They created bureaucracies to oversee all of these school activities. In short, these early twentieth century educational entrepreneurs copied a successful business model and used findings from the latest scientific studies to change public school goals, governance, organization, staffing, and curricula. Many of those changes lasted for decades; others still exist.

I suspect that many contemporary entrepreneurs (and readers) would challenge the link I make between progressives a century ago and today's risk-takers, even if I pointed out that both generations have been part of broad, politically powerful coalitions that are pressing schools to prepare youth for a changing economy. Or that both generations have used business practices in making changes in districts and schools. Or that both generations were deeply committed to expanding equal educational opportunity, albeit in different ways. I am sure that these facts would not dissolve doubts about comparing current with past entrepreneurs.

And that is because dissimilarities are too obvious to even suggest that both generations are alike. Yet as a historian, I know that establishment educators a century ago saw those bewhiskered progressives as uninformed outsiders, professors and businessmen who seldom stepped inside schools—just as many contemporary veteran educators see philanthropists funding jean-clad charter school entrepreneurs today. That kind of historical imagining is a tough leap to make for so many entrepreneurs who cherish the conceit that what they are doing has not been done before. For those readers who find it hard to picture that an earlier generation was as entrepreneurial as this one, consider each generation's commitment to transforming schools and view of equal educational opportunity.

A century ago, progressive entrepreneurs were concerned about poverty and slums eroding educational hopes. The solution that generation sought was to expand educational opportunity for immigrants and the poor beyond the age of twelve. Anyone could graduate high school—allowing for the racial, socioeconomic, and cultural segregation of those decades—if they completed the newly invented junior high school and entered high school, where job-linked vocational education had been added to the curriculum for those who wanted practical work after graduation. Progressives were willing to risk voters' anger in raising taxes and inventing new ways of making schools, curricula, and teachers available. They were willing to build institutions that sorted out those who would go on to college from those who would enter the labor market—all in the name of equal educational opportunity.[8]

Modern entrepreneurs reject the earlier generation's access and sorting definition of equal educational opportunity in favor of one that sees all students as capable of entering higher education. Entrepreneurs redesign recalcitrant urban middle schools into K–8 organizations and big urban high schools into small ones to get high test scores, low dropout rates, and admission to college. In language that condemns the "soft bigotry of low expectations," KIPP Academies, Teach For America (TFA), New Leaders for New Schools (NLNS), charter management organizations, and small high school pioneers such as Ted Sizer and Deborah Meier see opening college doors to poor and minority children as a virtual civil rights struggle. Thus, both generations of entrepreneurs were committed to equality of educational opportunity but defined it differently.[9]

Suppose my arguments still failed to persuade skeptical readers that these two generations are entrepreneurial. If so, indulge me and assume—for purposes of analysis—that I did convince doubters that in redefining equal educational opportunity and applying business ideology and practices to public schools in its goals, governance, organization, and curriculum, both generations sought to transform public schools. One area, however, is conspicuously absent from the list of successes: the classroom. Hence, another similarity between the two generations of educational entrepreneurs has been limited success in altering historic patterns in teaching practice and low-income students' performance.

Assertion #2: With all of these major changes in schools, educational entrepreneurs, past or present, have seldom altered substantially or permanently classroom regularities and low-income students' academic achievement.

Because the overall aim of most school reform past and present has been to produce literate and engaged students who could live and work in communities, entrepreneurs have sought the best policy levers to reach that goal. At the beginning of the twentieth century, progressives thought that large centralized school districts with elected school boards efficiently providing well-equipped buildings, ample textbooks, modern curriculum, and qualified staff would yield both economies of scale and desired student outcomes. Since then, reformers have turned to other levers such as decentralization, community control, site-based management, whole-school reform, systemic change, professional preparation, new technologies, more parental choice, and competition among schools to improve student achievement and behavior.

But the vital irreplaceable link between more choice and competition among schools, between whole-school reform and districtwide change, between efficient districts, superb textbooks, and a demanding curriculum is what happens daily between teachers and students. And that relationship, that slippery policy lever of change, has been tough to grasp, much less pull. The classroom connection is the Holy Grail of student learning, academic achievement, and moral behavior—everything else is secondary.

So it comes as a mild surprise that with so many successes to their credit, both generations of entrepreneurs have had a hard time substantially and permanently altering classroom regularities and students' outcomes.

By classroom regularities, I mean common patterns in classroom practices such as teachers putting desks in rows, lecturing, asking questions, and assigning homework. I mean students using textbooks, doing worksheets at their desks, answering teacher questions, and taking tests.

Over a century ago, for example, progressive entrepreneurs set out to transform these traditional teacher-centered practices by replacing rows of bolted-down desks with movable ones and dumping lectures, recitations, and worksheets for teacher-guided discussions, small-group work, and project-based curricula. These pedagogical entrepreneurs believed that their ways of teaching would produce well-rounded human beings who would be critical thinkers and independent decisionmakers as they worked and lived in their communities. How successful were they?

By the 1950s, progressive reformers had adopted progressive curriculum and textbooks. They added new words and concepts to their vocabulary. Except for kindergarten and the primary grades, however, only a few progressive classroom practices seeped into the upper grades of elementary schools and even less at the high school level except for vocational education, where students built real-life projects and worked outside of school. Yes, bolted-down desks disappeared. Teachers became less authoritarian and more informal in dress and language. Grouping students for instruction did occur. But traditional practices of teachers lecturing, using textbooks, assigning homework, doing worksheets in class, and students taking notes for tests continued to dominate classrooms, leaving unanswered the key question of whether this intended progressive pedagogy ever yielded the desired student outcomes.[10]

Turn now to the current entrepreneurs seeking to create high-performing urban schools in which the achievement gap between white and minority students shrinks and all students attend college. If anything, this generation side-steps debates over pedagogy and focuses on outcomes, assuming pragmatically that varied classroom practices can produce the desired academic achievement and behaviors. The majority of contemporary entrepreneurs will try any approach that seems to work with children.

Most evident in Teach For America, New Leaders for New Schools, and nearly all charter schools is a pragmatic indifference to any particular pedagogy or curricula. One promoter of charter schools echoed this pragmatic view of teaching practices: "In every way, shape and form, in cities around the country, charter schools are serving students' varied learning styles and customizing services for students who need something different than what is offered. You can't educate all of them well in the same manner."[11]

Some entrepreneurs, however, are adamant on the kind of instruction they want. KIPP schools, for example, use direct instruction, choral chants, and prescribed rewards and penalties for behavior—including many of the classroom regularities mentioned above. Others, such as Boston's Mission Hill School, New York City's Urban Academy, San Diego's High Tech High, The Big Picture Company, and Minnesota's New Country School, champion the active learning progressives sought decades ago. And even others like the Edison Schools and Aspire charter schools prize blended pedagogies. Both Edison and Aspire are committed to project-based learning and direct instruction, cooperative groups and worksheets, plus instructional practices tailored to children's differences.[12]

The agnostic view of pedagogy can be seen in Teach For America, an organization founded in 1990 that has recruited about twelve thousand teachers for two-year tours of duty in urban districts. While terms like "rigorous" and "engaging teaching" are often used in TFA's five-week summer training, specifying how novices should teach is of less importance than individual teachers getting a grip on classroom discipline and their students doing well on state and district tests.

I do not wish to enter the debates over TFA effectiveness in reducing the test-score gap, or attrition rates as compared to regular teacher education graduates. My point is that TFA has no particular name-brand pedagogy to inculcate in their trainees. If particular classroom practices can maintain classroom control and spur students who have large deficits in academic skills to achieve, great. But if not, chuck those practices and try others.

When I add up all of the differences among entrepreneurs on which forms of pedagogy work best with low-income minority students in producing high academic achievement, I found only the practical principle that a broad repertoire of teaching approaches is needed for students with varied abilities. While there are particular charter schools and small high schools mentioned above that are committed to traditional, progressive, or hybrids of both practices in classrooms, they are a minority of start-up schools. Unlike the earlier generation of educational entrepreneurs who approached classrooms with a progressive ideology, a no-nonsense belief in doing what seems to work—not dogma—drives current approaches to teaching and learning.

With a range of parental choices among programs, a one-school-at-a-time strategy, and an eclectic approach to instructional practice, current educational entrepreneurs will hardly alter pedagogy in most public schools, considering the small fraction of public school students in for-profit schools, charters, alternative principal-training programs, and TFA classrooms. No transformation is about to occur, but one unanticipated consequence for classroom teaching is predictable.

In the face of state and federal penalties for low test performance, entrepreneurial pragmatism toward pedagogy for largely poor and minority students gives way to preserving familiar classroom regularities, whether or not they find these practices worthwhile. Unintended to be sure, traditional practices of controlling classroom behavior and habitual teacher-directed patterns of classroom instruction easily trump other pedagogies. Even after scores of studies comparing students' achievement test scores in voucher and nonvoucher schools, charter and regular public schools, TFA and non-TFA classrooms, the answer to the question of whether time-honored pedagogies—the classroom regularities described above—will raise or lower the academic achievement of those students who have historically been ill served by public school is, to put it bluntly, we don't know.[13]

Thus, this generation of educational entrepreneurs is caught in a trap. They practice pedagogical agnosticism—a sensible approach in light of the sheer diversity among students in motivation, interests, and performance—yet these entrepreneurs have unintentionally preserved a form of teacher-centered pedagogy that dominated schooling for nearly a century and may or may not bear any causal link to achievement. They have done so by accepting without question existing organizational structures and school regularities that undercut the deep and lasting institutional changes in urban districts they so frequently call for. Worse yet, the trap that entrepreneurs have backed into strengthens the status quo they seek to overturn—the point of my third claim.

Assertion #3: Current educational entrepreneurs' efforts toward making radical changes in the governance and preparation of school leaders have ended up preserving present organizational structures and school practices in urban schools.

A century ago, entrepreneurs radically changed school governance and staffing by copying corporate boards of directors and creating institutions that would produce professional administrators and teachers. They transformed corrupt, politically partisan school boards into ones where elected civic and business leaders determined policy. They created university preparation programs for teachers out of what were then called "normal" schools and, for administrators, invented higher education courses for principals and superintendents, which soon became state-approved university programs certifying practitioners. And it is these systems of school governance and state-accredited university preparation programs that the present generation of entrepreneurs has challenged.

Current entrepreneurs welcome mayoral control of schools in various cities and lobby for broad chartering authority being given to state and local officials. They believe that basic changes in district and school governance, in concert with recruiting strong teachers and administrators, will unload inept managers and remove bureaucratic barriers that prevent academic improvement more effectively than efforts to work closely with parents and community institutions. Such a belief, of course, springs from the policy assumption that urban school districts have created their own mess and only a radical overhaul of governance and staffing will erase the test score gap.

Moreover, entrepreneurs have celebrated district-based preparation programs such as Teach For America, New Leaders for New Schools, and similar alternative ventures. Entrepreneurs see state licensing procedures and university programs as inflexibly rule bound, and out of touch with talented, energetic, and idealistic teacher candidates and the gritty realities of urban schools. Alternative credentialing taps pools of smart young college graduates and mid-career principal candidates who want to help children but also want to avoid the course-taking and extended time periods university study requires. Teach For America, the New York City Teaching Fellows, and New Leaders for New Schools attract such novices to work in hard-to-staff urban schools.

As someone who has had extensive experience in school-based licensing programs in the 1960s and 1970s and spent nine years in the most bureaucratic of urban systems—the D.C. schools—I endorse some of the rigorous alternative programs undertaken by the present generation. Nonetheless, I see a few issues that gnaw at the heels of innovators and just won't go away. Consider leadership.

Anyone reading the literature published by contemporary educational entrepreneurs cannot avoid such phrases as "teacher leaders" (TFA), "change agents" (NewSchools Venture Fund), "passionate and results-focused individuals" (NLNS), and "dynamic entrepreneurs and risk-takers who challenge the status quo to lead urban school systems" (The Broad Foundation). One is bombarded with happy visions of peppy young teacher leaders replacing tired, ineffective staff, assertive change agents swapping places with pedestrian principals, and charismatic CEOs taking over from hapless superintendents. The words entrepreneurs use become another trap they stumble into.[14]

The problem is that the rhetoric of individual gallant leaders and change agents is ahistorical, antiorganizational, and narrowly individualistic. In the early 1960s, for example, federally funded district programs trained returned Peace Corps volunteers to teach in slum schools. These programs used similar inflated rhetoric and even the same phrases to describe those novices and their supposed achievements. Contemporary entrepreneurs have ignored these programs' strengths (e.g., innovative alternative schools, strong supervision while learning to teach) and significant flaws (e.g., high attrition, few innovations lasted) and the limited successes of those teachers who did spend a few years in classrooms.[15]

Similarly, the historical record of school-based management since the early 1970s has offered many lessons about teacher decisionmaking that go unnoted by the present generation of reformers. For example, were urban teachers to be school leaders they would have to make decisions about textbooks, school curriculum, standards for student behavior, tracking plans, professional development, and other schoolwide matters. However, most teachers in urban schools do not decide these matters now. "Teacher leader" is an empty phrase in nearly all urban schools, save for a few small high schools, certain whole-school reform projects, and particular charter schools (see below).[16]

Here is the point. The popular business-inspired rhetoric and covert message that idealistic and energetic young teachers and principals get is that the system, its bureaucracy, and its leaders are the enemy, the source of all problems—except in those supposedly entrepreneurial-friendly districts such as New York City, Philadelphia, Chicago, and San Diego, and isolated islands of innovation elsewhere. In less-friendly districts, as a top official at New Leaders for New Schools said, "You do what you need to do to get the job done, then apologize to the district later." So individual teachers and principals have to be mavericks tough enough to fight the system on behalf of their students.[17]

This macho message—underscored by the metaphor of a war and a vocabulary of trenches, fighting faceless bureaucratic enemies, and guerilla warfare over district office rules—is embedded in the rhetoric of so many urban school entrepreneurs. These top-gun notions of heroic teacher and principal leadership are as common as metal detector gates in urban high schools. Such metaphors and vivid language reinforces a highly individualistic image of teachers and principals as leaders who seldom ask such tough questions as why schools are organized by age and grade and in what ways schools are connected to the community. Such shallow analysis invites incremental and faddish changes. Even worse, cowboy notions of personal autonomy undermine collaboration with veteran educators within schools, across schools, and between schools and district offices—all essential for sustaining reform.

There are, of course, other forms of school leadership that reside in adults and youth, teachers and parents collectively working together. Some charters, whole-school reforms, and independent entrepreneurs such as EdVisions teacher-run New Country School (in Minnesota), Camino Nuevo Charter Academy (in Los Angeles), Mission Hill (in Boston), and the Comer schools have connected with parents, reorganized the age-graded school through teacher and principal joint action, or done both. Other schools in Newark, Chicago, Los Angeles, Oakland, and Austin, Texas, organized their parents and community to deal with neighborhood and family issues (e.g., crime, tardiness, and absence from school) and boosted student achievement.[18]

In these schools, the leadership on display went far beyond recruiting individual heroes. In these entrepreneurial ventures, the assumption is that schools cannot do the work of school improvement alone; collective adult action inside and outside the school is essential for students to perform well academically. Such schools, however, are at the periphery, not the center, of current entrepreneurial thinking about leadership of charters, for-profit ventures, and recruiting of teachers and principals.

Many educational entrepreneurs continue to frame failing urban schools in terms of ineffective teachers, inept principals, and rigid district bureaucracies. The solution is to import young blood to cure the wretched system. The ahistorical, individualistic, and antiorganization message diverts attention from doing anything about traditional school structures, specifically, the commonplace age-graded school, which is the basic organizational building block of U.S. schooling.

The age-graded school (e.g., K–5, K–8, 6–8, 9–12), a mid-nineteenth century innovation imported from Prussia by educational reformers like Horace Mann and Henry Barnard—entrepreneurs of their day—was eventually institutionalized by the early 1900s. Since then it has become the unquestioned mainstay of school organization in the twenty-first century. Today, most taxpayers and voters have gone to kindergarten at age five, learned cursive writing in the third grade, studied Egyptian mummies in the sixth grade, took algebra in the ninth grade, and then exited from twelfth grade with a diploma.[19]

Overlooking the age-graded school's ordinariness is one blind spot of today's entrepreneurs. The age-graded school, to be brief, created a "grammar of schooling," organizational arrangements that touched teachers and students daily and that Americans have come to take for granted. It divides teachers into separate classrooms called "grades" and prescribes a curriculum carved up into 36-week chunks for each grade. Teachers and students cover each chunk, assuming that all children will move through the 36 weeks uniformly to be annually promoted. And, yes, those traditional classroom patterns of teaching practice mentioned above—what I call regularities—are intimately connected to the age-graded school.[20]

Americans have come to expect that six year olds will learn to read in the first grade, students will take U.S. History in the tenth or eleventh, and parents will receive report cards with letter grades signaling how their son or daughter has performed each semester. Schools that lack these arrangements, according to most parents and voters, are not "real schools." These institutional structures have efficiently processed millions of students over the past century, sorted out achievers from nonachievers, and now graduate nearly three-quarters of those entering high school—except in urban high schools where the percentages are much lower.

The age-graded school is also the institution that isolates teachers from one another, perpetuates teacher-centered pedagogy, and prevents a large fraction of students from achieving academically. It is also the institution that continually frustrates contemporary entrepreneurs who have wired schools, bought computers, and drum their fingers waiting for teachers to seamlessly integrate new technologies into daily lessons. It is also the institution that aggravates reformers seeking to convert large comprehensive high schools into smaller ones. This form of school organization has become the one best system for schooling the young. It is the sea in which teachers, students, principals, and parents swim, yet most entrepreneurs have seldom questioned this one-size-fits-all organization. Why?

Certainly, dominant social beliefs of parents and educators about a "real" school (i.e., learn to read in first grade, receive report cards, get promoted) and external constraints (e.g., college admissions, standardized tests, No Child Left Behind) have narrowed considerably entrepreneurial options to transform schools. For example, if a charter school applicant proposes a new school, the chances of receiving official approval and parental acceptance increase if it is structured as a familiar age-graded one. Surely there are start-up schools that reject age-graded structures, such as cyber-schools and particular community schools, but they are outliers.[21]

External pressures such as standards-based testing, college entrance requirements, and No Child Left Behind mandates requiring testing in third through eighth grade also strengthen the age-graded structure. These external demands constrict innovative impulses to only those that fit self-contained classrooms, coverage of the standardized curriculum, use of approved textbooks, and bringing children up to speed in thirty-six weeks.

What is the connection between the cowboy style of leadership, pervasive social beliefs about "real" school, and external pressures and the preservation of the age-graded school structure? Start-up schools using public funds may begin with lots of enthusiasm behind them, but sustaining the momentum while locating or building a facility, budgeting funds, recruiting staff, and seeing that curriculum and classroom instruction occurs as planned is no gentle stroll in the park, even for those schools that survive infancy. No surprise, then, that many entrepreneurs cobble a school together by hiring energetic but novice principals and lively but inexperienced teachers, and then give them plenty of autonomy while praying that both will stay long enough to get the school to work well. Little time and energy are left for anyone to consider why persistent classroom and school regularities shove these well-intentioned principals and teachers into making so many charter schools look like the traditional school down the block.[22]

The unintended (and ironical) consequence of earnest calls for radical changes in school governance bureaucracy and preparation of school leaders is to preserve the age-graded school and freeze the classroom practices that so many entrepreneurs want to alter. Also often lost in the entrepreneurial rhetoric of radical school change is any examination of the unrelenting focus on the economic purpose of schooling, while broader goals of the tax-supported public schools that historically have connected schools to the community are ignored.

Assertion #4: Current educational entrepreneurs' commitment to a narrow economic purpose for schooling has seriously neglected civic and social purposes that have historically integrated schools into community life.

The distilled message that business and civic leaders (including entrepreneurs) repeat endlessly to the nation's parents, educators, and students goes like this:

> We are entering the Information Age. It is a time of change equivalent to the shift from an agricultural to an industrial society. The global economy is deregulated and bringing freedom, democracy, and technological marvels to the rest of the world. But if Americans want to enjoy it, they will have to compete against six billion people out there, most of whom will work for a lot less money per hour.
>
> This economic revolution raises the bar for what skills and knowledge Americans will need to enter a labor market where every year new jobs are created and old jobs disappear. Advanced math and science knowledge plus hard skills such as problem-solving, reasoning, and communication now supplemented by soft social skills of working in small groups, taking initiative, and flexible decisionmaking begin in elementary school, get increasingly rigorous in high school, and now require a college degree. What Americans earn will depend upon what they learn.[23]

The essence of the message appears on public service ads in buses that warn youth to stay in school, in newspaper editorials, and is repeated by the nation's leaders—President George W. Bush called No Child Left Behind a "jobs bill." Both pervasive and unchallenged, the message is anchored in oft-quoted statistics of lifetime earnings linked to getting diplomas and advanced degrees. That going to college is an escalator to individual financial security and national economic growth is a widely shared belief.[24]

Questioning the dominant entrepreneurial rhetoric about the inexorable focus on economic ends of schooling, particularly when it is wrapped in expanding equal opportunity for low-income minorities, is hard because most Americans are predisposed to agree with this business-inspired language. Even were there more skeptics of this rhetoric, talk about civic engagement, community-building, reducing inequalities, and other purposes for urban public schools beyond the economic rationale sounds wimpy and out of touch with the realities facing the nation. When any analysis diverges from test scores, percentages of graduates going to college, and the importance of paper credentials, or even raises doubts about these indicators as useful ways to flag good schools, the argument and evidence are dismissed as politically liberal, softheaded, and impractical. So, readers, if you can—resist the impulse.

Facts contradicting the prevailing belief are often denied. Consider, for example, that only 30 percent of all occupations require a college degree, or that while developing human capital—more schooling—is important, economic growth depends far more on national policies (fiscal, monetary, regulatory, environmental), business practices, new technologies, and shifts in cultural norms around work and leisure.[25]

So within this unchallenged belief system of the private and public rewards of schooling, educational entrepreneurs press urban students to take rigorous academic subjects, perform well on tests, and go to college. The single-minded pursuit of economic benefits for both the individual and the nation freezes in amber the age-graded school and traditional teacher-centered practices into a narrow, pinched vision of a good school, thereby rejecting alternative versions of good schools. There are exceptions to this trend. Some charter elementary schools have character-building curricula, and some small high schools have service learning and advisory programs that give youth individual opportunities to serve communities and develop close bonds with adults.[26]

Many entrepreneurs would reject my claim and argue that all of these goals, including preparation for occupations, are not mutually exclusive. For example, those affiliated with KIPP schools, SEED (a Washington, D.C., public boarding school), High Tech High, and particular Edison and Aspire schools—to cite a few—can argue (and do) that they achieve these non–labor market goals. Yet anyone who has spent substantial time in schools can easily note the difference among classrooms and schools that give priority to goals of civic engagement, character, social justice, and building communities. In such schools, literacy is advanced and tests display solid gains in achievement, yet they differ palpably in school culture and practice. However, these schools face steady pressure from district and state authorities to raise test scores even further and have their students college ready, thereby pushing civic-minded entrepreneurs and district officials to either reduce efforts toward achieving these goals or abandon them. In the face of these unrelenting strains, they still meet those demands and persist in achieving other social and political goals. Consider community schools.[27]

Newark (N.J.) Quitman Street Community School has an extended day program and a full-service medical clinic, a Comer whole-school reform model that puts parents and teachers together to work for school improvement, and an afterschool parent program offering GED and computer classes. The neighborhood, initially skeptical of a community school, has embraced the services offered, and both parents and residents are involved in school activities. Quitman Street Community School is still a largely poor minority school, but through principal, teacher, and parent participation in the academic and social life of the school, the school plays an important role in strengthening both families and neighborhood.[28]

Schools as builders of community and civic engagement can be seen in the Industrial Areas Foundation in Texas creating the Alliance Schools, in Chicago's Logan Square Neighborhood Association, and in Los Angeles's Pueblo Nueva Development, where parents and community organizers joined teachers and principal to improve the neighborhood school, eventually starting a charter school.

Aimed at increasing equality of opportunity and reducing social injustice while improving academic achievement, these schools offer competing versions to the leading entrepreneurial model of a good school narrowly focused on preparing students for college and then the labor market. The constricted economic purpose driving the prevailing entrepreneurial vision is like an educational Gresham's Law, crowding out rival purposes even if historical evidence shows that such schools as described above can achieve strong literacy while pursuing purposes that build communities, reduce inequalities among students, invite democratic practices, and shape character within students.

SUMMARY

I made four claims about the growth and spread of educational entrepreneurs in the past decade. First, the phenomenon is not new. Since the early twentieth century, different generations of entrepreneurs have pursued similar ideologies in classrooms, schools, districts, states, and the nation. Inside and outside schools, there have been risk-takers who bet they could make a difference in children's lives.

Second, those entrepreneurs have altered the face of schooling in U.S. public schools. Goals, governance, organization, and curriculum have changed often and continue to change. Much less change has occurred in those teacher-centered practices established in classrooms since the late nineteenth century. While changes in classroom practices have occurred, progressive entrepreneurs were hardly the innovators they had hoped to be in the early twentieth century. The current generation, largely free of any ideological embrace of pedagogy—except for those few committed to particular practices—and pressed by frequent teacher turnover, harsh working conditions in urban schools, and accountability and testing rules, have drifted into the default pedagogy of traditional teacher-centered practices.

Third, even with radical calls for fundamental changes in governance and deregulated teacher and administrator preparation programs, an uncritical acceptance of the dominant form of school organization—the age-graded school—has ended up preserving the very structures that entrepreneurs have sought to overturn. In taking for granted the age-graded school, slipping into the default teacher-centered pedagogy, and uncritically accepting the goal of preparing workers, most educational entrepreneurs have reinforced status quo structures, practices, and a goal that undermines their desired transformation of schools.

The single-minded quest for occupational preparation and going to college has blinded most entrepreneurs to broader school goals of building children's character, communities, and civic participation that the mid-nineteenth-century entrepreneurial founders of public schools fought for and a small fraction of risk-takers acknowledge today.

SOME THOUGHTS FOR THIS GENERATION OF ENTREPRENEURS

As a historian of school reform, I have heard and read promoters' exaggerated claims of change over the past half-century, so I have been unpersuaded by educational entrepreneurs' flights of rhetoric. I have been, however, engaged by their ingenuity, commitment, and energy to improve urban schools. Inventiveness and dedication are admirable qualities. Were both to be attached to an energetic willingness to examine existing organizational structures, consider hybrid pedagogies, and question popular social beliefs about the purposes of schooling, this generation of educational entrepreneurs might well leave a deeper bootprint on the ground than the one they are leaving now.

How might they do that? Entrepreneurial pragmatism is a signal strength that furthers the agenda of urban school reform. Practical and realistic ideas borrowed from the military, business, medicine, philanthropy, private schools, and, yes, veteran educators applied to urban governance, organization, curricula, and classroom pedagogy is sensible, given the difficulties of reducing the achievement gap between minority and white students. Agnosticism toward pedagogies that work in urban classrooms, for example, is a decided plus in breaking away from the tired debates between progressives and traditionalists over the best way to teach, while recognizing that student differences demand a diverse portfolio of classroom approaches to learning. An openness to try different ways of solving school and classroom problems remains a defining feature of educational entrepreneurs and should be cultivated.

Yet as appealing as this pragmatic sensibility is toward pedagogy, the decided drift toward teacher-centered instruction under state and federal testing pressure and unexamined acceptance of the age-graded school runs counter to the entrepreneurial rhetoric of transformation and radical change. Reconciling the two requires at the least an open recognition of the tough choices entrepreneurs face in improving public schools.

Historically, fundamental changes in public schools have occurred as a result of social and political movements in the larger society that spilled over schools. Early twentieth-century progressives, the civil rights movement in the 1950s and 1960s, and the business-inspired surge of standards-based curriculum, testing, and accountability between the 1980s and the present all began outside of the schools. For the past quarter-century, business, civic, union, and foundation leaders formed political coalitions that lobbied successfully for state and federal intervention to improve schools. Educators seldom led but later joined these efforts. Without these external interventions, many of the deep and lasting changes within schools, from vocational education to the comprehensive high school to desegregation to accountability for student outcomes, would not have occurred. However, this is not the case with the present generation of entrepreneurs who largely work within urban schools.

While strong business and governmental pressure for standards-based reform has opened up schools to entrepreneurs, particularly in the past decade, with strong accountability legislation, most risk-takers have ended up working within urban systems providing new teachers and principals, establishing and operating charter schools, and offering services and products from tutoring to software to online instruction. As a result, entrepreneurs have learned to cooperate with district and school authorities at some level to achieve their goals. In short, today's entrepreneurs, unlike an earlier generation, are not in the business of fundamental or radical systemic reform but in the mundane practice of making incremental changes within resilient organizations to achieve their ends. They hope these small-bore changes will accumulate into larger improvements that eventually lead to students' higher test scores. For example, a top official for New Leaders for

New Schools reported that with urban superintendents he has negotiated changes in key personnel policies to place NLNS-trained principals. Constant haggling over rules with district officials and unions to make changes that permit more daily flexibility is part of the terrain that entrepreneurs inhabit. It is worthy, hard work that needs long-term commitments of seven to ten years from entrepreneurs.[29]

Thus, continued talk about radical change in schools may get foundations and venture capitalists to part with their money, but it is out of sync with the grinding small victories and defeats that entrepreneurs face daily in big-city districts. In California, for example, foundation-funded small high schools have to abide by the University of California admission regulations, district accountability requirements, and No Child Left Behind mandates. Securing waivers or bending requirements in just one of these areas is a victory. So exaggerated rhetoric about entrepreneurs transforming schools and making radical changes is false advertising. After all, the age-graded school, the basic structure of public schooling, remains untouched by entrepreneurial actions. Over time, then, rhetorical over-promising increases educator cynicism and saps entrepreneurial energy from the daily slog that marks incremental change within urban school systems. Abandoning flashy rhetoric for realistic language about making significant incremental changes and making longer time commitments to students and schools is a choice that entrepreneurs need to make.

Another tough choice is to reach beyond the familiar design of a college prep urban elementary or secondary school and seek other kinds of good schools. Many urban charters, magnets, for-profits, and small high schools are works in progress toward the ideal of a private preparatory school. Only a handful of entrepreneurs have either copied other models (e.g., community-based school, democratic school) or invented entirely new ones. Reading and math literacy come in all sorts of combinations and can be bent to community development, democratic practices, and social justice. Moreover, there are many ways to integrate literacy and achieve satisfactory test scores in schools that are organized differently than the age-graded model. Some have been mentioned above. Few entrepreneurs risk inventing new ways of organizing schools and wrapping civic, economic, technological, and community literacy into nontraditional schools without sacrificing academic achievement. Humility and imagination are not unfriendly to risk-taking. Yet the range of entrepreneurial inventions that I see in districts forms narrow rather than broad innovations. That is unfortunate for both children and the nation.

These thoughts and suggestions play to the strengths of entrepreneurial spirit so visible and vibrant in improving urban schools. For a larger footprint to be left, however, much less pseudo-radical rhetoric needs to be heard, there must be less copying of safe college prep models for urban schools, and more aggressive action in accumulating significant incremental changes may well make a more permanent mark in the soil.

CHAPTER 12

Politics, Policy, and the Promise of Entrepreneurship

Frederick M. Hess

For all the excitable prose that business books devote to entrepreneurs and their triumphs, the truth is that entrepreneurship is a headache. It demands that we take risks. It ensures that some children and families will endure bouts of subpar schooling or poor service, and that some schools or providers will be shuttered at inconvenient times. It presumes that even smart, thoughtful, well-trained experts cannot anticipate needs, develop solutions, and ensure progress in an orderly fashion. Is it really worth the hassle? In fact, the hassle is largely an illusion. Every day, our nation's schools fail millions of children and inadequately serve tens of millions more. If forced to compete on performance, many schools and districts might well find themselves out of business. Much of the "hassle" of entrepreneurship, then, is that it makes transparent the mediocrity and failure we can otherwise ignore.

Ultimately, entrepreneurship is a bet on the power of imaginative, creative, and talented people. The secret of successful entrepreneurial sectors— whether journalism in the late nineteenth century, automobile manufacturing in the early twentieth century, or high tech in recent decades—has always been their ability to summon energy and talent. Bold new opportunities attract and inspire talented, motivated risk-seekers in a way that professional hierarchies—much less public bureaucracies—do not. An entrepreneurial system encourages and allows these individuals to build large-scale organizations to deliver the benefits of their handiwork. None of this should be taken to romanticize entrepreneurship or imply that it's easy to devise useful enterprises. Most proposed ideas are flawed or pedestrian, and most would-be entrepreneurs are ill equipped for the task. I am, however, suggesting that opening the door to entrepreneurship is valuable in its own right, without illusions as to what lies beyond. The entrepreneurial promise lies not only in its capacity to unearth a Henry Ford, Fred Smith, Michael Dell, Bill Gates, or Ted Turner, but also in its ability to improve the quality of life for tens or hundreds of millions by encouraging these pioneers to build new organizations that make high-quality, affordable automobiles, parcel delivery, computers, software, and news available to all.

Today, programs like Teach For America (TFA), The New Teacher Project (TNTP), and New Leaders for New Schools are enjoying unparalleled success recruiting well-educated, highly motivated individuals to enter public schooling. Organizations like the Sedona Charter School, the EdVision cooperatives in Minnesota, Edison Schools, and the Aspire Public Schools are attracting and retaining educators who might otherwise depart public education for more hospitable environs. These ventures are placing large bets on people with great energy, creativity, and entrepreneurial habits of mind—the kind of people who historically have found public bureaucracies, such as school districts, a stifling place to work. Philanthropic givers and private investors are scrutinizing these individuals and their handiwork and are supplying the most promising with the resources to expand and build upon their successes.

The assumption that this entrepreneurial process will improve education is not uncontroversial. It is contested by professional educators and education scholars who believe that the entrepreneurial premise is counterproductive and misguided. These critics hold that the potential benefits of entrepreneurial activity are outweighed by its attendant risks and pale beside the advantages of coordinated efforts to improve the current system of educators, training, and resources. In this volume, several authors offer thoughtful, critical appraisals rooted in history, organizational analysis, and social science. Larry Cuban argues that educational entrepreneurs are repeating the mistakes of a generation of earlier reformers, Henry Levin that entrepreneurship has encountered insuperable obstacles, and Alex Molnar that educational management companies have failed to produce profits or results.

There are various ways to marry a faith in professional authority with a call for entrepreneurship. For instance, entrepreneurial ventures frequently consult with professional authorities or employ second strategies devised by recognized experts. The larger truth, however, is that the two perspectives are rooted in fundamentally distinct worldviews. One is skeptical of bureaucratic processes, the capacity of formal structures to support creative problem-solving, the value of conventional expertise, and consensus; the other places its trust in educational authorities and their corpus of knowledge.

In surveying this dispute, those inclined to endorse the entrepreneurial perspective are compelled to acknowledge the mixed record of educational entrepreneurship to date. In chapter 7, Bob and April Maranto highlight a further dilemma: The most effective new educational ventures may be those most limited in their capacity to grow rapidly. In the end, those who embrace the entrepreneurial presumption must do so with their eyes wide open to its costs, challenges, and track record.

AVOIDING INNOVATION FOR INNOVATION'S SAKE

For decades, a ceaseless tide of innovation has swamped schooling. It has rolled out and in and out again, with little attention to implementing new proposals or ensuring that schools and school systems are serious about them. A body of research, including my own volume *Spinning Wheels*, has critiqued the endless reform initiatives that sweep education.[1] Are the kinds of entrepreneurial efforts examined here simply more of the same?

In short, the answer is "no." The "spinning-wheels" problem is caused not by innovation per se, but by the failure to embed innovations in organizations characterized by intense fidelity to the change or to couple them with meaningful consequences for outcomes. While entrepreneurs can engage in faddism, they have strong incentives to instead focus on controlling costs and delivering results. In fact, some of today's most prominent ventures, like National Heritage Academies and the KIPP Academies, are resolutely "old school" in their program design, emphasizing features like high expectations, respect, and discipline. The cycle of entrepreneurial "creative destruction" is fundamentally different from the political cycle of reform and leadership change that has long characterized so many major school districts.

Historically, the spinning-wheels dilemma has been driven by the constant pressure on district officials to adopt promising reforms in order to reassure their communities that things are getting better. In organizations peopled by autonomous teachers and led by officials unable to compel cooperation, implementation tends to be half-baked and its results disappointing. As Larry Cuban has wryly noted in an earlier work, "Policymakers and others who set out to overhaul schools encounter a fundamental paradox: teachers and principals who block changes sought by reformers are supposedly the problem, yet these very same educators . . . are the people who connect with more than fifty million children daily and do the essential work of schooling."[2]

Successful entrepreneurs sidestep Cuban's paradox by building organizations populated by team members and staff committed to the innovation in question. The ability to build coherent cultures that foster commitment and trust is a critical determinant of entrepreneurial success. Sumantra Ghoshal and Christopher Bartlett have explained, "On the organizational trapeze, individuals will take the entrepreneurial leap only if they believe there will be a strong and supportive pair of hands at the other end to catch them."[3] The absence of such hands goes a long way in explaining the plight of so many conventional school reforms.

To maintain focus and cultural integrity, entrepreneurs need enough freedom from strictures that they are able to grow without having to wrestle a resistant bureaucracy. In education, to date these conditions have rarely been met, especially when it comes to the "intrapreneurs" described by Joe Williams in chapter 6. Forced to struggle against existing rules and within hostile or indifferent organizations, they have typically been unable to effect sustained change.

Ultimately, for entrepreneurs to matter, their efforts must be anchored in coherent organizations committed to a clear vision (though that vision will likely evolve). In that light, Steven Wilson's finding that educational management organizations have compromised designs in the face of political resistance is telling. Whether educational entrepreneurs are able or willing to build organizations that resist the temptations of trendiness remains an open question.

REJECTING A NEW "ONE BEST SYSTEM"

Since the 1974 publication of education historian David Tyack's seminal *The One Best System*, much education debate has proceeded from the premise that the factory-inspired urban school systems need to be redesigned.[4] Much of the furor has centered on efforts to uncover or design the "best practices" that could provide the template for a new, improved model of schooling. In many ways, the struggle has been to replace the twentieth-century "one best system" with one redesigned for the twenty-first century.

The entrepreneurial presumption rejects that aim. It dictates not that we determine what a good school "should" look like in 2040, but that we develop a flexible system that welcomes talent, focuses on results, rewards success, removes failures, and doesn't stifle the emergence of new and better solutions. This requires recognizing the critical difference between loving the process of entrepreneurship and loving the winners and "best practices" that have emerged thus far. Because today's winners are by definition the best of the "old way," seeking to enshrine today's best practices in statutes, regulations, or policies can serve to impede new providers and hinder the next generation of problem-solvers. For instance, Harvard business professor Clay Christensen, author of *The Innovator's Dilemma*, has pointed out that revolutionary change is typically wrought by "disruptive" innovations that result in products that are worse—but also cheaper, simpler, or more convenient— than the status quo. Stepping back from overbuilt models permits producers to revisit basic assumptions and build a new product on a new platform. Frequently, improvements in quality are not initially apparent, only coming later.[5] Efforts to construct a new "best system" or institute new "best practices" will hamper the search for new efficiencies and deny the possibility of disruptive innovation.

Rather than trying to identify the "best" models for schooling or school governance, reformers should promote measures that identify, reward, and disseminate effective models, while holding the door open for others to improve upon current practice. There are five essential principles in designing such a system.

First, the system must be dynamic, agile, and responsive to the challenges presented by a changing world. This requires the dissolution of familiar monopolies and a movement toward systems that are flexible and that do not erect exhausting barriers in the way of new providers. A dynamic system demands new knowledge, produced by rigorous models of research and development and supported by public and private capital markets. This "R&D" model has worked well in areas like medicine and technology, where products and services we deemed state-of-the-art in 1986 are now regarded as hopelessly antiquated.

Second, the system should strive to attract and retain teachers and leaders who are committed to and rewarded for excellence. Whereas today's school systems too often favor seniority, obedience, and uniformity, we should work toward a culture of meritocracy and promote organizations in which school leaders have the responsibilities, opportunities, and tools for effective leadership. The training pipeline for educators should be rethought accordingly, so as to reduce the emphasis on formal certification while focusing on selecting quality candidates and adding discernible value.

Third, education funding should be configured to support new ventures and foster creative problem-solving. Today's static funding systems discourage the emergence of cost-effective niche providers and the search for new efficiencies. State and federal regulations require nearly every district to provide similar bundles of services, while districts rarely move to strategically exploit the opportunity to hire specialized providers to improve efficiency when it comes to services like human resources, special education, facilities, or remedial instruction. Meanwhile, the absence of rewards for educators who identify cost savings mean there is little impetus to seek cheaper solutions. Education finance should be configured to accommodate nonprofit and for-profit providers of niche instructional services, enable all providers to compete for capital and operational funds, and reward cost-effective performance.

Fourth, a healthy entrepreneurial environment is highly transparent, with readily available performance data that compel providers to compete on cost and quality, while expanding access to the data needed to make sensible decisions. Student performance data should not only be readily accessible, but they must be usable by policymakers, educators, entrepreneurs, and parents. The various inputs into the system—money, people, and other resources—must be tracked and aligned toward services, permitting the cost-effectiveness of competing providers to be gauged in various ways. Parents must have the tools and information that permit them to make good choices and communicate their needs, and they must be encouraged to take responsibility for doing so.

Finally, the system must move from one designed around inputs and institutional needs to one designed around individuals and student outcomes. This requires recognizing students' varying needs and conceding that education is not a one-size-fits-all enterprise. For instance, restricting the ability of "cyber" charter schools to receive state per-pupil funding has benefits, but it also constricts the scope of entrepreneurial activity. NCLB-style accountability, premised on tracking average student performance across conventionally organized grades similarly limits entrepreneurial problem-solvers. In each case, statutes and rules create new obstacles for nontraditional providers, without regard to their promise or performance. Opportunities for customization should be encouraged and coupled with a valid and reliable set of competency-based achievement measures that can be utilized outside of conventional, grade-based environments.

The challenge is to design a system in which, twenty-five years from now, tomorrow's entrepreneurs are able to focus on solving problems rather than struggling to dismantle the roadblocks that we have unwittingly strewn in their path. Tomorrow's breakthroughs are likely to come from thinkers who are now in junior high school or in playpens, who are coming of age amid technologies and habits of mind that will always be an acquired taste for those born in 1940, 1960, or 1970. The goal ought not be to erect the "best" educational system, with new "twenty-first century" buildings and policies that will serve as a monument a half century from now, but one that is flexible and capable of growing and evolving with those it exists to serve.

To that end, it is worth noting William Bygrave and Andrew Zacharakis's preface to the *Portable MBA in Entrepreneurship*, which reminds us, "Entrepreneurship is what America does best. No other advanced industrial nation comes close. U.S. entrepreneurial companies created the personal computer, biotechnology, fast food, and overnight package delivery industries; transformed the retailing industry; overthrew AT&T's telecommunications monopoly; revitalized the steel industry . . . and the list goes on."[6] It would be remarkable if we could say something similar about K–12 schooling. Fortunately, education reformers have a profound tradition of American entrepreneurship to draw upon, even if it has historically stopped at the schoolhouse door. The challenge, for those persuaded by the entrepreneurial presumption, is to throw open that door.

CREATING AN ENTREPRENEURIAL ENVIRONMENT

Broadly speaking, there are three sets of obstacles blocking the door: barriers to the entry of new providers, a lack of venture capital, and a pinched human capital pipeline. The discussion below is not intended to be exhaustive, but to sketch out the shapes of potential reforms and some relevant considerations. While iconic management thinker Jim Collins has appropriately noted that it's possible to build a "pocket of greatness" even in a brutal environment, the failure to address these challenges will significantly limit the scope and success of educational entrepreneurship. [7]

Barriers to Entry

Barriers to entry are the laws, rules, and practices that make it harder or more costly to launch a new venture. Such barriers include everything from regulations hindering the opening of a charter school to textbook approval systems so onerous that only the largest publishers are able to compete. Three barriers worth particular attention are those measures that inhibit the opening of new schools, impose restraints on how new providers can operate, and put obstacles in the path of niche providers.

New charter schools face enormous difficulties in gaining access to venture capital and facilities. Because current practices presume that local districts will own and manage school buildings, it is frequently difficult for entrepreneurs to secure appropriate facilities.[8] New entrants find themselves forced to plead with their ostensible competition or scramble to make do with nontraditional facilities. State efforts have been modest to help providers finance facilities or otherwise circumvent local opposition. The Education Commission of the States has reported, in its most recent report on the question, that just eight states and the District of Columbia provide start-up or planning grants for charter schools and that barely half of all states with charter school laws provide any support for facilities at all.[9] Meanwhile, state regulations and codes help to make school facilities more expensive than is probably sensible. For instance, Joe Williams has reported previously that in New York, school construction codes are "so stifling that they invariably ended up inflating the final building price." A New York City school commission reported in 2002 that it cost about forty-percent more per square foot for a city school than to build local office towers, luxury condos, or hospitals.[10]

One step that might significantly level the playing field for entrepreneurs would be to take control of school facilities away from local school districts and hand it over to a special-purpose entity. One promising approach is to support the development of independent real estate trusts in which the construction and management of school facilities is separated from the traditional school district. Such an arrangement could ensure that the facilities will be professionally managed while enabling alternative providers to compete more readily for suitable facilities.[11] Similarly, state efforts to treat new providers more equably when it comes to capital expenditures would better allow new entrants to stand or fall on their merits.

Formal barriers to entry may be highly visible, but they are coupled with less obvious obstacles that can prove equally burdensome. For instance, state financing systems consistently fund charter schools at lower levels than traditional district schools, while roughly two-thirds of charter laws formally cap the number of charter schools allowed. The ability of new entrants to recruit talent and build their teams is also hindered by regulations on staffing. The Education Commission of the States has reported that, of the thirty-nine states with charter school laws in 2003, seventeen required full certification for all charter school teachers and another thirteen mandated that at least a portion of charter school teachers be certified. Only nine states allowed charter schools to freely hire unlicensed teachers or to apply for a waiver to do so.[12]

Finally, the No Child Left Behind Act's (NCLB) supplemental services provision—which makes available federal dollars to support private tutoring—has created new chances for purposive innovation, creating opportunities for new entrants and for existing organizations to expand. Particularly hostile to entrepreneurship, however, is the NCLB requirement that would-be supplemental service providers negotiate terms of access with the local school district—which is itself free to operate as a competing provider. As others have noted, this requirement is akin to requiring a new bookstore to obtain permission from the local Barnes & Noble before setting up shop. One potential remedy would be to provide for an independent agency, whether state-run or independent, to negotiate terms and conditions with all aspiring supplemental service providers—including school districts. Another way to address the conflict of interest is to allow school districts to monitor and supervise providers but not to serve as a supplemental service provider.

As a general rule, making schools more hospitable to entrepreneurship requires improving the clarity and rigor of outcome expectations, as appropriate, while reducing regulations and practices that impede charter schools, supplemental service providers, and other new ventures. In the case of reading programs, instructional technology, texts, and other products and services, this recommends giving schools and districts increased freedom to make purchases—and then holding them responsible for student outcomes. In today's environment of accountability, this shift is feasible to a degree inconceivable even a decade ago.

Venture Capital

New ventures can neither launch nor grow without money. There are three general sources that can be tapped to support educational start-ups: profit-seeking investors, nonprofits, and public agencies. Historically, in most sectors, profit-seeking dollars have driven the entrepreneurial engine. Most of that money is provided either by venture capital funds or by wealthy individuals. In K–12 schooling, on the other hand, aside from a burst of interest in educational management organizations during the mid-1990s, such investment has been rare.

The K–12 sector is dominated by public spending. State, local, and federal governments spent over $500 billion in 2005 on K–12 schooling—about ninety percent of all money expended on public and private schools. However, the vast majority of this spending is dedicated to salaries, benefits, school operations, and other routine line items. Vanishingly little is available for research, development, or new ventures. In fact, researchers have calculated that 40 to 70 percent of district money is formulaically allocated as soon as it arrives in the central office and never even appears in school budgets.[13] Outside of the limited funding for charter school facilities and start-up costs, almost no public spending supports entrepreneurial activity.

As University of Washington professor Paul Hill has concluded, "Public school systems can be fully open to entrepreneurship only if money that is now tied up can be released and reallocated."[14] A few ambitious public officials have begun experimenting with such efforts in very limited ways. Bart Peterson, the mayor of Indianapolis, is exploring the possibility of a public-private partnership in which the city would develop an incubator and support entrepreneurs for a year or two while they plan and launch new charter schools. New York City schools chancellor Joel Klein has relied on a mixture of public and private funds to recruit new leaders and develop new schools. However, meaningful change will require much more. Promising measures to reallocate public funding to support entrepreneurial efforts might include providing loan guarantees for new ventures, helping finance start-up costs, and financially assisting public-private partnerships.

For-profit investment has been rare because investments flow to ventures that offer an attractive, risk-adjusted return, and this has generally not been the case in schooling. First, because for-profit investors seek a competitive return, they will only invest in nonprofits in the most extraordinary of circumstances. In education, of course, many ventures are nonprofit. Second, there have been few especially promising for-profit enterprises, and those that do exist have struggled to attain profitability. More generally, for-profit investors are concerned not only with the innate attractiveness of a venture but also with whether the business climate is expected to remain hospitable in future years. Today, even in states where market conditions are stable and the climate is relatively receptive to for-profit ventures, investors can rarely take for granted that they will remain so.

There are steps that would make K–12 schooling more attractive to for-profit investment, triggering a significant infusion of money to support research, development, and creative problem-solving. For one, imposing clear standards for judging educational effectiveness would reassure investors that ventures will be less subject to political brickbats and better positioned to succeed if demonstrably effective. A more performance-based environment enables potential investors to assess risk in a more informed, rational manner. Eliminating laws that impede the types of ventures likely to attract for-profit investment, such as statutes curbing the involvement of for-profit firms in school management, would also help attract private capital.

Given the dearth of private investment and the constrained nature of public spending, entrepreneurial ventures to date have been disproportionately funded by the tiny sliver of money philanthropies contribute—especially the funds contributed by younger foundations with roots in the new economy. Such support has proven instrumental in the launch or expansion of the KIPP Academies, New Leaders for New Schools, Aspire Public Schools, the SEED Foundation, and other prominent efforts. Traditionally, philanthropic givers have been encouraged to avoid controversy, pay heed to professional

direction, and foster consensus—providing little succor to more entrepreneurial efforts. Today, however, several of the most influential educational
philanthropies—including the Gates Foundation, The Walton Family Foundation, and The Broad Foundation—have made the conscious decision to
support riskier, less conventional endeavors. Perhaps the most interesting
case is that of the NewSchools Venture Fund, discussed by Kim Smith (its former CEO) and Julie Petersen in chapter 1. NewSchools is a "venture philanthropy" that secures investments from both for-profit and nonprofit sources
and then seeks to provide start-up capital to ventures—both nonprofit and
for-profit—that comport with its strategic vision, are designed to achieve
scale over time, and promise to be sustainable.

These new funders accept the challenge posed by Harvard professor Ronald Heifetz, author of *Leadership without Easy Answers*, and his colleagues,
who have argued, "For foundations [to assert public leadership] they must
become accustomed to setbacks, uncomfortable public pressures, and . . .
view[ing] controversy and conflict as allies rather than obstacles in achieving reform."[15] Both philanthropists and the broader public must accept that
it's okay for investments to fail, so long as the failure is in pursuit of results-
oriented solutions. As Broad Foundation officials Wendy Hassett and Dan
Katzir have explained, "At The Broad Foundation, we do not regard our
grantmaking as charity work. Instead, we think of our work as making investments in areas in which we expect a healthy return . . . some [investments]
will be winners, others moderate successes, and others will fail."[16]

Human Capital Pipeline

Reducing barriers to entry and increasing available capital are all good and
well, but they will matter little unless there are people able and willing to
take advantage of new opportunities. The challenge is to attract a mass of
talented and energetic individuals, retain and cultivate promising problem-
solvers, and develop an infrastructure than can help support their efforts to
launch new ventures.

Today, licensing requirements deter many potential principals and teachers—especially those with limited tolerance for bureaucracy or procedural
niceties—from pursuing employment in K–12 schooling. Hiring practices in
many large districts are painfully slow, alienating and deterring potentially
attractive candidates.[17] Inflexible compensation systems penalize mobile
workers, do little to reward high performers, and provide expansive benefits
that are most attractive to those who stay in place for twenty years or more.
In short, schools are organized much like America's major industries were
in the 1950s—rewarding loyal service while discouraging entrepreneurial

behavior. Reforms necessary to foster more entrepreneur-friendly environs include loosening certification barriers, basing compensation and working conditions more on performance than on seniority, and creating opportunities for growth and advancement.

Some of the greatest successes in expanding the talent pipeline have been the result of entrepreneurial activity. Teach For America has brought more than fourteen thousand high-achieving college graduates into schooling since 1990. These new faces have, in turn, fueled a wave of entrepreneurship. TFA alums launched the KIPP Academies; high-achieving schools like the HEROES Academy in the Rio Grande Valley, Texas, and the Bronx Preparatory Charter School in New York City; and The New Teacher Project (TNTP), itself a program for recruiting teachers into urban school systems. Since 1997, TNTP has in turn recruited and prepared over thirteen thousand new teachers in twenty states.[18]

While TFA, TNTP, and similar efforts have piped individuals with an entrepreneurial bent into schooling, there is no guarantee that even a few of them will be prepared or equipped to successfully navigate the rigors of entrepreneurship. Potential entrepreneurs require a mixture of seasoning and experience on the one hand, and energy and a fresh perspective on the other. Effective entrepreneurship is rarely the work of those unacquainted with a sector. Most would-be entrepreneurs get their ideas through their previous employment and experience; a 2004 study of the nation's five hundred fastest growing companies found that more than half of the founders got the idea for their new venture while working in the industry, and another quarter while working in a field related to their current effort.[19] At the same time, launching an entrepreneurial venture typically requires enormous energy and time, and can be hard to reconcile with the demands of family. These realities suggest the value of a pipeline of energetic young veterans, who have worked in the sector, gained experience, and accumulated contacts.

Today, little machinery exists to cultivate would-be educational entrepreneurs, allow them to grow, or bring them into contact with potential funders. Young educators work alone in their classrooms, gain little nonclassroom experience, develop networks that are largely restricted to fellow teachers, and obtain no insight into team management or the demands of launching a new enterprise. In other entrepreneurial fields, twenty- and thirty-somethings move easily among multiple ventures, gain experience and responsibility, build expansive networks of mentors and peers, and learn how to conceive of new ventures. The cultivation of a new generation of entrepreneurs would be aided by structures that offered young educators similar opportunities outside the classroom. This might entail creating new roles, inside or outside of school districts, where qualified candidates work with teams on improving processes or practices in areas like curricular design, professional training, data management, technology integration, instructional design, or personnel management.

Networks that allow potential entrepreneurs to see education from various vantage points, find mentors and potential backers, and link up with kindred spirits are a critical link in any entrepreneurial ecosystem. Organizations like KIPP, TFA, and the NewSchools Venture Fund are working to forge networks of members and alumni. While such efforts are a vital first step, much more is needed. It may be natural to imagine that entrepreneurial personalities, given their desire for autonomy and tolerance for risk, can be successful without support or mentoring—but such is rarely the case. A vital step is for philanthropists and investors to recognize that much of the new-venture infrastructure in the private sector that they take for granted needs to be erected in education.

A handful of philanthropists have sought to take matters into their own hands, aggressively involving themselves in the planning and management of ventures that they support. NewSchools Venture Fund, for instance, taps its staff and network of expertise to provide management assistance that includes strategic planning, growth planning, business planning and financial modeling, team-building, fundraising, and strategic partnering. In a truly entrepreneurial sector, there would be dozens of organizations engaged in some variation of what NewSchools is doing, creating competition, increasing the pool of expertise, and enabling each to specialize by region or niche.

Reformers should seek to emulate the NewSchools approach and make such support accessible to a broader swath of potential entrepreneurs. One such model is for philanthropic or for-profit investors to establish "incubators" to nurture new ventures.[20] Today there are more than one thousand incubators around the country, typically providing cheap office space, business services, and access to mentoring and necessary expertise. Incubators, like Nokia's Innovent in Annapolis or Panasonic's Linux Collaboration Center in San Jose, are intended for companies in the very beginning stages. Eventually, successful ventures "graduate" and move out, creating room for a next wave. The managing director of the Houston Angel Network explains: "Incubators take companies that are missing something, and give them the resources they need to get to the [next] stage."[21] One option for the K–12 sector might be to take fuller advantage of the national network of federally supported small business development centers, many of which operate in partnership with state universities. The centers offer guidance on strategic planning; market analysis and strategy; product feasibility and development;

organizational analysis; financial control; and some offer specialized centers in areas like government contracting or technology transfer.

FOR-PROFITS VS. NONPROFITS

At this juncture, it is appropriate to offer a final word on the role of for-profit ventures. Nonprofits have been relatively successful, have enjoyed glowing press, and have captured the imagination of funders and management professionals. Ventures like High Tech High in San Diego or the EdVisions cooperative in Minnesota are relatively popular, in part because they avoid the unpleasant questions of profitability and self-interest implicit in profit-seeking ventures.

The desire to embrace nonprofits is an understandable and healthy one. Education, like health care, is a complex sector marked by tangled notions of the private and the public good. In such an environment, nonprofits able to marry idealistic passion and entrepreneurial energy are a welcome force. Educational nonprofits also enjoy some significant advantages over for-profits. They face fewer obstacles under state charter laws, can more readily pursue philanthropic support, and are typically less likely to encounter organized opposition from teachers unions, progressives, and the minority community.

While acknowledging the virtues of nonprofits is sensible, this appreciation ought not morph into a bias against for-profits. Profit-seeking enterprises also have unique strengths. For-profits seek to earn competitive returns for investors, allowing them to attract investors and tap the private equity markets. For-profit management also has an imperative to minimize expenses by seeking and adopting cost efficiencies that nonprofits might find excuses to reject. Given self-interested reasons to expand more rapidly than nonprofits, for-profits are also much quicker to respond to increasing demand by entering a field or expanding their services. Conversely, driven by a focus on the bottom line, for-profits are more willing to reduce output or withdraw from an industry when circumstances warrant, allowing them to more rapidly reallocate resources.

Nonprofits have little incentive to become "early adopters" of a cheaper, inferior process. Even if substituting technology for teaching staff proves to be cost-effective, it is also sure to upset parents and community members. Meanwhile, because there are no investors to reap the benefits of new efficiencies or cost savings, there isn't much of a constituency for such measures. Similarly, scholars have noted that for-profits typically fare better than nonprofits at attracting managerial and technical talent and at competing for high-priced talent.[22]

Of course, the uneven record of for-profits in some segments of K–12, like education management, has cooled the interest of potential equity investors. While the unfriendly policy environment, unproven business models, and uneven financial results of early entrants have limited such investment, we ought not dismiss the potential of for-profit ventures or imagine that non-profits can readily match their capacity for scale, dexterity, and aggressive cost-cutting. In short, there are important roles for both nonprofits and for-profits, and the near-term advantages and positive press that accrue to non-profits ought not to blind us to that reality.

ENTREPRENEURSHIP AND PUBLIC POLICY

Educational entrepreneurs tend to be surprisingly reticent when it comes to policy: they prefer to avoid picking fights or issuing vocal challenges to the status quo. This poses something of a dilemma, given that public policy plays a crucial role in determining the future success of their ventures. As Henry Levin, author of chapter 8, has previously noted, entrepreneurs need to "understand the politics of education and the fact that, when public dollars are financing the enterprise, [politics] cannot be separated from political decision-making."[23]

Educational entrepreneurs operate on a public stage. They compete for public dollars, frequently seek to contract with public schools or districts in some fashion, and must answer to state laws and regulations. For-profit enterprises like National Heritage Academies and Edison Schools and non-profit entities like the KIPP Academies compete for the opportunity to operate charter schools that are regulated by state law and funded by tax dollars. Entrepreneurial staffing ventures, like New Leaders for New Schools, seek to place candidates in public schools. Tutoring firms like Kaplan or Catapult that provide supplemental services under NCLB compete for federal dollars, are monitored by state agencies, and must negotiate contracts with local public school districts. Every step of the way, the fate of entrepreneurial providers—both nonprofit and for-profit—is intertwined with federal, state, and local policy.

Nonetheless, it is rare that voices of the educational entrepreneurs are clearly heard when it comes to the heated policy debates over teacher preparation, collective bargaining, charter school restrictions, or the design of state accountability systems. Rather, the decision of The New Teacher Project to engage in such debates—through public advocacy and the research reports *Missed Opportunities: How We Keep High-Quality Teachers Out of Urban Classrooms* and *Unintended Consequences: The Case for Reforming the Staffing*

Rules in Urban Teachers Union Contracts—has been significant because it is so unusual.[24]

The reasons for this reticence are obvious. These entrepreneurs wish to preserve political capital, maintain working relationships with partners in state government and public school districts, and avoid stirring antipathy that could impede efforts to expand existing operations. These are considerations that entrepreneurs are typically loathe to discuss in public, but only too happy to candidly enumerate behind closed doors and off the record. Their caution is understandable and warranted. The danger, however, is that it can result in their successful ventures coming to serve as Potemkin villages enlisted in the service of the status quo—with districts and traditional educators accepting them, so long as they agree to muzzle themselves, keep their head down, and mute criticism of the structural impediments that obstruct possible imitators and hinder their own efforts.

Reformers consistently express frustration that most citizens and educators expect less of poor, minority children. In that light, it was newsworthy when a 2005 survey of two thousand Teach For America teachers showed that 91 percent thought schools should expect inner-city students to achieve academically at the same level as students from wealthier backgrounds.[25] The results drew much attention, and TFA staff actively promoted the finding. In doing so, however, the TFA leadership was careful not to indict traditional colleges of education or district officials for failing to prepare or recruit more such teachers. The multipage press releases announcing the results included not one sentence even glancingly critical of anyone with a hand in the status quo. Indeed, while TFA's track record itself may constitute the sharpest existing indictment of teacher licensure systems and conventional teacher preparation, TFA officials have taken care to avoid publicly critiquing teacher preparation or advocating the removal of licensure barriers.

The same sensible caution is on display in Edison Schools founder Chris Whittle's influential 2005 book *Crash Course*, a volume promoted as a "revolutionary" treatise on school reform. Business pundit James Glassman has wryly noted that in the book Whittle takes care to assure teachers unions and educators that "they have nothing to fear from him."[26] Whittle, a scarred veteran of the entrepreneurial trenches, has learned to eschew harsh language and employ feel-good rhetoric, writing in an open letter to union leaders, "Though teachers are your primary constituency, I know that your organizations care deeply about children, too."[27] Whittle takes pains to promise that, under his reforms, "union 'profit margins' would actually improve."[28] Avoiding divisive proposals, his major recommendations are for the federal government to spend more on education research and to open a few new programs to train teachers and principals—though, even there, Whittle is careful to explain that he doesn't mean to imply any criticism of existing programs. While "there are those who believe that America's teachers colleges are part of the problem," he notes, he will "leave that to others to debate."[29]

In truth, it's neither fair nor constructive to criticize Whittle or any other entrepreneur on this count. Entrepreneurs are in a bind. They are focused on building organizations, and public proclamations may very well inflame political opposition while alienating potential allies. Consequently, they can hardly be criticized for avoiding public fights whenever possible. Meanwhile, even when they remain silent, entrepreneurs can have an enormous impact on the education debates simply by providing visions of what is possible and proof points that analysts and reformers can use in the course of public debate. TFA and the KIPP Academies, for instance, have fundamentally altered discussions about teacher recruitment and urban schooling and students.

However understandable, the reticence of entrepreneurs means they may be ill-suited to challenge the roadblocks posed by public policy and established practice. In fact, entrepreneurs have good cause to describe their accomplishments in broad strokes, to soft-pedal the problems they face, and to disavow those observers who would suggest that future organizational success hinged on the enactment of divisive reforms.

There is some evidence that some entrepreneurs may be starting to play more aggressively upon the policy landscape and that the reluctance to speak up is starting to change in healthful ways. The New Teacher Project, in particular, has launched the aforementioned research efforts. Meanwhile the influx of graduates into the ranks of school leaders, advocates, and researchers is changing the contours of the debate. The increase in the size of the entrepreneurial community, the role played by the maturing NewSchools Venture Fund and other entities in organizing summits and seeking to form a more coherent entrepreneurial community, and the reputations of the most successful entrepreneurs may be gradually positioning more of them to speak their piece.

NOTHING VENTURED, NOTHING GAINED

The paradox of entrepreneurship is that it forthrightly accepts the risk that some ventures and ideas will fail so as to address a larger risk—the likelihood that systems will otherwise find themselves mired in a staid mediocrity. Entrepreneurship is frustrating to education specialists because it doesn't pose any hard-and-fast educational "solutions." The entrepreneurial promise doesn't come with particular brain-based theories of learning or pat guidance on instruction—rather, it seeks to extract excellence by keeping the field open to fresh ideas, whether they be a skillful application of an old model or an effort to leverage new knowledge, management practices, or technology. Next to this uncertain process, the jargon-laden programs crafted by authoritative educational experts may seem safer and more reputable. A wealth of human experience, however, suggests that such faith is misplaced.

In weighing the claims of those skeptical of entrepreneurship, it may be helpful to keep in mind Harvard business professor Clay Christensen's admonition that many widely accepted management principles "are, in fact, only situationally appropriate. There are times at which it is right *not* to listen to customers [and] right to invest in developing lower-performing products that promise *lower* margins."[30] The point is not that good managers routinely ignore their consumers, but that there are no universally applicable dogmas in a changing world. One response to such insights would be to call for an ever more omniscient science of management and organizational change. The "safer" systemic solution, however, may be to embrace dynamic problem-solving and allow new ventures to vie with established routines.

In the end, entrepreneurship is not about quick solutions to today's problems. In K–12 schooling, where we are quick to declare grandiose aims and then demand immediate solutions, such a stance approaches apostasy. Nonetheless, the greatest educational risk we confront today lies not in nurturing the nascent entrepreneurial sector but in continuing to cling to an inadequate and anachronistic status quo. Risk is the price of progress. Failed ideas, providers, and schools are indeed a high price to pay. They are only worth paying when compared to the alternative, to the stagnation and the ceaseless, pointless tinkering that have for so long been the face of school reform.

Notes

INTRODUCTION
Entrepreneurship, Risk, and Reinvention
Frederick M. Hess

1. Peter F. Drucker, *Innovation and Entrepreneurship* (New York: HarperBusiness, 1985), 21.
2. Joseph A. Schumpeter, *Capitalism, Socialism, and Democracy* (New York: Harper, 1975).
3. Drucker, *Innovation and Entrepreneurship*.
4. W. Chan Kim and Renee Mauborgne, "Value Innovation," in *Harvard Business Review on Breakthrough Thinking* (Boston: Harvard Business School Press, 1999), 200.
5. Clayton M. Christensen and Michael E. Raynor, *The Innovator's Solution: Creating and Sustaining Successful Growth* (Boston: Harvard Business School, 2003), 73.
6. Chris Whittle, *Crash Course: Imagining a Better Future for Public Education* (New York: Riverhead Books, 2005); Wendy Kopp, *One Day, All Children: The Unlikely Triumph of Teach For America and What I Learned Along the Way* (New York: PublicAffairs, 2003); Marilyn L. Kourilsky and William B. Walstad, eds., "Social Entrepreneurship," special issue, *International Journal of Entrepreneurship Education* 2, no. 1 (2003): 85–111; Paul T. Hill and James Harvey, ed., *Making School Reform Work: New Partnerships for Real Change* (Washington, DC: Brookings Institution Press, 2004).
7. Chris Swanson (director of the Editorial Projects in Education Research Center), e-mail correspondence with author, February 23, 2006.
8. Fifty-nine percent of fourth graders in Atlanta, 63 percent in Los Angeles, and 67 percent in Washington, D.C., scored "below basic" in reading in 2005. U.S. Department of Education, National Center for Education Statistics, data accessed online using NAEP data explorer search tool, www.nces.ed.gov/nationsreportcard/nde/.
9. Frederick M. Hess, *Common Sense School Reform* (New York: Palgrave Macmillan, 2004); Abigail Thernstrom and Stephan Thernstrom, *No Excuses: Closing the Racial Gap in Learning* (New York: Simon & Schuster, 2003).
10. Paul T. Hill, "Entrepreneurship in K–12 Public Education," in Kourilsky and Walstad, "Social Entrepreneurship," 67.
11. J. Gregory Dees and Beth Anderson, "For-Profit Social Ventures," in Kourilsky and Walstad, *Social Entrepreneurship*, 13.
12. Carl J. Schramm, *The Entrepreneurial Imperative* (New York: HarperCollins, 2006); Paul A. London, *The Competition Solution: The Bipartisan Secret Behind American Prosperity* (Washington, DC: AEI Press, 2005).

13. John Thornhill, "The View of the Future from Davos," *Financial Times*, January 31, 2006, p. 13.

14. U.S. Census Bureau, "Computer Use in the United States," *Current Population Survey (CPS) Reports* (Washington, DC: U.S. Census Bureau, October 1993), table A.

15. Motion Picture Association of America Worldwide Market Research, *US Entertainment Industry: 2004 MPA Market Statistics* (Los Angeles: Motion Picture Association of America, March 2005), 41, available online at www.mpaa.org/researchStatistics.asp.

16. Matthew Yi, "Apple Cuts iPod Prices," *San Francisco Chronicle*, February 8, 2006, p. C1.

17. The figure on homeschooled children comes from National Center for Education Statistics, *Homeschooling in the United States: 2003* (Washington, DC: U.S. Department of Education, February 2006), table 2; National Center for Education Statistics, *Distance Education Courses for Public Elementary and Secondary School Students: 2002–03* (Washington, DC: U.S. Department of Education, March 2005), 4, 10.

18. John F. Watson, *Keeping Pace with K–12 Online Learning: A Review of State-Level Policies and Practices* (Naperville, IL: Learning Point Associates, October 2005).

19. Jay P. Greene, "Buckets into the Sea: Why Philanthropy Isn't Changing Schools, and How It Could," in *With the Best of Intentions: How Philanthropy Is Reshaping K–12 Education*, ed. Frederick M. Hess (Cambridge, MA: Harvard Education Press, 2005), 49–76.

20. Christensen and Raynor, 221.

21. Whittle, *Crash Course*, 129.

22. For a more comprehensive history of entrepreneurship in America, see chapters 9 and 15 of Peter Drucker's *Innovation and Entrepreneurship*.

23. BizMiner, "BizMiner Startup Business Risk Index: Detailed Industry Report" (Camp Hill, PA: Brandow Company, May 2005).

24. Drucker, *Innovation and Entrepreneurship*, 120.

25. Book sales figures are from Jim Milliot, "Top Five Pubs Take Half of Sales," *Publishers Weekly*, April 25, 2005, available online at www.publishersweekly.com/article/CA527260.html. Percentage of titles figure is reported by PMA, the Independent Book Publishers Association, on Para Publishing's website, www.parapublishing.com/sites/para/resources/statistics.cfm.

26. Motion Picture Association of America Worldwide Market Research, *US Entertainment Industry: 2004 MPA Market Statistics* (Los Angeles: Motion Picture Association of America, March 2005), 12–17, available online at www.mpaa.org/researchStatistics.asp.

27. William T. Bielby and Denise D. Bielby, "Controlling Prime-Time: Organizational Concentration and Network Television Programming Strategies," *Journal of Broadcasting & Electronic Media* 47 (December 2003): 373–396.

28. Author's calculation based on the National Association of Television Program Executives, *2004 Pilot Bible* (Los Angeles: Author, May 2004) and two television database websites, www.tv.com and www.imdb.com.

29. James R. Walking and Douglas A. Ferguson, *The Broadcast Television Industry* (Boston: Allyn & Bacon, 1998), 111, 120.

30. Robert B. Laughlin, "Reinventing Physics: The Search for the Real Frontier," *Chronicle of Higher Education*, February 11, 2005, p. B6.

31. Whittle, *Crash Course*, 88.

32. William D. Bygrave, "The Entrepreneurial Process," in *The Portable MBA in Entrepreneurship*, 3rd ed., ed. William D. Bygrave and Andrew Zacharakis (Hoboken, NJ: John Wiley, 2004), 1–27.

33. Thomson Venture Economics and the National Venture Capital Association, "Private Equity Enjoyed Record Fundraising Year in 2005," news release, January 2006, available online at www.nvca.org/pdf/FundraisingQ42005final.pdf.

34. Zoltan J. Acs et al., *Global Entrepreneurship Monitor: 2004 Executive Report* (Babson Park, MA: Global Entrepreneurship Monitor, May 2005), tables 1, 3, available online at www.gemconsortium.org/download.asp?fid=364.

35. Anne Dumas, "What's American and Envied by France?" *Washington Post*, June 5, 2005, p. B2.

36. Diego Comin and Thomas Philippon, "The Rise in Firm-Level Volatility: Causes and Consequences," forthcoming, *National Bureau of Economic Research Macroeconomics Annual 2005* (Cambridge, MA: MIT Press). Working paper version (July 2005) is available online at pages.stern.nyu.edu/~tphilipp/papers/diego.pdf.

37. Dorothy Leonard and Jeffrey F. Rayport, "Spark Innovation Through Empathic Design," in *Harvard Business Review on Breakthrough Thinking* (Boston: Harvard Business School Press, 1999), 33.

CHAPTER 1
What Is Educational Entrepreneurship?
Kim Smith and Julie Landry Petersen

1. "Maxims for Revolutionists," in *Man and Superman* (Cambridge, MA: The University Press, 1903).

2. Howard Stevenson et al., *New Business Ventures and the Entrepreneur*, 5th ed. (Boston: Irwin McGraw-Hill, 1999).

3. Martin Seligman, *Learned Optimism: How to Change Your Mind and Your Life* (New York: Knopf, 1991).

4. J. Gregory Dees, "The Meaning of 'Social Entrepreneurship'" (Durham, NC: Fuqua School of Business at Duke University, 1998), available online at www.fuqua.duke.edu/centers/case/documents/dees_SE.pdf.

5. Clayton M. Christensen, *The Innovator's Dilemma* (Cambridge, MA: Harvard Business School Press, 1997).

6. Howard H. Stevenson and William A. Sahlman, *Entrepreneurship: A Process, Not a Person* (Working Paper 87–069) (Cambridge, MA: Harvard Business School, 1987).

7. U.S. Census Bureau, *National Estimates by Age, Sex, Race: 1900–1979*, available online at www.census.gov/popest/archives/pre-1980/PE-11.html.

8. *Digest of Education Statistics 2004* (Washington, DC: U.S. Department of Education, National Center for Education Statistics, 2005), available online at http://nces.ed.gov/programs/digest/d04/index.asp.

9. Jay P. Greene and Marcus A. Winters, *Public High School Graduation and College-Readiness Rates: 1991–2002* (New York: Manhattan Institute, February 2005).

10. Center for Education Reform. See www.edreform.org.

11. The MoneyTree Survey. See www.pwcmoneytree.com/moneytree/index.jsp.

12. Eduventures, Inc., *The Education Quarterly Investment Report, Year-End Report 2000: Venture Capitalists Seek Reality, Revenues and Rational Business Models*, 2001, available online (by subscription only) at www.eduventures.com.

13. This is known as Moore's Law, and was first posited by Gordon Moore, co-founder of semiconductor technology firm Intel, in 1965. For more on Moore's Law, see www.intel.com/technology/mooreslaw/index.htm.

14. As cited in Peter F. Drucker, *Innovation and Entrepreneurship* (New York: HarperBusiness, 1985).

15. Eric Bassett, Catherine Burdt, and J. Mark Jackson, *The Education Investor: 2004 Year-End Review and Outlook* (Boston: Eduventures, 2005).

16. *The PRI Directory* (New York: Foundation Center, 2003).

17. Jim Collins, *Good to Great: Why Some Companies Make the Leap . . . and Others Don't* (New York: HarperBusiness, 2001).

18. Chris Whittle, *Crash Course: Imagining a Better Future for Public Education* (New York: Riverhead Books, 2005), 30.

19. As quoted in Bill Shore, *The Cathedral Within: Transforming Your Life by Giving Something Back* (New York: Random House, 1999).

CHAPTER 2
Entrepreneurs at Work
Paul Teske and Aimee Williamson

1. Gifford Pinchot, *Intrapreneuring: Why You Don't Have to Leave the Corporation to Become an Entrepreneur* (New York: Harper & Row, 1985).

2. Although the term is perhaps most associated with nonprofit ventures, the concept spans sectors and has also been applied to for-profit organizations with a focus on a social mission. See J. Gregory Dees and Beth Anderson, "For Profit Social Ventures," *International Journal of Entrepreneurship Education* 2, no. 1 (2002): 21–39.

3. Joseph A. Schumpeter, *Capitalism, Socialism, and Democracy* (New York: Harpers, 1942), 82–85.

4. Other psychological work probed more carefully the "need for control" that entrepreneurs seem to possess: James Rotter, "Generalized Expectations for Internal versus External Control of Reinforcement," *Psychological Monographs* 80 (1966): 609–623; and Robert Brockhaus and Pamela Horwitz, "The Psychology of the Entrepreneur," in *The Art and Science of Entrepreneurship*, ed. Donald L. Sexton and Raymond W. Smilor (Cambridge, MA: Ballinger, 1986), 25–48. Building on this work, Welsh and White could then list eleven common characteristics of entrepreneurs: James Welsh and John White, "Converging of Characteristics of Entrepreneurs," in *Frontiers of Entrepreneurship Research*, ed. Kenneth Vesper (Wellesley, MA: Babson College, 1981), 29–58.

5. Schneider and Teske provide evidence of this in their search for entrepreneurs in local government organizations. See Mark Schneider and Paul Teske, *Public Entrepreneurs: Agents for Change in American Government* (Princeton, NJ: Princeton University Press, 1995).

6. Robert Brown and Jeffrey R. Cornwall, *The Entrepreneurial Educator* (Lanham, MD: Scarecrow Press, 2000), 11.

7. In a February 2004 Gallup poll, 86 percent of adults surveyed indicated that education was extremely/very important in influencing their vote for president, tying the economy for top choice. See www.pollingreport.com/prioriti.htm.

8. See Richard Lee Colvin, "A New Generation of Philanthropists and Their Great Ambitions," in *With the Best of Intentions: How Philanthropy Is Reshaping K–12 Education*, ed.

Frederick M. Hess (Cambridge, MA: Harvard Education Press, 2005); and Tamar Lewin, "Young Students Are New Cause for Big Donors," *New York Times*, August 21, 2005.

9. Morris and Jones argue against such a line and characterize entrepreneurship in terms of "intensity," which is a function of the "frequency" of entrepreneurial activities and the "degree" to which activities are entrepreneurial: Michael H. Morris and Foard F. Jones, "Entrepreneurship in Established Organizations: The Case of the Public Sector," *Entrepreneurship: Theory and Practice* 24, no. 1 (Fall 1999): 71–91.

10. Paul T. Hill, "Entrepreneurship in K–12 Public Education," in "Social Entrepreneurship," ed. Marilyn L. Kourilsky and William B. Walstad, special issue, *International Journal of Entrepreneurship Education* 2, no. 1 (2003): 85–111.

11. Subsequent work has provided support for this perspective; for example, Morris and Jones, in "Entrepreneurship in Established Organizations," argue that the primary characteristics of public entrepreneurship are "innovativeness," "risk taking," and "proactiveness," with proactiveness referring to the implementation phase.

12. *21st Century Schools Project Bulletin* 4, no. 24 (December 21, 2004), www.ppionline.org (e-newsletter of the Progressive Policy Institute).

13. Douglas McGray, "Working with the Enemy," *New York Times*, January 16, 2005.

14. Tamar Lewin, "Options Open, Top Graduates Line Up to Teach to the Poor," *New York Times*, October 2, 2005, p. A1.

15. Wendy Kopp, *One Day, All Children* (New York: Public Affairs, 2001), 40.

16. Kopp, *One Day, All Children*, p. 23, italics in original.

17. Debra Viadero, "Study Finds Benefits in Teach For America," *Education Week* 23, no. 40 (June 2004): 1.

18. See Adriane Williams and Watson S. Swail, *Focus on Results: An Academic Impact Analysis of the Knowledge Is Power Program (KIPP)* (Virginia Beach, VA: Education Policy Institute, August 2005), available online at www.educationalpolicy.org/pdf/KIPP.pdf.

19. See Jay Mathews, "School of Hard Choices: In the KIPP Academy Program, It's Motivation That's Fundamental," *Washington Post*, August 24, 2004.

20. See Jennifer Vilaga, "Social Capitalists," available online at www.fastcompany.com/social/2004/profiles/newleaders.html.

21. See Cheryl Dahle, "The Change Masters," *Fast Company* no. 90 (January 2005): 47, available online at www.nlns.org/resources/FastCompany.pdf.

22. Jonathan Schnur, "A Recipe for Successful Schools" (Washington, DC: Alliance for Excellent Education, 2004), available online at www.all4ed.org/publications/ProfilesInLeadership/Schnur.pdf.

23. See company website: www.washpostco.com.

24. Lynn Olson, "For-Profit Writes Mandatory Courses for Phila. High Schools," *Education Week* 24, no. 22 (2005): 1–4.

CHAPTER 3
The Policy Landscape
Patrick McGuinn

1. See Terry Moe, "A Union by Any Other Name," *Education Next* 1, no. 3 (Fall 2001): 40–45; Tom Loveless, ed., *Conflicting Missions? Teachers Unions and Educational Reform* (Washington, DC: Brookings Institution Press, 2000); Myron Lieberman, *The Teacher*

Unions: How the NEA and the AFT Sabotage Reform (New York: Free Press, 1997); and Peter Brimelow, *The Worm in the Apple: How the Teacher Unions Are Destroying American Education* (New York: HarperCollins, 2003).

2. Andrew J. Rotherham and Sara Mead, "Back to the Future: The History and Politics of State Teacher Licensure and Certification," in *A Qualified Teacher in Every Classroom?* ed. Frederick M. Hess, Andrew J. Rotherham, and Kate Walsh (Cambridge, MA: Harvard Education Press, 2004), 11–47.

3. National Center for Education Information (NCEI), "Alternative Routes to Teacher Certification: An Overview" (2005), available online at www.ncei.com.

4. For more on the curriculum of schools of education, see David Steiner with Susan Rozen, "Preparing Tomorrow's Teachers," in Hess et al., *A Qualified Teacher in Every Classroom?*

5. Thomas B. Fordham Foundation, "The Quest for Better Teachers: Grading the States," 1999, available online at www.edexcellence.net.

6. NCEI, "Alternative Routes to Teacher Certification: An Overview."

7. Forty percent of new teachers hired in New Jersey come through alternative certification programs, while one-third of Texas's and California's new hires come through alternate routes. C. Emily Feistritzer, "State Policy Trends for Alternative Routes to Teacher Certification: A Moving Target" (Washington, DC: National Center for Alternative Certification, 2005).

8. Emily Feistritzer has noted, however, that there has recently been "a shift away from emergency and other temporary routes to new routes designed specifically for nontraditional populations of post-baccalaureate candidates, many of whom come from other careers." Feistritzer, "State Policy Trends."

9. Since 2001, Louisiana has also permitted nontraditional providers of teacher candidates, though as of 2003 only three had been approved (a school district and two nonprofits). Bryan C. Hassel and Michele E. Sherburne, "Cultivating Success through Multiple Providers," in Hess et al., *A Qualified Teacher in Every Classroom?*, 201–222.

10. Data from the National Center for Alternative Certification, available online at www.teach-now.org.

11. Andrew J. Rotherham and Sara Mead, "Back to the Future."

12. Frederick M. Hess, "A License to Lead? A New Leadership Agenda for America's Schools" (Washington, DC: Progressive Policy Institute's 21st Century Schools Project, January 2003), available online at www. ppionline.org.

13. Susan M. Gates et al., "Who Is Leading Our Schools? An Overview of School Administrators and Their Careers" (Arlington, VA: RAND Education, 2003).

14. As Feistritzer has noted, school administrators are generally viewed and trained as instructional leaders rather than CEOs. C. Emily Feistritzer, "Better Leaders for America's Schools: A Manifesto" (Washington, DC: Thomas B. Fordham Foundation, May 2003), available online at www.edexcellence.net.

15. Hess, "A License to Lead?"

16. Feistritzer, "Better Leaders for America's Schools."

17. For additional detail on the specific requirements of individual states in the area of principal and superintendent licensure, see the National Center for Education Information website at www.ncei.com/publications.html.

18. U.S. Department of Education, "Innovative Pathways to School Leadership" (Washington, DC: U.S. Department of Education, Office of Innovation and Improvement, December 2004), available online at www.ed.gov/admins/recruit/prep/alternative/report.pdf.

19. U.S. Department of Education, "Innovative Pathways to School Leadership."

20. Education Commission of the States, "What Governors Need to Know: Highlights of State Education Systems" (February 2005), available online at www.ecs.org.

21. Gregg Vanourek, "State of the Charter Movement 2005: Trends, Issues, and Indicators" (Washington, DC: Charter School Leadership Council, May 2005).

22. In a 2002–03 national survey by the Center for Education Reform, 14 percent of charter schools reported using a Core Knowledge approach, 13 percent college prep, 13 percent science/math prep, 13 percent direct instruction, 12 percent thematic instruction, 9 percent back to basics, 6 percent arts, and 6 percent school to work. Center for Education Reform, "Charter Schools Today" (Washington, DC: Author, 2004), 12, available online at http://edreform.com/-upload/CSTRecordSuccess2003.pdf.

23. As cited in Vanourek, "State of the Charter Movement 2005."

24. Vanourek, "State of the Charter Movement 2005."

25. As cited in Scott Elliot, "Public Schools, Private Markets" (Washington, DC: Education Writers Association of America, 2005), available online at www.ewa.org.

26. Vanourek, "State of the Charter Movement 2005."

27. Louann Palmer and Rebecca Gau, "Charter School Authorizing: Are States Making the Grade?" (Washington, DC: Thomas B. Fordham Foundation, June 2003), available online at www.edexcellence.net/doc/charterauthorizing_fullreport.pdf.

28. Vanourek, "State of the Charter Movement 2005."

29. Chester E. Finn Jr. and Eric Osberg, "Charter School Funding: Inequity's Next Frontier" (Washington, DC: Thomas B. Fordham Foundation, August 2005), available online at www.edexcellence.net/institute/charterfinance.

30. Finn and Osberg, "Charter School Funding."

31. Shaka Mitchell and Jeanne Allen, "Solving the Charter School Funding Gap" (Washington, DC: Center for Education Reform, 2005), available online at www.edreform.com/_upload/CER-CSFundingGap2005.pdf.

32. Kim Smith and James Willcox, "A Building Need," *Education Next* 4, no. 2 (Spring 2004): 44–51.

33. These funds are dispersed through eighteen different federal programs, with the majority coming through Title I and special education grants. Other programs include the Charter Schools Grant Program ($218 million in 2005), State Charter School Facilities Incentives grants ($200–300 million), and the Credit Enhancement for Charter School Facilities program ($37 million). Vanourek, "State of the Charter Movement 2005."

34. Vanourek, "State of the Charter Movement 2005."

35. Vanourek, "State of the Charter Movement 2005."

36. Vanourek, "State of the Charter Movement 2005."

37. Policy and Program Studies Service, "Evaluation of the Public Charter Schools Program: Final Report" (Washington, DC: U.S. Department of Education, 2004).

38. Finn and Osberg, "Charter School Funding."

39. As cited in Elliot, "Public Schools, Private Markets."

40. Center on Education Policy, *From the Capitol to the Classroom: Year 3 of the No Child Left Behind Act* (Washington, DC: Author, 2005), 131.

41. Siobhan Gorman, "Selling Supplemental Services" *Education Next* 4, no. 4 (Fall 2004): 31–36.

42. Jeffrey Cohen, testimony provided at the U.S. House Committee on Education and the Workforce hearing on April 26, 2005, available online at www.house.gov/ed_workforce.

43. Steven Pines, "Remarks before the Center on Education Policy Forum on Supplemental Education Services," May 16, 2005, available online at www.cep-dc.org.

44. For more on the implementation of NCLB in urban districts, see Michael Casserly, "Choice and Supplemental Services in America's Great City Schools," in *Leaving No Child Behind? Options for Kids in Failing Schools*, ed. Frederick M. Hess and Chester E. Finn Jr. (New York: Palgrave Macmillan, 2004).

45. U.S. Department of Education, "Creating Strong Supplemental Educational Services Programs" (Washington, DC: U.S. Department of Education, Office of Innovation and Improvement, May 2004), available online at www.ed.gov/admins/comm/suppsvcs/sesprograms/report.pdf.

46. The number of SES providers in operation has witnessed considerable growth over the program's first two years, rising from four to eleven providers on average at the state level, and from an average of seven to thirty-one in very large school districts. Center on Education Policy, *From the Capitol to the Classroom*. While many approved SES providers operate in a single district or state, by the end of 2004, ten for-profit companies (led by Plato Learning, Kaplan, and Catapult Learning) had been approved as SES providers in twenty-five or more states. Paul Peterson, "Making Up the Rules As You Play the Game," *Education Next* 5, no. 4 (Fall 2005): 43–48.

47. For more on the state takeover, see Catherine Gewertz, "It's Official: State Takes Over Philadelphia Schools," *Education Week*, January 9, 2002, available online at www.edweek.org/ew/articles/2002/01/09/16philly.h21.html.

48. For more on the evolution of the federal role in education, see Patrick McGuinn, *No Child Left Behind and the Transformation of Federal Education Policy, 1965–2005* (Lawrence: University Press of Kansas, 2006).

49. Center on Education Policy, *From the Capital to the Classroom*, available online at www.ctredpol.org/pubs/nclby3/press/cep-nclby3_21Mar2005.pdf.

50. Center on Education Policy, *From the Capital to the Classroom*. "Title I schools" are high poverty schools that receive funds from Title I of the Elementary and Secondary Education Act. The distinction between Title I and non-Title I schools is very important because the mandatory corrective actions spelled out in the new law for failing schools only apply to Title I schools. The other provisions of the law (such as those regarding standards, testing, and school report cards) apply to Title I and non-Title I schools alike.

51. For more on the implementation of NCLB's school choice provisions in the states, see Hess and Finn, *Leaving No Child Behind?*

52. E. E. Schattschneider, *Politics, Pressures and the Tariff* (Hamden, CT: Archon Books, 1963).

CHAPTER 4

Mapping the K–12 and Postsecondary Sectors

Adam Newman

1. J. L. Hammett Co. website, www.hammett.com/custserv/customerservicemain.jsp?cid=19.

2. *Webster's Ninth New Collegiate Dictionary* (Springfield, MA: Merriam-Webster, 1988).

3. Center for Education Reform, "All about Charter Schools" (Washington, DC: Author, November 2005), available online at www.edreform.com/index.cfm.

4. All private investment and merger and acquisition transactions and figures featured and referenced in this section reflect *publicly announced* transactions and *publicly disclosed* dollar amounts and investors.

CHAPTER 5
For-Profit K–12 Education: Through the Glass Darkly
Alex Molnar

1. Michael R. Sandler, *The Emerging Education Industry: The First Decade* (Potomac, MD: Education Industry Leadership Board, April 2002), available online at www.education industry.org/eilb/media/EmergingEducation.pdf.
2. "Crème in the News," available online at www.cremedelacreme.com/news.asp; "Child-care and Preschools by Crème de la Crème," available online at www.cremedelacreme. com/homepage.asp.
3. Karen Arenson, "Speedy Growth in Career Schools Raises Questions," *New York Times*, July 12, 2005.
4. John Hechinger, "Battle over Academic Standards Weighs on For-Profit Colleges," *Wall Street Journal*, September 30, 2005.
5. WIU video tour, available online at www.wintu.edu/video.htm.
6. Michael Winerip, "Billions for Schools Are Lost in Fraud, Waste and Abuse," *New York Times*, February 2, 1994.
7. Winerip, "Billions for Schools Are Lost in Fraud, Waste and Abuse."
8. Arenson, "Speedy Growth in Career Schools Raises Questions."
9. Eryn Brown, "Can For-Profit Schools Pass an Ethics Test?" *New York Times*, December 12, 2004.
10. Alex Molnar, David Garcia, Carolyn Sullivan, Brendan McEvoy, and Jamie Joanou, *Profiles of For-Profit Education Management Organizations, 2004–2005* (Tempe: Arizona State University, Education Policy Studies Laboratory, Commercialism in Education Research Unit, 2005). The report defines an EMO as a company that is for-profit, manages a school that receives public funds, and has an open enrollment policy. It is important to note that while the annual *Profiles* report labels education management companies as "profitable" and "not profitable," in the case of privately held companies the designation is based on the companies' self-reports. Unlike publicly traded companies, privately held companies are not required to make their earnings statements public. Finally, it is likely that a substantial number of EMOs that operate a small number of schools are not included in the *Profiles*. At this point there is no way to systematically track such small providers.
11. NACSA Educational Service Provider Information Clearinghouse, updated March 2005, available online at www.charterauthorizers.org/esp/esp.php.
12. NACSA Educational Service Provider Information Clearinghouse, updated March 2005, available online at www.charterauthorizers.org/esp/esp.php. The GEO Group is also known as ABS School Services. Its parent company is the publicly traded Matrix Bancorp. It is *not* connected to another organization, also called the GEO Group, which is an international operator of privately held correctional services.
13. Molnar et al., *Profiles of For-Profit Education Management Organizations*.

14. Laura Fording, "Education 21st Century-Style," *Newsweek Technology & Science*, March, 30, 2004, available online at http://msnbc.msn.com/id/4633126/site/newsweek.

15. Scott Stephens, "Ohio Virtually Booming with Cyber Schools," *Plain Dealer,* June 27, 2004.

16. RPP International, *The State of Charter Schools: 2000* (Washington, DC: U.S. Department of Education, Office of Educational Research and Improvement, 2000), available online at www.ed.gov/pubs/charter4thyear/index.html.

17. Craig Hawley, "Small Schools" in Alex Molnar, ed., *School Reform Proposals: The Research Evidence* (Tempe: Arizona State University, Education Policy Studies Laboratory, 2002), available online at www.asu.edu/educ/epsl/EPRU/documents/EPRU%202002-101/Chapter%2003-Howley-Final.htm.

18. Molnar et al., *Profiles of For-Profit Education Management Organizations.*

19. Sharon Nichols, Gene V. Glass, and David C. Berliner, *High-Stakes Testing and Student Achievement: Problems for the No Child Left Behind Act* (EPSL-0504-105-EPRU) (Tempe: Arizona State University, Education Policy Studies Laboratory, Education Policy Research Unit, 2005).

20. Alex Molnar, *Virtually Everywhere: Marketing to Children in America's Schools: The Seventh Annual Report on Trends in Schoolhouse Commercialism, Year 2003–2004* (Tempe: Arizona State University, Education Policy Studies Laboratory, 2004).

21. Hal R. Varian, "Putting a White House Annual Report to a Test," *New York Times,* June 2, 2005, p. C2. White House *Economic Report of the President 2005* (Washington, DC: U.S. Government Printing Office, February 17, 2005).

22. "Company Profile," Edison Schools, Inc., available online at www.edisonschools.com/overview/ov0.html; Molnar et al., *Profiles of For-Profit Education Management Organizations.*

23. Stephanie Banchero, "Schools Told to Outsource Tutoring," *Chicago Tribune*, December 9, 2004.

24. Susan Saulny, "A Lucrative Brand of Tutoring Grows Unchecked," *New York Times*, April 4, 2005.

25. Association of Community Organizations for Reform Now and American Institute for Social Justice, *Accountability Left Behind—While Children and Schools Face High Stakes Testing, Tutoring Companies Get a Free Ride* (Washington, DC: Authors, 2004).

26. Anne Wick, "Edison Plans to Exploit NCLB Funding," *Heller Report on Educational Technology Markets* 14, no. 3 (2003); Tungsten Learning, available online at www.tungstenlearning.com/whatweoffer.html.

27. Robert Broomfield, "High-Stakes Cheating Spawns New Market," *School News*, March 9, 2005, available online at www.eschoolnews.com/news/pfshowStory.cfm?ArticleID=5564; "Caveon Test Security to Apply Its Test Cheating Detection Services to the Texas Assessment of Knowledge and Skills," news release for Caveon.com, July 19, 2005, available online at www.caveon.com/pr/press7-19-05.htm.

28. Bruce Nichols, "Houston ISD Mixes Business, Education," *Dallas Morning News*, May 12, 2005.

29. Gerald Bracey, *Charter Schools' Performance and Accountability: A Disconnect* (Tempe: Arizona State University, Education Policy Studies Laboratory, May 2005).

30. Brian P. Gill, Laura S. Hamilton, J. R. Lockwood, Julie A. Marsh, Ron W. Zimmer, and Deanna Hill, *Inspiration, Perspiration and Time: Operations and Achievement in Edison*

Schools (MG-351-EDU) (Santa Monica, CA: RAND Corp., October 2005), available online at www.rand.org/publications/MG/MG351/.

31. Alex Molnar, Glen Wilson, and David Allen, *Profiles of For-Profit Education Management Companies 2003–2004* (Tempe: Arizona State University, Education Policy Studies Laboratory, Commercialism in Education Research Unit, February 2004), available online at www.asu.edu/educ/epsl/EPRU/epru_2004_Research_Writing.htm.

32. Alec MacGillis, "Pitching the Quick Fix," *Baltimore Sun*, September 19, 2004.

33. Banchero, "Schools Told to Outsource Tutoring."

34. Tracy Dell'Angela and Jodi S. Cohen, "Tutoring Firm Expelled from Seven of City's Schools," *Chicago Tribune*, March 7, 2005.

35. Don Babying, "Urban Districts Get Flexibility on Tutor Programs," Associated Press, reprinted in the *Chicago Sun Times*, September 1, 2005.

36. Association of Community Organizations for Reform Now and American Institute for Social Justice, *Accountability Left Behind*.

37. Bracey, *Charter Schools' Performance and Accountability*.

38. Sam Dillon, "Collapse of 60 Charter Schools Leaves Californians Scrambling," *New York Times*, September 17, 2004; see also Jennifer Coleman, "California Charter Academy Closes Remaining Two Schools," *San Francisco Chronicle*, August 11, 2004.

39. Coleman, "California Charter Academy Closes Remaining Two Schools."

40. Josh Cornfield, "C-U '04 Report Card: Needs Improvement," *Daily Times* (Chester, PA), September 9, 2004, available online at www.zwire.com/site/news.cfm?newsid=1288520 2&BRD=1675&PAG=461&dept_id=18171&rfi=6.

41. "Board of Control Members Should Resign," *Daily Times* (Chester, PA), October 5, 2005, available online at www.zwire.com/site/news.cfm?newsid=15329460&BRD=1675&PAG =461&dept_id=18171&rfi=8.

42. Lisa Kim Bach, "818 Students Opt to Switch from Struggling Schools," *Review-Journal* (Las Vegas) September 9, 2004, available online at www.reviewjournal.com/lvrj_ home/2004/Sep-09-Thu-2004/news/24729463.html.

43. Molnar et al., *Profiles of For-Profit Education Management Organizations*.

44. Susan Snyder and Martha Woodall, "Panel Denies Two Charters' Renewal Bids," *Philadelphia Inquirer*, March 13, 2003.

45. Michael R. Wickline, "State Gets Estimate on Virtual School Cost: Price Tag Would Have Been $6.8 Million," *Arkansas Democrat-Gazette*, June 12, 2004, available online at http://epaper.ardemgaz.com/WebChannel/ShowStory.asp?Path=ArDemocrat/2004/06/ 12&ID=Ar01502.

46. "Our View: Keep Eye on Relationship between Schools, Contractors," *Idaho Statesman*, July 16, 2004, available online at www.idahostatesman.com/apps/pbcs.dll/article? AID=/20040716/NEWS0501/407160311/1001/NEWS.

47. Jason Embry, "Line Separating School, Private Firm Is Blurred," *Austin American-Statesman*, September 17, 2004.

48. Rachel May Proctor, "Virtually Inviolable: TEA to Resurrect Online Charters," *Austin Chronicle*, January 16, 2004.

49. "Our View: Keep Eye on Relationship between Schools, Contractors."

50. Robert Digital, "Bennett Plugs Online School's Virtues," *Press Democrat* (Riverside, CA), July 17, 2004.

51. Natalie Arbulu, "Sabis School Surplus Sparks Fiscal Dispute," *Springfield Republican*, November 12, 2004.

52. See Lawrence O. Picas, "Setting Budget Priorities," *American School Board Journal* 187, no. 5 (May 2000): 30; Henry Levin, "Bear Market," *Education Next* 1, no. 1 (Spring 2001); Glen E. Robinson and Nancy Protheroe, "Budget Comparisons for Local School Districts," *Education Digest* 57 no. 8 (April 1992): 11.

53. Christopher Whittle, *Crash Course: Imagining a Better Future for Public Education* (New York: Riverhead Books, 2005).

54. Doug Oplinger and Dennis J. Willard, "Online Students Missing Exams," *Akron Beacon Journal*, June 3, 2005.

55. Henry Levin, "The Public-Private Nexus in Education," *American Behavioral Scientist* 43, no. 1 (March 2000), available online at www.ncspe.org/publications_files/publications_files/31_OP01.pdf.

CHAPTER 6
Entrepreneurs within School Districts
Joe Williams

1. For a more detailed look at Fritsche Middle School during the 1999–2000 school year, see Joe Williams, "Independence Inspires MPS Charter School; Fritsche Seems to Thrive in Its First Year Free of Many Traditional Constraints," *Milwaukee Journal Sentinel*, July 16, 2000; and Joe Williams, "Having Pushed for Charter School Status, MPS School Must Now Prove Itself," *Milwaukee Journal Sentinel*, October 3, 1999.

2. Williams, "Independence Inspires MPS Charter School."

3. Williams, "Independence Inspires MPS Charter School."

4. Frederick M. Hess, *Revolution at the Margins* (Washington, DC: Brookings Institution Press, 2002).

5. John Gardner, "How School Choice Helps Public Education," unpublished paper, 1997.

6. Remarks by William Andrekopoulos before the National Association of Charter School Authorizers, Denver, Colorado, October 24, 2005.

7. Jim Smith, "Executive Decision: Kids Are the Bottom Line," *New York Newsday*, March 3, 2003.

8. Abby Goodnough, "At Baruch, Levy Urges Heedig to Altruism," *New York Times*, June 2, 2001.

9. Linda Darling-Hammond et al., "Does Teacher Preparation Matter? Evidence about Teacher Certification, Teach For America, and Teacher Effectiveness," paper presented at the annual meeting of the American Educational Research Association, April 2005.

10. Paul T. Decker, Daniel P. Mayer, and Steven Glazerman, "The Effects of Teach For America on Students: Findings from a National Evaluation" (MPR reference no. 8792-750) (Princeton, NJ: Mathematica Policy Research, Inc., June 9, 2004), available online at www.mathematica-mpr.com/publications/pdfs/teach.pdf.

11. Chuck Lavaroni, "The Creative Teacher and the Entrepreneurial Process," prepared for the International Academy for Educational Entrepreneurship, available online at www.edentrepreneurs.org/paper.phtml.

12. Joe Williams, *Cheating Our Kids: How Politics and Greed Ruin Education* (New York: Palgrave Macmillan, 2005).

13. Robert Kolker, "Mike Bloomberg Goes to the Principals Office," *New York Magazine*, October 6, 2003.

14. See Carl Campanile, "530 Teachers Given an F," *New York Post,* July 1, 2004.
15. See Carl Campanile, "530 Teachers Given an F."
16. See Carl Campanile, "530 Teachers Given an F."
17. Kathleen Lucadamo, "Passions Erupt at Hearing on Teachers Deal," *New York Sun,* November 14, 2003.
18. Williams, *Cheating Our Kids.*
19. Greg Hinz, "It's Back to School for Aspiring Principals: Northwestern, Biz Leaders to Launch Academy," *Chicago Tribune,* November 24, 1997.
20. Joe Williams, "Principal School Flunks Finance," *New York Daily News,* October 15, 2003.
21. Joe Williams, "Welch Gets Ed Job: Ex-GE Boss to School Principals in Leadership," *New York Daily News,* January 14, 2003.
22. Interview with the author.
23. Remarks by California secretary of education Alan Bersin to the National Association of Charter School Authorizers, Denver, Colorado, October 24, 2005.
24. Marsha Sutton, "Four San Diego Schools Earn Charter Status," *Voice of San Diego,* March 2, 2005.
25. Alan Greenblatt, "The Impatience of Paul Vallas," *Governing Magazine,* September 2005.
26. Alan Greenblatt, "The Impatience of Paul Vallas."
27. Joe Williams, "Teacher Seniority Rules Nixed for Summer Hires," *New York Daily News,* June 17, 2005.
28. Bersin remarks to NACSA; see note 23.
29. Remarks by William Andrekopoulos to NACSA, Denver, Colorado, October 24, 2005.

CHAPTER 7

Markets, Bureaucracies, and Clans: The Role of Organizational Culture

Robert Maranto and April Gresham Maranto

1. John E. Chubb and Terry M. Moe, "Politics, Markets, and the Organization of Schools," *American Political Science Review* 82, no. 4 (December 1988); John E. Chubb and Terry M. Moe, *Politics, Markets, and America's Schools* (Washington, DC: Brookings Institution Press, 1990).
2. William G. Ouchi, Bruce S. Cooper, Lydia G. Segal, Tim DeRoche, Carolyn Brown, and Elizabeth Galvin, *Organization Configuration and Performance: The Case of Primary and Secondary School Systems* (Los Angeles: UCLA, Anderson School of Management, 2003); William G. Ouchi, "Academic Freedom," *Education Next* 4, no. 1 (Winter 2004): 21–25.
3. William G. Ouchi, "Markets, Bureaucracies, and Clans," *Administrative Science Quarterly* 25, no. 1 (March 1980); Ouchi borrows from Oliver E. Williamson, *Markets and Hierarchies* (New York: Free Press, 1975).
4. Stephen Goldsmith and William D. Eggers, *Governing by Network: The New Shape of the Public Sector* (Washington, DC: Brookings Institution Press, 2004).
5. Anthony Downs, *Inside Bureaucracy* (Boston: Little, Brown, 1967); Ouchi, "Markets, Bureaucracies, and Clans."
6. Karen M. Hult and Charles Walcott, *Governing Public Organizations* (Pacific Grove, CA: Brooks/Cole, 1990); Ouchi, "Markets, Bureaucracies, and Clans"; Ouchi et al., *Organization Configuration and Performance;* Ouchi et al. borrow heavily from Williamson, *Mar-*

kets and Hierarchies; Oliver E. Williamson, "Comparative Economic Organization: The Analysis of Discrete Structural Alternatives," *Administrative Science Quarterly* 36, no. 2 (June 1991): 269–296.

7. Ouchi, "Markets, Bureaucracies, and Clans," 136.

8. Downs, *Inside Bureaucracy.*

9. Coalition of Essential Schools, "About the Coalition of Essential Schools," 2003, available online at www.essentialschools.org/pub/ces_docs/about/about.html.

10. James Nehring, *Upstart Startup: Creating and Sustaining a Public Charter School* (New York: Teachers College Press, 2002).

11. North Central Regional Educational Laboratory, "The Coalition of Essential Schools" (Naperville, IL: Author, 2004).

12. Core Knowledge Foundation, "Core Knowledge" (Charlottesville, VA: Author, 2005), available online at www.coreknowledge.org/CK/index.htm.

13. Core Knowledge Foundation; see note 12.

14. Core Knowledge Foundation, "Filling the Curriculum Void: Lessons from Core Knowledge Schools" (Charlottesville, VA: Author, 2005).

15. E. D. Hirsch Jr., *The Knowledge Deficit* (Boston: Houghton Mifflin, 2006).

16. Edward J. Dirkswager, *Teachers as Owners* (Lanham, MD: ScarecrowEducation, 2002); Eric Rofes, "Teachers as Communitarians: A Charter School Cooperative in Minnesota," in *Inside Charter Schools,* ed. Bruce Fuller (Cambridge, MA: Harvard University Press, 2000); Doug Thomas, Walter Enloe, and Ronald J. Newell, *The Coolest School in America* (Lanham, MD: ScarecrowEducation, 2005).

17. EdVisions Schools, "Overview of EdVision Schools," 2005, available online at www.edvisions.com/html/edvisions_schools.shtml.

18. Dirkswager, *Teachers as Owners,* 2, 20, 25.

19. EdVisions Cooperative, "Ryzin Charts," available online at www.edvisions.com/html/ryzin_charts_0.shtml.

20. Ronald J. Newell, "EdVisions Schools Found to Provide Most Instruction per Dollars Spent!" 2005, available online at www.edvisions.coop/2005_02_01_archive.html.

21. Ronald J. Newell and Irving H. Buchen, *Democratic Learning and Leading* (Lanham, MD: ScarecrowEducation, 2004), 48.

22. C. Descry, *Crow Canyon* (Prescott, AZ: SRES Press, 1993). Ed Berger writes under the name C. Descry.

23. Descry, *Crow Canyon;* Robert Maranto, "Did the Teachers Destroy the School? Public Entrepreneurship as Creation and Adaptation," presented at the annual meeting of the American Society for Public Administration, Phoenix, March 24, 2002.

24. Henry M. Levin, "Thoughts on For-Profit Schools," *Occasional Paper 14* (New York: Columbia University, National Center for the Study of Privatization in Education, 2001); Henry M. Levin, "Potential of For-Profit Schools for Educational Reform," *Occasional Paper 47* (New York: Columbia University, National Center for the Study of Privatization in Education, 2002).

25. Alex Molnar, David Garcia, Carolyn Sullivan, Brenden McEvoy, and Jamie Joanou, *Profiles of For-Profit Education Management Organizations 2004–2005* (Tempe: Arizona State University, Education Policy Studies Laboratory, Commercialism in Education Research Unit, 2005), available online at www.asu.edu/educ/epsl/CERU/CERU_2005_emo.htm; RAND Education, *A Decade of Entrepreneurship in Education,* 2005, available online at www.rand.org/news/press.05/10.11.html.

26. Chris Whittle, *Crash Course: Imagining a Better Future for Public Education* (New York: Riverhead Books, 2005), 68.
27. John E. Chubb, "Lessons in School Reform from the Edison Project," in *New Schools for a New Century,* ed. Diane Ravitch and Joe Viterirri (New Haven, CT: Yale University Press, 1997), 86–123; John E. Chubb, "The First Few Years of Edison Schools: Ten Lessons in Getting to Scale," in *Expanding the Reach of Education Reforms,* ed. Thomas K. Glennon Jr., Susan J. Bodilly, Jolene R. Galegher, and Kerri A. Kerr (Santa Monica, CA: RAND, 2004); Whittle, *Crash Course.*
28. Jane Hannaway and Nancy Sharkey, "Does Profit Status Make A Difference? Resource Allocation in EMO-Run and Traditional Public Schools," *Journal of Education Finance* 30 (Summer 2004): 27–50; Whittle, *Crash Course.*
29. RAND Education, *A Decade of Entrepreneurship.*
30. Chubb, "The First Few Years."
31. Maranto, "Tale of Two Cities"; Whittle, *Crash Course.*
32. Lizz Pawlson, *KIPP: Life Lessons* (San Francisco: KIPP Foundation, 2005).
33. Brian Lamb, "Afterwards: An Interview with David Levin," CSPAN, 2005.
34. North Star Academy, "College Placement Results," 2005, available online at www.northstaracademy.org/results.html; Abigail Thernstrom and Stephan Thernstrom, *No Excuses: Closing the Racial Gap in Learning* (New York: Simon & Schuster, 2003).

CHAPTER 8
Why Is This So Difficult?
Henry M. Levin

1. The author is thankful to Heather Schwartz for her valued assistance.
2. Peter F. Drucker, *Innovation and Entrepreneurship* (New York: HarperBusiness, 1985).
3. *Goals 2000: Educate America Act,* U.S. Code 20 (1994), §§ 5801 et seq.
4. Larry Cuban, "Reforming: Again, Again, and Again," *Educational Researcher* 19, no. 1 (January 1990): 3–13.
5. Jeffery Henig and Steven Sugarman, "The Nature and Extent of School Choice," in *School Choice and Social Controversy: Politics, Policy, and Law,* ed. Steven Sugarman and Frank Kemerer (Washington, DC: Brookings Institution Press, 1999).
6. Larry Cuban, *How Teachers Taught: Constancy and Change in American Classrooms, 1890–1990* (New York: Teachers College Press, 1993).
7. Seymour Sarason, *The Predictable Failure of Educational Reform: Can We Change Course Before It's Too Late?* (San Francisco: Jossey-Bass, 1990).
8. All three of these strategies are included in a vision of what education will be like in 2030 by Chris Whittle, founder and CEO of Edison Schools, in his book *Crash Course: Imagining a Better Future for Public Education* (New York: Riverhead Books, 2005).
9. William J. Baumol, "Macroeconomics of Unbalanced Growth: The Anatomy of Urban Crisis," *American Economic Review* 57, no. 3 (June 1967).
10. Byron Brown, "Why Governments Run Schools," *Economics of Education Review* 11, no. 4 (December 1992): 287–300; Richard Rothstein, Martin Carnoy, and Luis Benveniste, *Can Public Schools Learn from Private Schools?* (Washington, DC: Economic Policy Institute, 1999).

11. See, for example, Matthew Andrews, William Duncombe, and John Yinger, "Revisiting Economies of Size in American Education: Are We Any Closer to a Consensus?" *Economics of Education Review* 21, no. 3 (June 2002): 245–262.

12. More recently Edison Schools has reduced the number of schools that it is managing and substantially expanded its provision of supplementary services, including summer school, afterschool programs, and tutoring. Although it is privately held and does not need to report its financial status, these changes have reportedly made it a profitable entity.

13. Jane Hannaway and Nancy Sharkey, "Does Profit Status Make a Difference? Resource Allocation in EMO-Run and Traditional Public Schools," *Journal of Education Finance* 30, no. 1 (Summer 2004): 27–49; William Ratchford II, "Going Public with School Privatization," *Abell Report* 18, no. 3 (May/June 2005): 1–8.

14. Ratchford II, "Going Public with School Privatization."

15. Gary Miron and Christopher Nelson, *What's Public about Charter Schools?* (Thousand Oaks, CA: Corwin Press, 2002); Brian P. Gill, Laura S. Hamilton, J. R. Lockwood, Julie A. Marsh, Ron W. Zimmer, and Deanna Hill, *Inspiration, Perspiration, and Time: Operations and Achievement in Edison Schools* (MG-351-EDU) (Santa Monica, CA: RAND Corp., October 2005), available online at www.rand.org/publications/MG/MG351/.

16. Gill et al., *Inspiration, Perspiration, and Time,* xxvi–xxvii. To Edison's credit, it sponsored this rigorous evaluation. A search of major sources and requests to EMOs found no evaluations of this quality for any of the other EMOs.

17. Natalie Lacireno-Paquet, Thomas T. Holyoke, Jeffrey Henig, and Michele Moser, "Creaming versus Cropping: Charter School Enrollment Practices in Response to Market Incentives," *Educational Evaluation and Policy Analysis* 24, no. 2 (Summer 2002): 145–158.

18. Ohio has the largest number of online charter schools in the country. The majority of such schools were in "academic emergency" or "academic watch," the two lowest categories in the rating system of the State of Ohio. Doug Oplinger, "Charter Schools Take Step Back in Ohio Ratings," *Akron Beacon Journal,* August 17, 2005.

19. See a comprehensive summary of studies in Clive R. Belfield and Henry M. Levin, *Privatizing Educational Choice: Consequences for Parents, Schools, and Public Policy* (Boulder, CO: Paradigm Publishers, 2005), chap. 6.

20. See the details available online at www.cde.ca.gov/re/lr/wr/index.asp.

21. Personal conversation with Dr. Gerry House, October 27, 2005.

22. Christopher Lubienski, "Charter School Innovation in Theory and Practice: Autonomy, R&D, and Curricular Conformity," in *Taking Account of Charter Schools,* ed. Katrina E. Bulkley and Priscilla Wohlstetter (New York: Teachers College Press, 2004); Christopher Lubienski, "Innovation in Education Markets: Theory and Evidence on the Impact of Competition and Choice in Charter Schools," *American Educational Research Journal* 40, no. 2 (2003).

23. Luis Huerta, Maria Fernanda Gonzalez, and Chad d'Entremont, "Cyber and Home School Charter Schools: Adopting Policy to New Forms of Public Schooling," *Peabody Journal of Education* 81, no. 1 (forthcoming 2006).

24. Doug Oplinger and Dennis J. Willard, "Online Students Missing Exams," *Akron Beacon Journal,* June 3, 2005.

25. Christopher Nelson and Gary Miron, "Professional Opportunities for Teachers: A View from Inside Charter Schools," in Bulkley and Wohlstetter, *Taking Account of Charter*

Schools; Brian P. Gill, Michael Timpane, K. E. Ross, and Dominick J. Brewer, *Rhetoric versus Reality: What We Know and What We Need to Know about Vouchers and Charter Schools* (Santa Monica, CA: RAND Corp., 2001); Martin Carnoy, Rebecca Jacobsen, Lawrence Mishel, and Richard Rothstein, *The Charter School Dust-Up: Examining the Evidence on Enrollment and Achievement* (New York: Teachers College Press, 2005).

26. Cuban, *How Teachers Taught*; Larry Cuban, *Oversold and Underused: Computers in the Classroom* (Cambridge, MA: Harvard University Press, 2001).

27. Deborah Meier, *The Power of Their Ideas: Lessons for America from a Small School in Harlem* (Boston: Beacon Press, 1995).

28. Elissa Gootman and David M. Herszenhorn, "Getting Smaller to Improve the Big Picture: Trying to Lift Performance by Shrinking City Schools," *New York Times*, May 3, 2005.

29. Robert Evans, *The Human Side of School Change: Reform, Resistance, and the Real-Life Problems of Innovation* (San Francisco: Jossey-Bass, 1996).

30. Evans, *The Human Side of School Change*.

31. Milbrey W. McLaughlin, "The RAND Change Agent Study Revisited: Macro-Perspectives and Micro Realities," *Educational Researcher* 19, no. 9 (December 1990): 11–16.

32. David Tyack and Larry Cuban, *Tinkering toward Utopia: A Century of Public School Reform* (Cambridge, MA: Harvard University Press, 1995).

33. Jennifer Mrozowski, "Charters Have High Turnover," *Cincinnati Enquirer*, July 3, 2005.

34. Lubienski, "Charter School Innovation."

35. David B. Tyack, *Turning Points in American Educational History* (Waltham, MA: Blaisdell, 1967).

36. Paul J. DiMaggio and Walter W. Powell, "The Iron Cage Revisited: Institutional Isomorphism and Collective Rationality in Organizational Fields," *American Sociological Review* 48, no. 2 (April 1983).

37. John W. Meyer and Brian Rowan, "Institutionalized Organizations: Formal Structure as Myth and Ceremony," *American Journal of Sociology* 83, no. 2 (September 1977): 147–160.

38. Karl E. Weick, "Educational Organizations as Loosely Coupled Systems," *Administrative Science Quarterly* 21, no. 1 (March 1976): 340–363.

39. Tyack, *Turning Points*.

40. Samuel Bowles and Herb Gintis, *Schooling in Capitalist America* (New York: Basic Books, 1976); Martin Carnoy and Henry M. Levin, *Schooling and Work in the Democratic State* (Stanford, CA: Stanford University Press, 1985).

CHAPTER 9

Opportunities, but a Resistant Culture

Steven F. Wilson

1. Sean Gallagher and Eric Bassett, "Postsecondary Institutions: Learning Markets and Opportunities 2004" (Boston: Eduventures, December 2004).

2. See www.schwab.com.

3. Stephen D. Simpson, "Apollo Looking a Bit Less Godlike," *TheMotleyFool.com*, September 19, 2005.

4. Howard Block, an analyst at Banc of America Securities, in Eryn Brown, "Can For-Profit Schools Pass an Ethics Test?" *New York Times,* December 12, 2004.

5. Eduventures, Inc., *K–12 Market Overview 2005* (Boston: Author, March 2005).

6. Alex Molnar, David Garcia, Carolyn Sullivan, Brendan McEvoy, and Jamie Joanou, *Profiles of For-Profit Education Management Organizations, 7th Annual Report, 2004–2005* (Tempe: Arizona State University, 2005).

7. J. Mark Jackson, Catherine Burdt, Eric Bassett, and Matthew Stein, "K–12 Solutions: Learning Markets and Opportunities 2004" (Boston: Eduventures, December 2004).

8. Gallagher and Bassett, "Postsecondary Institutions."

9. Apollo Group, *2004 Annual Report,* available online at www.apollogrp.edu.

10. Bright Horizons Family Solutions, *2005 Annual Report* (Cambridge, MA: Author).

11. Score! Educational Centers, "About Us," available online at www.escore.com/about/.

12. Eduventures, *K–12 Market Overview.*

13. George Cigale, chief executive officer of Tutor.com, interview with the author, January 31, 2005.

14. See www.growingstars.com; Saritha Ray, "A Tutor Half a Mile Away, but as Close as the Keyboard," *New York Times,* September 26, 2005.

15. Eduventures, *K–12 Market Overview.*

16. See Riverdeep website, www.riverdeep.net.

17. For the number of users, see the Blackboard Academic Suite Brochure, available online at www.blackboard.com/docs/as/bb_academic_suite_brochure_single.pdf.

18. Larry Berger, chief executive officer of Wireless Generation, interview with the author, January 30, 2005.

19. Thomas L. Friedman, "Still Eating Our Lunch," *New York Times,* September 16, 2005.

20. See www.heymath.net.

21. See www.headsprout.com.

22. Lesley Heilman, deputy director of communications of the Center for Education Reform, cited in "Cyber Education Gains in Tucson," *Arizona Daily Star,* May 28, 2005.

23. See www.K12.com.

24. Tim Wiley and J. Mark Jackson, "Professional Development Management Systems Poised for Growth" (Boston: Eduventures, September 2005).

25. See College Coach website, www.getintocollege.com/corporate/index.html.

26. Kate Stone Lombardi, "College Guidance, Now Part of a Parent's Job," *New York Times,* August 18, 2004.

27. Nobel Learning Communities, Form 10-K, filed September 19, 2005, p. F-3, available online at www.nasdaq.com/asp/quotes_sec.asp?symbol=NLCI&selected=NLCI&page=filings.

28. Eric Bassett, Eduventures, interview with the author, October 31, 2005.

29. Berger, see note 18.

30. George Cigale, see note 13.

31. See Steven F. Wilson, *Learning on the Job: When Business Takes On Public Schools* (Cambridge, MA: Harvard University Press, 2006).

32. J. C. Huizenga, interview with the author, July 10, 2003.

33. CSR Research Consortium, "What Have We Learned about Class Size Reduction in California?" September 2002, available online at www.classize.org; Caroline M. Hoxby, "The Effects of Class Size on Student Achievement: New Evidence from Population Varia-

tion," *Quarterly Journal of Economics* 115, no. 4 (2000); Ludger Wössmann and Martin West, "Class-Size Effects in School Systems around the World: Evidence from Between-Grade Variation in TIMSS," Harvard University, Program on Education Policy and Governance, working paper no. 02–02, 2002.

34. Octavio Visiedo, interview with the author, February 12, 2003.
35. Imagine Schools, "Imagine Schools Initiates Conversion to Nonprofit Status," news release, September 7, 2005.
36. Quoted in Abigail Thernstrom and Stephen Thernstrom, *No Excuses* (New York: Simon & Schuster, 2003).
37. Steven G. Rivkin, Eric A. Hanushek, and John F. Kain, "Teachers, Schools, and Academic Achievement," *Econometrica* 73, no. 2 (2005): 417–438; Jonah E. Rockoff, "The Impact of Individual Teachers on Student Achievement: Evidence from Panel Data," *American Economic Review* 94, no. 2 (2004), cited in Andrew Leigh and Sara Mead, "Lifting Teacher Performance," Policy Report, Progressive Policy Institute, April 2005.
38. Leigh and Mead, "Lifting Teacher Performance."

CHAPTER 10
The Bias against Scale and Profit
John E. Chubb

1. Center for Education Reform, news release, October 27, 2005.
2. Estimated from National Center for Education Statistics, *Digest of Education Statistics 2004* (Washington, DC: U.S. Department of Education, 2005), table 86.
3. The Center for Education Reform, the most widely cited evaluator of charter school laws, rates only six laws an A and fourteen laws a B, judging them along various dimensions of support for charter school openings. Center for Education Reform, *The Simple Guide to Charter School Laws: A Progress Report* (Washington, DC: Author, 2005).
4. The political battles associated with new charter legislation and the compromises emerging from those battles have been widely documented. See, for example, Chester E. Finn Jr., Bruno V. Manno, and Gregg Vanourek, *Charter Schools in Action: Renewing Public Education* (Princeton, NJ: Princeton University Press, 2001).
5. The development of the modern school system is well explained in David B. Tyack, *The One Best System: A History of American Urban Education* (Cambridge, MA: Harvard University Press, 1974).
6. Augmenting these arguments were concerns about schools falling under the control of waves of immigrants flooding the cities.
7. On the impact of school and district consolidation see Paul E. Peterson, "Consolidate Districts Not Schools," in *Reforming Education in Arkansas,* ed. Koret Task Force (Stanford, CA: Hoover Institution Press, 2005).
8. Estimated from National Center for Education Statistics, *Digest of Education Statistics 2004,* table 86.
9. See John E. Chubb, "Should Charter Schools Be a Cottage Industry?" in *Leveling the Playing Field for Charter Schools,* ed. Paul T. Hill (Stanford, CA: Hoover Institution Press, 2006). The analysis includes all EMOs or CMOs serving at least four schools—a minimal threshold for considering organizations to be attempting to get to scale.

10. At this writing, Imagine Schools was reportedly in the process of converting from for-profit to not-for-profit status. But because it built its school portfolio as a for-profit organization, it is considered for-profit here.

11. The average enrollment in K–12 schools exceeds nine hundred because these schools are virtual, attended via the Internet.

CHAPTER 11
Educational Entrepreneurs Redux

Larry Cuban

1. From NewSchools Venture Fund, "Entrepreneurs in Action," available online at www.newschools.org/portfolio/entrepreneurs.htm.

2. I thank Eric Bredo and David Tyack for sharing their thoughts on our bike rides. Rob Reich helped me think through some differences between current and past educational entrepreneurs. Heather Kirkpatrick, Craig Peck, Kim Marshall, Jonathan Garfinkel, and Rick Hess provided many comments and constructive suggestions on a first draft. James Forman pushed me to fill in blanks in key arguments, for which I am grateful. Of course, I am responsible, not they, for the accuracy of text, interpretations, and conclusions in this chapter.

3. Frederick M. Hess, "Educational Entrepreneurship: Why It Matters, What Risks It Poses, and How to Make the Most of It," prospectus for Harvard Education Press (April 2005).

4. I use "educational entrepreneur" and "reformer" interchangeably for those individuals in schools, districts, universities, and private for-profit companies, past and present, who saw opportunities, were willing to take risks, and started new programs or invented new processes to improve public schools. Although the word "entrepreneur" was hardly used in that early twentieth century burst of school reform that profoundly shaped U.S. education for the next hundred years, figures like Ellwood P. Cubberley (professor, Stanford University), Jane Addams (founder of Hull House, Chicago), and Pierre DuPont (businessman) worked in different venues and for different reasons to improve schooling in the early twentieth century. A similar listing of academics, school leaders, and corporate figures could be assembled for the 1960s, the second time that business interest in education and entrepreneurial activity spilled over public schools. Although in the late 1960s and early 1970s a few years of frantic entrepreneurial activity spread over urban schools, it soon dissolved in scandals and failure, leaving little residue from their efforts—the main reason I do not include this generation of entrepreneurs in the chapter. In these years, a few individuals and companies left a temporary mark with "performance contracting" projects, corporate ventures into schooling the disadvantaged, "turnkey" programs, and alternative schools. A third full-fledged generation of entrepreneurs could be compiled into a list for the first decade of the twenty-first century of individuals, for-profit companies, and nonprofit companies engaged in actively reforming public schools. It is this generation that I discuss. See David Tyack and Elisabeth Hansot, *Managers of Virtue* (New York: Basic Books, 1982) and Raymond E. Callahan, *Education and the Cult of Efficiency* (Chicago: University of Chicago Press, 1962) for the earlier generations. For the 1960s and early 1970s, see David Tyack and Larry Cuban, *Tinkering toward Utopia* (Cambridge, MA: Harvard University Press, 1995), 114–120; and

Francis Keppel, "New Relationships between Education and Industry," *Public Administration Review* 30 (July–August 1970): 353–359.

5. In the classic intellectual history of the progressive education movement, *Transformation of the School* (New York: Anchor Books, 1961), Lawrence Cremin divided progressive education into three wings: the scientific, the child-centered, and the reformist. Cremin used the term "pedagogical progressives" for child-centered reformers, which I use. I also use a similar typology that David Tyack worked out in *The One Best System* (Cambridge, MA: Harvard University Press, 1974) with his addition of the phrase "administrative progressives," which remains both useful and relevant three decades later. In *Managers of Virtue*, Tyack and Hansot elaborate further who administrative progressives were and what they did in Part II, "Schooling by Design in a Corporate Society," 105–179. Also see Ellen Condliffe Lagemann, *An Elusive Science: The Troubling History of Education Research* (Chicago: University of Chicago Press, 2000), chaps. 2 and 3. On the importance of tests to administrative progressives, see Daniel Resnick, "History of Educational Testing," in *Ability Testing: Uses, Consequences, and Controversies,* ed. Alexandra Wigdor and Wendell Garner (Washington, DC: National Academy Press, 1982); Jerome D'Agostino, "Achievement Testing in American Schools," in *American Education: Yesterday, Today, and Tomorrow*, 99th Yearbook of the National Society for the Study of Education, Part II, ed. Thomas L. Good (Chicago: National Society for the Study of Education, 2000). For the rhetorical and policy impact of scientific management that administrative progressives sought to apply to public schools, see Callahan, *Education and the Cult of Efficiency*.

6. Tyack, *The One Best System*.

7. Quote is from Ellwood P. Cubberley, professor of education at Stanford University in 1907, in Tyack and Hansot, *Managers of Virtue*. Tyack and Hansot called the scientifically inclined wing of the progressives "scientific educational entrepreneurs."

8. Diane Ravitch, *Left Back: A Century of Failed School Reforms* (New York: Simon & Schuster, 2000); David Labaree, *How to Succeed in School: The Credentials Race in American Education* (New Haven, CT: Yale University Press, 1997); Herbert Kliebard, *The Struggle for the American Curriculum, 1893–1958* (Boston: Routledge & Kegan Paul, 1986).

9. Much of this analysis comparing two generations of educational entrepreneurs is drawn from Tyack and Hansot, *Managers of Virtue*; Norton Grubb and Marvin Lazerson, *The Education Gospel* (Cambridge, MA: Harvard University Press, 2004); Larry Cuban, *The Blackboard and the Bottom Line: Why Schools Can't Be Businesses* (Cambridge, MA: Harvard University Press, 2004).

10. Larry Cuban, *How Teachers Taught*, 2nd ed. (New York: Teachers College Press, 1993); Arthur Zilversmit, *Changing Schools: Progressive Education Theory and Practice, 1930–1960* (Chicago: University of Chicago Press, 1993). The interpretations that I and Zilversmit offer about the limited entry of progressive practices in classrooms differ from what Diane Ravitch offers in *Left Back*.

11. V. Dion Haynes, "Charter Schools Expand in Several New Directions," *Washington Post*, August 25, 2005.

12. See the Edison Schools website, www.edisonschools.com/design/d04.html; Aspire website, www.aspirepublicschools.org/design/curric.html; The New Country website, www.mncs.k12.mn.us/; KIPP website, www.kipp.org/. I could not find any information on pedagogy for New Leaders for New Schools, implying that they are agnostic on what works best with low-income minority children. Also, RAND just published a

study of twenty-three Edison schools, which showed mixed results in comparison with a matched set of non-Edison schools. While there were both absolute and relative test-score gains in reading and math for Edison schools during the study, RAND researchers pointed out the variations in implementation and that results were not "uniformly positive." See www.rand.org/publications/MG/MG351/.

13. For charter schools, see Martin Carnoy, Rebecca Jacobsen, Lawrence Mishel, and Richard Rothstein, *The Charter School Dust-Up: Examining the Evidence on Enrollment and Achievement* (New York: Teachers College Press, 2005); Frederick M. Hess, *Revolution at the Margins* (Washington, DC: Brookings Institution Press, 2002). TFA's impact on academic achievement is contested. For an independent, largely negative assessment of its impact, see Ildiko Laczko-Kerr and David C. Berliner, "The Effectiveness of 'Teach For America' and Other Under-Certified Teachers on Student Academic Achievement: A Case of Harmful Public Policy," *Education Policy Analysis Archives* 10, no. 37 (September 6, 2002), available online at http://epaa.asu.edu/epaa/v10n37/. For an independent, largely positive assessment, see www.teachforamerica.org/tfa/Mathematica.html#Mathematica. I could not find any independent assessments of New Leaders for New Schools, Success For All, Comer Schools, and other whole-school reform models. All have a raft of studies that show achievement gains, plateauing of scores, and occasional losses in elementary schools.

14. I have taken quotes from websites of these organizations: www.teachforamerica.org/; www.newschools.org/; www.nlns.org/NLWeb/Index.jsp; www.broadfoundation.org/

15. Bethany Rogers, "Social Policy, Teaching and Youth Activism in the 1960s: The Liberal Reform Vision of the National Teacher Corps" (Unpublished doctoral dissertation, New York University, 2002). I also taught in and eventually directed a school-based program training returned Peace Corps volunteers to teach in Washington, D.C., public schools between 1963 and 1967.

16. Jane David, "Synthesis of Research on School-Based Management," *Educational Leadership* 46 no. 8 (May 1989); Lori Jo Oswald, "School-Based Management," *ERIC Digest* 99 (July 1995).

17. Thomas B. Fordham Foundation, "Better Leaders for America's Schools: A Manifesto," available online at www.edexcellence.net/institute/publication/publication.cfm?id=1. "Entrepreneurship with a Difference," NewBusiness, 2001, available online at www.hbs.edu/entrepreneurship/newbusiness/2001summer_5.html.

18. Mark R. Warren, "Communities and Schools: A New View of Urban Education Reform," *Harvard Educational Review* 75 no. 2 (2005). For the Industrial Areas Foundation work in Texas, see www.industrialareasfoundation.org/iafaction/iafactionschools.htm. For Comer Schools and evaluations, see http://info.med.yale.edu/comer/, and for evaluations of Comer schools by Thomas Cook, see http://info.med.yale.edu/comer/research_evaluation/externalevals.html.

19. Tyack, *The One Best System*.

20. Tyack and Cuban, *Tinkering toward Utopia*.

21. Chris Whittle lays out fresh new design ideas for elementary and secondary schools in *Crash Course: Imagining a Better Future for Public Education* (New York: Riverhead Books, 2005). What is striking about these ideas, some of which early twentieth-century progressives would cheer, is that they are rooted in the age-graded school. Time and again, Whittle recommends independent work, children tutoring, students doing school chores. All of these recommendations refer to which grade these design features should

begin in. So even Whittle, who rails at the unchanging nature of schools, accepts the one basic structure that shapes much of the adult and student behavior that he seeks to change (see chapter 5 of this volume).

22. Teaching approaches in charter schools often resemble regular schools, according to one study. Christopher Lubienski, "Innovation in Education Markets: Theory and Evidence on the Impact of Competition and Choice in Charter Schools," *American Educational Research Journal* 40 no. 2 (2003).

23. The core issues analyzed in this paragraph are taken from Jeff Faux, "Can Liberals Tell a Credible Story?" *The American Prospect* 8 no. 35 (November/December 1997); and Grubb and Lazerson, *The Education Gospel*. I have adapted the language.

24. President Bush's quote is in his "State of the Union" address in the *New York Times*, January 30, 2002. One reader of an earlier draft questioned this statement about educational entrepreneurs using the rhetoric about schools and labor markets. The reader argued that the rhetoric is more often stated by state and federal officials and policy folk than risk-taking educators. I agree that much of the language entrepreneurs use seldom mentions preparing graduates for the labor market or occupational preparation as a goal of public schools. But I do see the fevered concentration on college preparation and "success in life," however, as verbal proxies for occupational preparation and financial security. For one example, see epigraph for this chapter.

25. Grubb and Lazerson, *The Education Gospel*.

26. For examples of the exceptions I mention in this paragraph, see The Met (The Metropolitan Regional Career and Technical Center in Rhode Island), available online at www.metcenter.org/; The Urban Academy in New York City, available online at www.urbanacademy.org/. Also see Michelle Fine, "Not in Our Name," *Rethinking Schools* 19 no. 4 (Summer 2005).

27. Schools that do achieve in the areas mentioned in the paragraph, as well as traditional measures of academic achievement, are described in Warren, "Communities and Schools," and endnote 23. One founder of an urban charter school told me that "we have a wonderful supply of afternoon enrichment classes from dance to yoga to drama to public speaking. The pressure to take the kids out of those and put them in extra literacy and numeracy blocks is powerful. The bottom line is that there are only so many hours in the day and time spent in yoga . . . is not time spent in front of a book."

28. Warren, "Communities and Schools."

29. Jon Schnur, New Leaders for New Schools, at a conference on educational entrepreneurship held at the American Enterprise Institute, Washington, DC, November 14, 2005.

Chapter 12
Politics, Policy, and the Promise of Entrepreneurship
Frederick M. Hess

1. Frederick M. Hess, *Spinning Wheels: The Politics of Urban School Reform* (Washington, DC: Brookings Institution Press, 1999).

2. Larry Cuban, *The Blackboard and the Bottom Line: Why Schools Can't Be Businesses* (Cambridge, MA: Harvard University Press, 2005), 5.

3. Sumantra Ghoshal and Christopher A. Bartlett, *The Individualized Corporation: A Fundamentally New Approach to Management* (New York: Harper Books, 1999), 93.

4. David B. Tyack, *The One Best System: A History of American Urban Education* (Cambridge, MA: Harvard University Press, 1974).

5. Clayton M. Christensen, *The Innovator's Dilemma* (New York: HarperBusiness, 2003).

6. William D. Bygrave and Andrew Zacharakis, preface to *The Portable MBA in Entrepreneurship*, 3rd ed., ed. William D. Bygrave and Andrew Zacharakis (Hoboken, NJ: John Wiley and Sons, 2004), viii.

7. Jim Collins, *Good to Great and the Social Sectors: A Monograph to Accompany Good to Great* (Boulder, CO: Jim Collins, 2005), 30.

8. Sara Mead, *Capital Campaign: Early Returns on District of Columbia Charter Schools* (Washington, DC: Progressive Policy Institute, October 2005).

9. Education Commission of the States, "Charter School Finance" (Denver: Education Commission of the States, April 2003).

10. Joe Williams, *Cheating Our Kids: How Politics and Greed Ruin Education* (New York: Palgrave Macmillan, 2005), 23–25.

11. Michael DeArmond, "Getting Out of the Facilities Business: A Public School Real Estate Trust," in *Making School Reform Work: New Partnerships for Real Change*, ed. Paul T. Hill and James Harvey (Washington, DC: Brookings Institution Press, 2004), 26–40.

12. Education Commission of the States, "Charter Schools and the Teaching Quality Provisions of No Child Left Behind" (Denver: Education Commission of the States, 2003).

13. Marguerite Roza and Karen Hawley Miles, *A New Look at Inequities in School Funding: A Presentation on the Resource Variations Within Districts* (Seattle: Center on Reinventing Public Education, May 2002), 9.

14. Paul T. Hill, "Entrepreneurship in K–12 Public Education," in "Social Entrepreneurship," ed. Marilyn L. Kourilsky and William B. Walstad, special issue, *International Journal of Entrepreneurship Education* 2, no. 1 (2003): 71.

15. Ronald A. Heifetz, John V. Kania, and Mark R. Kramer, "Leading Boldly: Foundations Can Move Past Traditional Approaches to Create Social Change through Imaginative—and Even Controversial—Leadership," *Stanford Social Innovation Review* (Winter 2004): 28.

16. Wendy Hassett and Dan Katzir, "Lessons Learned from the Inside," in *With the Best of Intentions: How Philanthropy Is Reshaping K–12 Education*, ed. Frederick M. Hess (Cambridge, MA: Harvard Education Press, 2005), 240.

17. Jessica Levin and Meredith Quinn, "Missed Opportunities: How We Keep High-Quality Teachers Out of Urban Classrooms" (New York: The New Teacher Project, 2003), available online at www.tntp.org/report.html.

18. As reported on The New Teacher Project website, "Who We Are" section by Grove and Zacharakis, available online at www.tntp.org.

19. William D. Bygrave, "The Entrepreneurial Process," in *The Portable MBA in Entrepreneurship*, 1–27, 4.

20. See Abigail Winger, "Incubators for New Schools," in Hill and Harvey, *Making School Reform Work*, 41–51.

21. Michael Patterson, "Hatching for Success," *Business Week Online*, Winter 2005, available online at www.businessweek.com/magazine/content/05_49/b3962458.htm?campaign_id=rss_smlbz.

22. J. Gregory Dees and Beth Anderson, "For-Profit Social Ventures," in Kourilsky and Walstad, *Social Entrepreneurship*, 1–26.

23. Henry M. Levin, "Potential of For-Profit Schools for Educational Reform," in Kourilsky and Walstad, *Social Entrepreneurship*, 82.

24. Levin and Quinn, "Missed Opportunities"; Jessica Levin, Jennifer Mulhern, and Joan Schunck, "Unintended Consequences: The Case for Reforming the Staffing Rules in Urban Teachers Union Contracts" (New York: The New Teacher Project, 2005).

25. Abigail Smith, "Equity within Reach: Insights from the Front Lines of America's Achievement Gap" (New York: Teacher For America, 2005), 6, available online at www.teach foramerica.org/documents/equitywithinreach.pdf.

26. James K. Glassman, "An Entrepreneur Goes to School," *Wall Street Journal*, September 7, 2005.

27. Christopher Whittle, *Crash Course: Imagining a Better Future for Public Education* (New York: Riverhead Books, 2005), 241.

28. Whittle, *Crash Course*, 128.

29. Whittle, *Crash Course*, 222.

30. Christensen, *The Innovator's Dream*, xv.

About the Contributors

John E. Chubb is founding partner, executive vice president, and chief education officer of Edison Schools. He is also a distinguished visiting fellow at the Hoover Institution and a member of the Koret Task Force on K–12 Education. Since 1984, he has been a nonresident senior fellow at the Brookings Institution, where he has authored numerous studies. His books include *Within Our Reach*; *Bridging the Achievement Gap*, edited with Tom Loveless; and *A Lesson in School Reform from Great Britain* and *Politics, Markets, and America's Schools*, both coauthored with Terry Moe. He has taught at Stanford University, Princeton University, and Johns Hopkins University, and served as a consultant for the White House and many state governments.

Larry Cuban is professor emeritus of education at Stanford University. A former urban high school teacher, administrator, and superintendent, Cuban spent twenty-five years in public schools before becoming a professor and researcher at Stanford. His most recent books are *The Blackboard and the Bottom Line: Why Schools Can't Be Businesses* and *Why Is It So Hard to Get Good Schools?*

Frederick M. Hess is director of education policy studies at the American Enterprise Institute and executive editor of *Education Next*. His many books include *Common Sense School Reform, Revolution at the Margins, Spinning Wheels, No Child Left Behind: A Primer, Tough Love for Schools,* and *With the Best of Intentions*. He serves as advisor to the Ash Institute at Harvard University and on various boards, including the review board for the Broad Prize in Urban Education. His research has appeared in scholarly journals including *Social Science Quarterly, American Politics Quarterly, Urban Affairs Review, Educational Policy, Journal of Teacher Education,* and *Teachers College Record*. He formerly taught high school in Baton Rouge, Louisiana.

Henry "Hank" M. Levin is the William Heard Kilpatrick Professor of Economics and Education at Teachers College, Columbia University, and the David Jacks Professor of Education and Economics, emeritus, at Stanford University. He is also the director of the National Center for the Study of Privatization in Education. From 1986 to 2000, Levin served as director of the Accelerated Schools Project, a national school reform initiative for accelerating the education of at-risk youth. He specializes in the economics of education and human resources and has published twenty books and nearly three hundred articles on these subjects. His most recent books are *Cost-Effectiveness Analysis, Privatizing Education*, and *Readings in the Economics of Higher Education*.

April Gresham Maranto is a researcher, mother, and volunteer. She coedited *School Choice in the Real World: Lessons from Arizona Charter Schools* with her husband, Robert Maranto, and her work has appeared in journals including *Phi Delta Kappan, Family Law Quarterly*, the *Journal of Applied Psychology, Social Behavior and Psychology*, and the *Journal of Traumatic Stress Studies*. She has previously taught at Lafayette College, Furman University, and the University of Minnesota.

Robert Maranto teaches political science and public administration at Villanova University and taught previously at the University of Pennsylvania, James Madison University, and Southern Mississippi University. He has done extensive research on political appointees in government, civil service reform, and school reform, producing more than forty scholarly publications. His op-eds have appeared in the *Washington Post, Washington Times, Philadelphia Inquirer, Baltimore Sun*, and *Hartford Courant*. Maranto and his wife, April Gresham Maranto, coedited *School Choice in the Real World: Lessons from Arizona Charter Schools*. He also wrote *Beyond a Government of Strangers* and coedited two forthcoming books, *Charter Schools and Educational Reform*, with Myron Kayes, and *The Second Term of George W. Bush*, with Douglas M. Brattebo and Tom Lansford.

Patrick McGuinn is assistant professor of political science at Drew University. He was previously a visiting assistant professor at Colby College, a postdoctoral fellow at the Taubman Center for Public Policy and American Institutions at Brown University, and a predoctoral fellow at the Miller Center for Public Affairs, University of Virginia. His work on education policy has been published in *The Journal of Policy History, Publius: The Journal of Federalism, The Public Interest, Teachers College Record*, and *Educational Policy*, and his book *No Child Left Behind and the Transformation of Federal Education Policy, 1965–2005*, was published in 2006. McGuinn is a former high school teacher.

Alex Molnar is professor of education policy and director of the Education Policy Studies Laboratory at Arizona State University. He previously taught at the School of Education at the University of Wisconsin-Milwaukee and served as chief of staff for the Wisconsin Department of Public Instruction's Urban Initiative, a project that resulted in the creation of the state's Student Achievement Guarantee in Education program. Molnar's work has appeared in newspapers like the *New York Times*, the *Wall Street Journal*, and *Education Week*, and in scholarly journals including *Educational Evaluation and Policy Analysis, Phi Delta Kappan*, and *Educational Leadership*. His most recent books are *School Commercialism: From Democratic Ideal to Market Commodity, Giving Kids the Business: The Commercialization of America's Schools*, and *Vouchers, Class Size Reduction, and Student Achievement*.

Adam Newman is vice president for research and client services at Eduventures, where he oversees the direction and operations of the company's research and advisory practices. He has worked on a wide range of research projects and growth-oriented advisory engagements for K–12, postsecondary, and corporate clients. His published research includes *Closing the Equity Gap: Addressing NCLB Compliance with Access Infrastructure Software, What Can Virtual Learning Do for Your School?* and *Charting the Course: Postsecondary E-Learning Providers Respond to New Market Conditions.* Before joining Eduventures, he was senior manager at the Corporate Executive Board, a membership-based research organization delivering best practices analysis to Global 2000 companies. He has also taught and coached in middle and secondary schools.

Julie Landry Petersen is communications manager at NewSchools Venture Fund, where she oversees publications strategy and the writing and editing of articles and papers in support of the fund's network and intellectual capital development. Before joining NewSchools, Petersen was a senior writer at the business and technology magazine *Red Herring*, where she covered venture capital as well as a range of other beats, including education, entrepreneurs, and start-ups. In 2001, she was named one of the "30 Under 30" business journalists in the country by the TJFR Group for her online and print writing at *Red Herring*.

Kim Smith is cofounder and executive chairman of NewSchools Venture Fund, which she established in 1998 to transform public education by supporting education entrepreneurs. She began her career as a business-education consultant, later becoming a founding team member of Teach For America and founding director of BAYAC Ameri-Corps, a consortium of nonprofits in the San Francisco Bay Area. She also held marketing positions with Silicon Graphics' Education Industry Group, where she focused on online learning. In 2001, Smith was featured in *Newsweek*'s report on the "Women of the 21st Century" as "the kind of woman who will shape America's new century." She is also a member of the 2002 Class of Henry Crown Fellows of the Aspen Institute.

Paul Teske is professor of public affairs and director of the Center for Education Policy Analysis at the University of Colorado. He previously was a professor of political science at SUNY Stony Brook. He is coauthor of *Choosing Schools: Consumer Choice and the Quality of American Schools* and has written numerous articles on aspects of education policy, including school choice, charter schools, parental involvement, school leadership, and teacher training. He has also coauthored a book on entrepreneurs in local government, *Public Entrepreneurs: Agents for Change in American Government.* His research has been widely discussed in the media, including the *New York Times, New York Post, Milwaukee Journal Sentinel, Education Week,* and on WBEZ (NPR) Chicago.

Joe Williams is a nonresident senior fellow with Education Sector. A New York-based writer, he covered the New York City school system for the *New York Daily News* from 2000 to 2005. From 1994 to 2000 he covered the Milwaukee Public Schools and that city's voucher program. Williams has won numerous national and local awards for education reporting and recently authored a book on education politics, *Cheating Our Kids: How Politics and Greed Ruin Education.*

Aimee Williamson is a PhD candidate in the Graduate School of Public Affairs at the University of Colorado at Denver. Her dissertation examines differences in human resource management policies in private, charter, and traditional public schools. She is coauthor of "School Choice" in the 2005 *Polling America: An Encyclopedia of Public Opinion*. Williamson is also a lecturer at the University of Colorado at Denver.

Steven F. Wilson is the Michael R. Sandler Senior Fellow at the Center for Business and Government at Harvard University's John F. Kennedy School of Government and a consultant to Edison Schools. He is author of *Learning on the Job: When Business Takes on Public Schools* and was founder and CEO of Advantage Schools, a charter school management company. Before founding Advantage, he was special assistant for Massachusetts Governor William Weld during the passage and implementation of the state's 1993 comprehensive education reform act. Wilson is the former executive director of the Pioneer Institute for Public Policy Research, and his book *Reinventing the Schools: A Radical Plan for Boston* led to the establishment of pilot schools in Boston and the state's charter school law.

Index